DCF Delaware Community Foundation™

Engaging Communities, Empowering Giving™

Stay Curious.

Please enjoy this book,
a gift from the
Delaware Community Foundation.

Praise for *I Never Thought of It That Way*

"This beautifully written book delivers a challenge wrapped in compassion for how hard it is to be curious and open-minded when we 'know' we are right! By being inspiring and intensely practical, Mónica Guzmán has written an essential guide for living in a pluralistic democracy."
—William Doherty, PhD, professor of marriage and family therapy at the University of Minnesota and cofounder of Braver Angels

"*I Never Thought of It That Way* is a critical read for critical times. Every word on every page reflects Mónica's ebullience, generosity, and sincere love for humanity. Her approach has a disarming vulnerability—and that's the point. It is difficult, it is disruptive, it may even be dangerous, but curiosity is how we undivide. Thankfully, Mónica's is contagious."
—Angel Eduardo, cultural commentator and writer for Idealist.org, Center for Inquiry, and the Foundation Against Intolerance & Racism (FAIR)

"In this rare book about our divided times that's neither doom and gloom nor empty platitudes, Moni does a masterful job of acknowledging and grappling with the immensity of our divides, while also offering hope and an actionable road map for crossing them. This is a clear-eyed and refreshing read that'll leave you craving more."
—Annafi Wahed, cofounder of cross-partisan newsletter *The Flip Side*

"In this perceptive, wise, accessible book, Mónica shows us how to ask more humane questions of our fellow Americans. She shows us that by seeking truly to understand rather than judge, every one of us can improve our country's civic culture. Curiosity cures. Read this book, then live it."
—Eric Liu, CEO, Citizen University and author of *You're More Powerful Than You Think*

"In this warm and thoughtful book, Mónica offers a wonderfully simple recipe to heal our partisan divide: curiosity and conversation. We should all give her approach a try."
—Bill Adair, creator of the Pulitzer Prize–winning website PolitiFact

"If you sense something 'wrong' in the way we've come to interact, Mónica shows that you're right—and offers actionable guidance. This book offers more than new ways of bridging divides. It sparks a curious, higher-level way of thinking that supports healthier thoughts, emotions, relationships, and decisions. Highly recommended."
—Ellen Petry Leanse, Stanford University instructor, leadership coach, and author of the *The Happiness Hack*

"Books like this don't come along very often—and neither do writers like Mónica Guzmán. She has authored a tour de force that takes the reader deep into the reasons we are polarized, gives life to these reasons through compelling human stories, and uses her own fascinating life and career to illuminate our path toward a democracy of conviction, compassion, and curiosity."

—John Wood, Jr., national ambassador for
Braver Angels and host of the *John Wood Jr. Show*

"There aren't many books you can instantly apply to every frustrating conversation you're having, but that's exactly what Moni has given us with this brilliant, approachable, and enjoyable book. If you feel trapped by a dead-end conversation, or too tired and disillusioned to enter the fray, this book will help you see others, and yourself, with more curiosity and compassion than before."

—Buster Benson, author of *Why Are We Yelling?*

"Mónica Guzmán offers us a practical guide for a path forward: reclaiming an appreciation of the basic humanity of our fellow citizens and remaining open to the possibility that we can learn from people we differ from. Anyone who cares about healing our national conversation should read this book."

—Alexandra Hudson, author, speaker, and founder of Civic Renaissance

"At a time when Americans feel overwhelmed with toxic polarization, Mónica gives us a book we desperately need. In *I Never Thought of It That Way*, she elucidates the transformational power of curiosity, coupled with empathy, to change hearts and shows us practical ways to adopt these vital principles for the sake of a more perfect union."

—Nathan Bomey, author of *Bridge Builders*

"A treasure trove of proven tips to ward off toxic polarization in our everyday lives, this book is a gift for Americans hoping to rise above division and unlock the riches of conversation and relationships across differences. Moni's own raw and humorous experiences bring her wisdom to life and illuminate a better path for all of us."

—Pearce Godwin, founder of Listen First Project and the #ListenFirst Coalition

"This book will inspire you and warm your heart. It's our best book on this topic. With great wisdom, Mónica teaches us the skills to become better people and more patriotic Americans."

—David Blankenhorn, cofounder and president of Braver Angels

"In clear and lively exposition, Mónica Guzmán lays out how we have become unlikely and increasingly not interested in talking to people with whom we don't agree. It's hard to run a family, a school, or a democracy that way. Here we get no simple remedy, but a sensible, straight-talk toolkit. We need to return to our basic curiosity about what other people think and feel. That's our most human, most empathic, starting point."

—Sherry Turkle, MIT professor, *New York Times* best-selling
author of *Reclaiming Conversation* and *The Empathy Diaries*

"Our polarization isn't a condition that descended upon us and we must accept. It emerged from behaviors and emotions we can redirect. Mónica's tools for understanding without judgment are precisely the ones we need to build a bridge over the chasm—a bridge we must build if we value our democratic republic and our relationships with people we love and disagree with."

—Bill Bryant, former WA Republican gubernatorial candidate

"A vivid account of polarization by someone who has experienced the fracturing of our country more intimately than most, this beautifully crafted narrative takes you inside the most vexing political divisions and makes them understandable. Readers will appreciate the depth of connections Mónica created with her subjects, and the book's excellent recommendations about how to begin to repair our national divide."

—Dr. Christopher Bail, head of the Polarization Lab at
Duke University and author of *Breaking the Social Media Prism*

"Lots of books explain how to have hard conversations about politics, but this is the one you need to read—right now. It's honest, funny, surprising, and actionable. Take it to the beach; bring it on the bus. Hand it out at family reunions; leave it in your office cafeteria. There's no time to waste."

—Amanda Ripley, author of *High Conflict:
Why We Get Trapped and How We Get Out*

"Everyone is losing their minds, but good news—Mónica Guzmán can help us find them. Whether you're left, right, center, or you have had it with the tribes and labels, this book is your map out of the madness. All it takes is a few questions and the commonsense courage to see people as people—*not* monsters."

—Bridget Phetasy, writer, stand-up comedian, and host of the
YouTube program *Dumpster Fire* and podcast *Walk-Ins Welcome*

"Mónica's love of personal connection underpins this gentle, persuasive, and effective guide to better communication with people across vast ideological and personal divides. The lessons of this book will improve all your personal and professional relationships, guaranteed, and might even save America."

—Markos Moulitsas, founder of Daily Kos

"Mónica invites wonder into the gulfs that divide us—a revolutionary kind of wonder that beckons us to listen beyond sound bites and slogans to the stories that carry our shared humanity. *I Never Thought of It That Way* is an accessible and practical guide for how to imagine a future that leaves no one behind."

—Valarie Kaur, author of *See No Stranger* and founder of the Revolutionary Love Project

"The question of how we can heal as a nation is the question of our time. In *I Never Thought of It That Way*, Mónica has given us the tools for the only way I can see that happening: if we the people do it ourselves. I cannot imagine anyone who will not learn from and rejoice in this book."

—Tom Rosenstiel, best-selling author and Eleanor Merrill Visiting Professor at the University of Maryland

I NEVER THOUGHT OF IT THAT WAY

I NEVER THOUGHT OF IT THAT WAY

HOW TO HAVE FEARLESSLY CURIOUS CONVERSATIONS IN DANGEROUSLY DIVIDED TIMES

MÓNICA GUZMÁN

BenBella Books, Inc.
Dallas, TX

BenBella Books, Inc.
10440 N. Central Expressway
Suite 800
Dallas, TX 75231
benbellabooks.com
Send feedback to feedback@benbellabooks.com

BenBella is a federally registered trademark

Printed in the United States of America
10 9 8 7 6 5 4 3 2 1

Library of Congress Control Number: 2021039364
ISBN 9781637740323 (trade cloth)
ISBN 9781637740330 (ebook)

Editing by Claire Schulz
Copyediting by Scott Calamar
Proofreading by Lisa Story and Doug Johnson
Indexing by WordCo Indexing Services, Inc.
Text design and composition by PerfecType, Nashville, TN
Cover design and illustrations by Faceout Studio, Molly von Borstel
Interior illustrations by Haley Weaver
Printed by Lake Book Manufacturing

Special discounts for bulk sales are available.
Please contact bulkorders@benbellabooks.com.

To my bold and beautiful city of Seattle

*May we never stop growing
in our understanding
of each other*

AUTHOR'S NOTE

Division can get personal, especially when it complicates your relationships. I'm hugely grateful to everyone who's ever shared their personal story of polarization with me and helped me see truths about the issue that I couldn't have seen any other way. I have used just first names and in some cases pseudonyms in the interest of confidentiality. In a few cases, identifying details have also been changed to protect individuals' privacy.

CONTENTS

INTRODUCTION

On the morning of Election Day 2020, I was driving east from Seattle to my parents' house in Redmond, Washington, wondering if I should turn around.

About a week earlier, I'd asked my parents if I could watch the results of the presidential election from their house. Mom blinked over her plate of carnitas tacos from the food truck down the way. She looked at Dad, then back at me.

"*Claro*, Moni," she said in Spanish. *Of course, Moni.* Then her eyes held mine a moment, asking what I was silently asking myself: *But are you sure you want to?*

After all, I'm a liberal who voted for Joe Biden, and Mom and Dad are conservatives who voted enthusiastically—and twice, now—for Donald Trump.

I drove their way in silence, my hands gripping the steering wheel of the sturdy 2004 black Nissan Altima they sold me for a dollar when my Civic felt too clunky for our kids, a mere four months before Trump's 2016 victory shook the world. I preferred the too-loud rumble of the Altima's wheels on the road to any music that could make the day feel too normal. Would my parents end the day happy and relieved, or would I? Who would feel at home in our country tomorrow?

Up ahead, a big American flag waved by the conifers along the highway. Seeing it brought me back to my mother's naturalization ceremony twenty years earlier. "Did you notice I dressed in red, white, and blue?" Mom had texted this past Independence Day when Dad dug up and shared a family photo from the New Hampshire state courthouse. In the photo, Mom's in a red cardigan with white buttons and a blue skirt, clutching a small American flag as she poses next to me, my younger brother, and my dad, who'd been naturalized a month prior. I was seventeen then, my long hair draped over a purple sweater. Being under eighteen meant my brother and I were automatically naturalized along with our parents. It was our first family photo as American citizens. We were beaming.

Later that year, I slung my high school backpack off my shoulders in our home office to see a Bush-Cheney sign tacked to the bulletin board above Mom's desk. *Republicans?* I thought. *Really?* We erupted about Clinton's welfare policy one night, the spoons rattling in our gray Tupperware ice cream saucers when my hand hit our tile-top wooden table too hard. And I'll never forget the drive home from Hoyt's Newington Cinema 12 after seeing the Michael Moore documentary *Fahrenheit 9/11*. "Liberal bias? It's the truth!" I yelled in Spanish from the back seat, frustrated that house rules meant I couldn't use my bigger English vocabulary to trounce their puny arguments once and for all. I remember thinking then, *How could they not see?*—echoes of that long-ago conversation now filling the silence in the Altima.

By November 3, 2020, I'd found myself a new, strange party trick in true-blue Seattle: admitting to roomfuls of fellow liberals (after a swig of whatever drink is in my hand) that my parents—who I see most every weekend and call about everything from cooking tips to the kids' latest swim lesson—are "Mexican immigrants who voted for Trump."

It would always stun the room for a second. People needed time to square this reality with what they know of the wall on the southern border, the talk of Mexico sending rapists and criminals, all that seemed to them like an endless string of hostility aimed at immigrants from Latin America.

I'd watch and wait for someone to ask the first question left hanging in the air: "So, why did they vote that way?"

Then I'd feel their eyes probing me as, silently, they asked the other: *And why are you still speaking to them?*

With the stars and stripes long faded from my rearview, I steered the Altima into my parents' cul-de-sac, wondering, one last time, if I should just go home.

I parked the car in the driveway of their two-story Craftsman, inches from the closed garage. Grabbing my phone and overnight bag from the passenger seat, I stepped out of the Altima, passing on my way to their covered front porch the faded "Choose Life" bumper sticker Mom had stuck proudly on its left back bumper years ago, and that I, for reasons I don't fully understand, refused to scrape off.

I took a deep breath and rang the doorbell.

If there's one thing that most people on the left and right can agree on, it's that the way we treat and talk to the other side is broken. We can't stomach the ideas across the political divide, let alone the people who hold them. In one 2021 poll, most Americans thought the biggest threat to our country's way of life was "other people in America." By June, US voters rated "division in the country" as the number one issue facing them personally.

If you're reading this book right now—whether you consider yourself conservative, liberal, something in between, or something off that spectrum altogether—I bet you've wondered, as I have, how long we can hold it together while our differences threaten to wreck our relationships, our country, and our ability to share our lives, really, at all.

Maybe you're like Sophia, a woman in Boston who lost several deep friendships when she switched from supporting Hillary Clinton in 2016 to Donald Trump in 2020. Having grown up in a communist country, she sees something dark and destructive in the Left's agenda and is convinced that Joe Biden is an illegitimate president. "The facts are different, the values are different," she told me as she described her preferred solution: a Conservative States of America and a Liberal States of America. "Peaceful divorce might be the only way."

Or you might be more like Marcus, a young man in Portland who feels a spiritual connection to his nation's ideals and its imperfect pursuit of them. The results of the 2016 election threw him into a state of confounded despair that made him want to both reach conservatives and fight like hell for a country he sees them shoving toward authoritarianism. "That's where there's two modes in me," he told me. "It's the political vigilance and the need to understand."

Or is it Eddie you relate to, a man in rural Kentucky who told me he's tired of turning on the news to "watch them lecture me on what kind of racist I am"? The way he sees it, the liberal mainstream media are responsible for the hate he sees tearing America apart, and he feels helpless to stop it. "They don't consider us human beings," he said.

I could hardly believe what I heard from Barbara in Knoxville, Tennessee, a mother of five grown men whose families got so fired up clashing over politics at her 2017 Thanksgiving dinner, it was like a bomb went off. One of her sons is very conservative, another very liberal, a third and fourth moderately conservative and liberal, respectively, and a fifth son is more centrist. Yes, really. "I think my family is a microcosm of the country," she told me.

Barbara, who describes herself as a conservative libertarian Christian, had tried to keep the peace that holiday. "Can't we just have a nice family dinner?" she'd begged. When she walked through her house to survey the damage, one young family was packing up to leave early, two of her sons had stormed off, a pair of her daughters-in-law were comforting each other in the kitchen, and a third, then six months pregnant, sat crying on a low brick wall out back while Barbara's two-year-old granddaughter patted her mother's hand, saying, "Everything's gonna be all right."

"I went out to the mom with the little girl, and you know what she said?" Barbara recounted to me. "She smiled and she said, 'You know, when anything happens to her, I hold *her* and pat *her* and say, *Everything's gonna be all right.* That's what I do for *her*!'"

I didn't meet Sophia, Marcus, Eddie, or Barbara thanks to friends or family. We connected instead through our shared determination to find some answer to the challenges these dangerously divided times present in our lives.

Determination can turn easily into desperation, which is how I opened my email one day to find a new message in my inbox from a man named Leo. Opening the email, I learned that Leo is liberal and that he lives in rural Montana. After a series of quickly escalating text messages from his conservative son about several heated political issues, he explained, his son had just told him that he didn't want him in his life anymore, that he was afraid he might indoctrinate his kids.

Leo had seen a talk I'd given about my politically divided family the day after the 2020 election and reached out. "I really don't know where to turn," he wrote.

But somehow, he'd found his way to me.

Each story I hear from Americans of all political stripes about the ways these divides are pulling them apart—each of the fallings-out, the declined invitations, the tweetstorms, the dialed-up villainy, *all* these ways that people are no longer speaking to people—brings me face-to-face with that question:

Why am *I still speaking to them?*

Even after the tense three-hour conversation about race and law enforcement with Mom in June 2020 where neither of us changed our minds. Even after the two-hour argument with Dad about how the White House handled the coronavirus pandemic where I definitely went too far and he was about as mad as I'd ever seen him. Even after all that, why am I not only *speaking* to my parents, who are way on the other side of a political divide, but listening to them, learning from them, and enjoying their company?

And why, when I say that my parents are Mexican immigrants who voted for Trump, do I not say the rest of it? Why am I both eager and afraid to tell my fellow Seattle liberals that I not only speak to my parents, but that I understand them? That if I were them, I would have voted for Donald Trump, too?

I hear people say the answer to all this division is more education and information—but *trustworthy* information, not that other junk. I hear them say the answer is persuasion, that no conversation is worth having with someone who disagrees with you if you're not challenging their ideas and trying to show them where they're wrong. I hear them say the answer is simply action: stop yammering and do something to build a more sensible world, ignoring or defeating whoever's standing in your way.

I say an answer, though it might include all these things, won't give us what we need. What we need are more questions.

As a journalist, I've asked a lot of those. I used to be awful at it; I still remember my terror as a kid the day Mom *made* me march up to the cashier at the Burger King near our house and ask for another packet of salt. What if I sounded stupid? It took all my courage at my first newspaper internship just to pick up the phone and call a stranger. My heart would stop when I heard their voice.

But then I fell in love with what they could show me.

Given the chance to ask anything I wanted about who people are, what they do, or what they think, I realized what for years I'd been too petrified to notice: everybody's so goddamn *interesting*. I stopped being afraid to ask questions; I was too impatient to hear the answers. Soon I developed an incurable addiction to people—our stories, our passions, the totally unique way each of us sees the world—and to conversation itself, that unpredictable meeting of minds where individuals with wildly different lives can surprise, delight, and ultimately learn from each other.

It didn't occur to me until recently, but every one of my now thousands of interviews was something everyone craves but rarely encounters: a conversation bent on understanding without judgment. In the best ones I was in a state of hyper-observation, desperate to see someone's perspective so fully—in an hour or two—that I might have a *chance* at passing it on, real and intact, to strangers. It didn't matter what side of an issue someone was on. I had to know why they saw their world in whatever way they saw it—whether it was the young Muslim girls in Michigan whose lives turned upside down after 9/11, the small business owner in New Hampshire who was obsessed with vintage lunch boxes, or the man in Texas who was con-victed of killing two taxicab drivers and told me, two weeks before I would witness his execution, that he didn't do it. I found myself walking alongside him, her, them, *everyone* through their vastly different stories—my heart so stunned, giddy, or broken I couldn't hide it; my initial judgments so distant, they grew faint; and my mind so locked on *learning* that it could take all my restraint, in the heat of conversation, not to shout a question like a demand.

One of my favorite questions to ask in any interview is, "Why *you*?" Why did *you* start a church in a bar, become your community's most beloved nurse, or decide to study crows for a living, and not, you know, somebody else? So I guess I should answer that question for myself. Why did *I* write this book about how to stay curious across divides, and why should you bother to read it?

If I can sum up the work I've done in my seventeen years of listening to people professionally, I'd say it's been one big, evolving experiment on how we can better understand each other. I don't do it for fun, though it's the most fun I've ever had. I do it because connecting with other humans is what makes our lives rich and meaningful. Especially when so much can pull us apart.

Seeing people across divides seems daunting, so I've tried over the years to make it inviting. In Seattle I fell in with the young, booming, all-things-are-possible tech crowd, demystifying its magic and mayhem in my jour-nalism. Then I pivoted as the runaway growth warped the city I'd grown to love and divided us over red-hot crises around class, density, homeless-ness, the works. I found myself joining eager partners to span what divides we could—young and old, rich and poor, local and transplant, housed and homeless—with stories, yes, but also dinners, outings, events, whatever might get us to see past the caricatures. When the political divide became too big to ignore, we organized a bus trip to bridge urban and rural America in a way that seemed impossible until it happened. That visit still echoes, years later, for several participants—and it changed everything for me.*

---

* And you'll read more about it in Chapter Eight!

I began to see political polarization as the problem that eats other problems, the monster who convinces us that the monsters are us. I saw its claws everywhere—in my city, in my networks, in the assumptions we were making about people we didn't know who'd made choices we didn't understand. I tried to call it out, but I could barely find the words. And with so much to fight for in the world—the movements and conflicts shaping and challenging us—who would listen?

But I wasn't alone. One after the other I stumbled onto fresh projects working to fix this—to name it, confront it, and find the tools to overcome it. I began to participate in ongoing conversations, workshops, and experiments about how to cross the political divide, then I began to advise them. I got to know a growing and downright inspiring network of people who also refuse to believe that we're helpless against this beast of a divide, who know that it's our job—*all* our jobs—to find a better way. And in 2021, I joined the leadership of a project that's become the largest grassroots, cross-partisan organization in the country dedicated to political *de*polarization—a project called Braver Angels.

Coming from the field of journalism, I feel like I'm supposed to be rah-rah for information as the cure for everything. But I'm not. I'm tired of us throwing out links and throwing up our hands. Ranting to *our* people, who get it, while raging at *those* people, who don't. I'm done, too, going along with the idea that if we could just rid the world of "misinformation," everything would be fine. As if mowing down weeds would keep new ones from sprouting. False stories soar because good people relate to something in them that's *true*: a fear or value or concern that's going unheard, unexplored, and unacknowledged. Every time? Yes, every time! Why do we ignore that?

I think of my mother, who was so afraid I'd lose my perfect Spanish living in the United States that too often, her first response to something heavy and vulnerable I'd tell her as a teenager was to correct something I'd gotten wrong in my grammar. I'd howl, "You're not hearing me!" She'd snap out of it, apologize, and try again—listening not for my words or how well I followed some rule but for my own unique *meaning*.

We know what happens when the people we love don't think we really see them: they go find someone who will. Someone who might exploit that basic need we all have to belong, to matter. We're desperate to correct the lies that make bad divisions worse. I get it; I am, too. But we're missing something big here. Misinformation isn't the product of a culture that doesn't value truth. It's the product of a culture in which we've grown too afraid to turn to each other and hear it.

None of this seems right to me. More to the point: none of it seems curious. I see us treat our curiosity—our built-in hunger for understanding—like it's a sweet little muse, like it just *happens* to us, flitting by when we're joyfully inspired. No. Curiosity is big and it is badass. At its weakest, it keeps our minds open so they don't shrink. At its strongest, it whips us into a frenzy of unstoppable learning. Take it from the once-shy inquirer at countless charged conversations. Nothing busts through the walls we've built between us like a question so genuine and perceptive it cannot be denied. Nothing.

Our monster of a divide, meet our brawny beast of curiosity.

I'll let you two take it from here.

✶✶✶

At my parents' place on Election Day 2020, the three of us watched the results of the presidential race stream in on Fox News, then CNN, then back and forth for hours. We had our first shouting match, about immigration, over sips of the sangrias Mom mixed. We had a bigger one, about race, late into the night, with me standing cross-armed in front of the TV, Mom taking my side for a fun, hot second, and usually reserved Dad leaning forward in his recliner, not giving an inch, his voice booming.

Earlier in the day, on a walk with Dad around their neighborhood, he told me about something that happened to him the previous week.

He'd gone out with his camera—he's a bird photographer, and a good one—and run into a fellow photographer he recognized from Instagram whose work he loves. They got to chatting, and out of nowhere the photographer insulted Trump in that buddy-buddy way that made it abundantly clear to my dad that the photographer assumed that he, too, couldn't stand him. A Seattle-area Latino with a Mexican accent? It wouldn't be the first time.

My Dad slowed down as he told me the next part: He nodded along with what the guy was saying. In fact, he said, looking down at the pebbled path, he heard himself mock his own conservative beliefs along with the other photographer.

This hung in the air between us a bit. I thought about how hard it must've been for Dad—a guy who will not be talked out of his midday nap, let alone any of his opinions—to hear himself *lie* like that.

"You know, Mónica," he said in Spanish, breaking the silence, "I've heard that some people who don't share their parents' politics . . . they stop letting them see their grandkids. And I've wondered if that'll ever happen to us."

I have two kids, now eight and six years old, and they see their grandparents all the time. My dad's written *songs* for them. Songs he plays on his guitar and they memorize then launch into singing at full volume from the back seat of my Altima when I least expect it. I didn't hesitate. *"Jamás,"* I told Dad. *Never.* "That'll never happen, Dad. That'll never, *ever* happen to us."

Back at their house, after all the night's results had been reported and we had one more political clash about . . . well, who *knows* what it was about, I was sitting at their kitchen island eating butter pecan ice cream Mom had served me in the same little gray Tupperware cups I'd used as a kid.

By the time I picked up the last bite, Mom had changed into her long red nightshirt. She sat down next to me, patted my hand, and said she was glad I'd come. I put down my spoon. I was glad I'd come, too. Neither of us knew who'd won, whose views would hold sway in the months and years to come. But I was grateful that for that moment, at least, it didn't matter.

So here we all are, folks. Crossing paths in a stuck world that's ready for something different—but what? I've been wrestling with the possibilities for years now without realizing it: stumbling onto people and their bottomless stories, following this compulsion to help us come together and understand each other precisely where it's hard, and always, in the background, loving and learning from parents whose politics are at constant war with my own.

All of that, plus watching our world lurch and stagger through its challenges, with everyone from leaders to neighbors weaving their disparate threads into *knots* but trying really hard not to—kept me coming back to one question: What is keeping us from *seeing* each other, and how do we get it (the hell) out of our way?

I've spent some time now studying—OK, *agitating* over this question, and gathering the tools and techniques we need to address it.

So here's my promise: This book will equip and inspire you to be *one level* more curious about people who disagree with you than you have ever been. It shares a set of tools I've developed and road-tested in countless conversations—tools to help you find more answers by asking more powerful questions. Questions that bridge the divides you want to span in your life—whether that's to the friend you've been afraid to talk to about a contentious issue, to your in-laws you know vote differently than you do, or to your acquaintances who share strong opinions on social media—and not the ones you don't.

How do we see different people around us more clearly?

We see people, first, by putting a check on three dynamics that make us turn away from anyone who's too different from us, even when we don't mean to. In Part I, **SOS**, we'll confront these dynamics—sorting, othering, and siloing—and explore a powerful way to overcome them.

We see people by talking *with* them, not just about them, and mining the boundary between our diverging perspectives for fresh angles on truth. In Part II, **Curiosity**, we'll learn how to notice and fill the gaps in our understanding by unleashing our curiosity in the context where it's most powerful—conversation. Whether you want to talk, text, video chat, or go at it on social media, I'll show you how to create the best conditions for an exchange worth having, and how to build enough traction with each other to discover mind-blowing insights together.

We see people by looking *past* our lazy guesses, pushy opinions, and overwhelming desire to win. In Part III, **People**, we'll explore what it looks like to turn your assumptions into questions, your opinions into starting points, and your no doubt unassailable capacity to reason your way to *your* views into an on-ramp for understanding how other people reason their way to *theirs*.

We see people by peering behind their views to the paths they walked to get to them. In Part IV, **Paths**, we'll learn how illuminating it can be to get curious about people's experiences and values. I'll show you how you can ask questions that turn people into storytellers—yourself included—and how to recognize the attachments to identities or beliefs that might keep you from seeing other perspectives fully.

Finally, we see people by getting their meaning *right*. In Part V, **Honesty**, I'll show you how to prioritize candor and clarity in your conversations so thoroughly that not even the most charged political trigger words can knock you off course. And when they do—there's always a way to get back on track. Especially with your own powerful question, which I'll show you how to ask anytime, anywhere.

Along with all these tools, I offer stories and insights that I hope can help you find *your own powerful reason* to have one more conversation with someone who confounds you, or ask one more bold, curious question. Maybe you choose just this once to join a risky exchange instead of sitting it out, to ask something you've always been afraid to ask, or to spend one more open-minded moment with opposing voices you'd normally dismiss or avoid.

My bet is that that one conversation, that one question, that one moment, will crack doors in your mind you'll want to do more to push open.

To be clear: This book is *not* about converting people to your side. It's not about persuasion or crafting better arguments—though it will help you hear and be heard better than you might have thought possible.

It'll be a bumpy ride, but a thrilling one. Even if you're already sold on everything curiosity offers, a lot of things—including your own hardwired human instincts—will do their darnedest to tell you that you already know everything you need to know about what *those other people* think. Curiosity is a bit of a rebellious act these days, but don't worry. This is a fight you can actually win.

If I've arrived at one conviction in all my work, it's that the barriers between us are lower than we think. Ultimately, this book is about *seeing*, and seeing clearly in divided times, *through* conversations with different people rather than in spite of them.

Where did that spite come from? That's where we begin . . .

Part I

SOS

OK, so here's the issue: you and I are stumbling around a confounding world because we are too divided to see it clearly.

I blame three things for this, three patterns in how we relate to each other. They come from human nature (so we'll never be rid of them, boo!). But we can totally hack them if we know what we're doing (so we're still the boss of them, yay!). They can get the better of us if we let them, and we need to know how they work to stop them from warping, well, everything.

The first pattern is about who we like to be around. There's no mystery to this—we like to be around people who are like us. People who share things in common with us. People who make us smile, keep us comfortable, and aren't getting us all mad or nervous.

The second pattern is about who we *don't* like to be around. These folks are opposed to us in some way. They annoy us, or stand against us, or disagree on something that matters. We push off from them, and the distance feels good, and right.

The third is about the things we say and hear. How we explain our worlds to each other, the signals that reach us and don't, and how we sink, over time, into a hole where our attitudes are reinforced instead of challenged, particularly about what those *other* people think.

Split up into steps, the patterns above go like this:

- We get together into groups. We'll call this **sorting**.

- We push off against groups that seem opposed to us. We'll call this **othering**.

- We sink deeper into our groups and our stories, where it's harder to hear anything else. We'll call this **siloing**.

Now I'm no fan of the mess these patterns are making, but I can't trash them outright. We humans are social creatures, and sorting, othering, and siloing give us comfort when things are crazy. We want affirmation. We want clear friends and enemies—who's with us and who's against us. Most of all, we want answers. Answers that let us move from one day to the next knowing that no matter what's breaking the world today, we're going to be fine tomorrow. Or at least, we'll still be in good company.

But there's just no question that sorting, othering, and siloing are an **SOS**. A call for help. They're blinding us to each other's perspectives, turning our neighbors, friends, and relatives into fools and monsters, and cranking up the volume way too high on what is already a cacophony of information that drowns out so much else.

To put it as plainly as I can, sorting, othering, and siloing are steering us away from reality. It's nice to be comfortable in a scary time and certain in an unsure one. But at what cost?

In Part I, I'm going to tell you why these three patterns in how we relate to each other make it harder for us to see the world around us. I'll tell you why they're built-in features of our very social lives, and how they can work against us, warping our gaze beyond our own limited perspective.

We'll start at ground zero for human relations: a simple little house party.

1

Sorting

I f there's one law of human nature that rules them all these days, it's that it's way, *way* easier to like people who are like us.

Every networking event, random get-together, or mixed-bag house party of friends, acquaintances, and total strangers is a game you win by finding your people. Or at least, a few folks to smile with for a while. That takes a little chitchat. The kind that starts on easy common ground (weather, traffic, the delicious chips and dip) and pokes and prods from there, probing for connection.

When you know and like someone, conversations pick up where you left off. You steer the discussion to topics and ideas you know will be interesting or useful. You remember what ground you've covered before and how fun it was (or wasn't). You have the benefit of a shared path and some trust. You've practiced.

When you don't know someone, conversations are all about one thing: discovery. They're one big mutual search. You're looking for interesting thoughts to pass the time, sure, but also for that bedrock slab of commonality on which you could build more than just some chatter. Every now and then, you'll find it. Most of the time, you won't.

Think about the last time you were in a social scene surrounded by strangers. You approach someone, and your brain makes a million silent assumptions based on how a person looks, moves, talks. You start with a baseline, something you know you have in common because you're both here, how: *How do you know the host? Did you try the pretzels?* Or: *It's chilly out there, right?*

When the cheap, easy chuckles die down, it's on to level two: original conversation. You strike a few matches, see what lights: *What keeps you busy? I like that jacket! Did you hear about [fill in carefully selected news headline]? What part of town are you in?*

At a friend's housewarming party, I'm on minute three of a chat with a woman I bumped into in the hallway. We're channel surfing from weather to traffic to nice things about the party host and nothing's catching on. I mention my kids; her eyes glaze over. She mentions her cats (I'm allergic to cats); we both shoot a glance at the snacks on the console table.

A burst of laughter from the kitchen breaks the growing awkwardness between us, and I'm grateful. Some people are too different to find common ground with quickly. My stamina wanes when I have to force a smile I don't feel, holding up the face muscles that takes,* because they won't hold up themselves. I mumble something about a drink, she mumbles something about the pretzels, and we drift off, each finding our way, within moments, to people who are easier to talk to.

OUR SORTED LIVES

Finding and huddling up around *our people* is, demographically, what social scientists call "sorting."

If you think of human interaction like our house party, with friends and strangers bumping into each other and either bonding or not, sorting is what happens at hour three, when everyone's found their favorite group and hasn't moved for at least twenty minutes. Conversations are flowing, drinks

---

* The main muscles that pull up your smile have a killer name: zygomaticus.

are emptying, and each group starts to build its own voice and culture. The clowns in the kitchen are trading jokes. The thinkers in the living room are onto their third brainy debate. Outside on the deck they're kicking a ball around, trading slow stories, and gazing at the stars.

We go near people who share our interests for reasons we feel and know and appreciate. Sorting makes us happier, less bothered, more content, and more linked.

Being alike connects us. The fancy term for one force behind this is "homophily," literally the love of sameness. Sociologists also refer to it as the "birds of a feather" phenomenon.

Good bonds are good for us. How good? We are twice as likely to die prematurely when we have weak relationships as when we have strong ones, according to one 2009 study. We bond more easily with people who are like us. So hey—we're going to hang with similarish people and it's no big deal. Think of everything it serves up: a fun chat at a party. Fast-forming friendships. Or the algorithmic efficiency of online dating. Yay.

Plus, when we surround ourselves with similar people, we get the benefit of facing fewer moments where we reckon with our judgment of other people's decisions—or their judgment of ours. We all know how that feels. You love all things meaty and spend time with someone who's a strict vegetarian—or vice versa. You might be close with that person, but every shared meal is a potential reminder of that difference between you, and you have to do a little work in the background to suppress the temptation to judge, doubt, or distance.

"I am because we are," goes the Ubuntu proverb. We crave community and connection. Sorting makes it easy. How could that possibly be bad?

~~~~

For an obvious, current example of sorting, mosey on over to your nearest US map. More specifically, any map of county-level electoral results from this millennium.

Urban areas lean more Democratic and are conventionally shaded blue. Rural areas lean more Republican and are conventionally shaded red. The color code is so familiar now we don't think about it. And sorting goes deeper than the state or county, all the way down to the neighborhood level. Just one in every eight of my thousand closest neighbors in Seattle is Republican, according to fascinating address-level research released in 2021. For 25 million voters around the country, daily life is even more politically segregated. Those voters—so about 12 percent of the American electorate—live in places like parts of blue Columbus, Ohio, and red Gillette, Wyoming, where just *one in ten* of their neighbors is with the other side. One in ten! It's the result of complex demographic shifts over decades, combined with that simple truth that like attracts like.

But as we know, the "red" and "blue" areas of these maps don't just show a difference in what political parties people vote for. Along with geography, loads of other identities—religion, race, ideology—fall unofficially under the banner of red and blue, not to mention a preference for things like walkable neighborhoods (trends Democrat) or bigger single-family homes (trends Republican). The associations aren't airtight, but we see them often enough to make assumptions: Republicans are more Christian, white, and conservative. Democrats are more non-Christian, nonwhite, and liberal.

To be clear, there's not a ton of hard evidence that people are straight-up *choosing* to live where their neighbors share their politics (or getting the heck out of Dodge when they don't), but it wouldn't make much difference. So much of who we are and what we like just so happens to line up with a certain party affiliation—like wanting to live in a dense neighborhood near plenty of coffee shops versus wanting to spread out in a roomier lot near plenty of churches—that we end up politically sorted anyway. This makes sorting a much more powerful force than we think: move closer to people who are like you in one way, and you'll find yourself surrounded by people who are like you in *all* the ways.

This is a big deal. I have said that we are "dangerously" divided. One reason we're dangerously divided is because when so many of the identities and preferences that matter to us line up with our politics, it changes how we *feel* our politics.

It makes politics way more personal.

Think back to how you felt when your side won or lost the last presidential election. If you're like a lot of Americans—particularly if your identities and preferences lined up more or less neatly with your politics—it probably felt either really good or really bad. Maybe even better or worse than you felt about elections with similar outcomes in the past. These red/blue identity stacks—what political scientists call "mega-identities"—play a part in that.

"Each election becomes, not just, you know, 'Well the Democrats lost, so what a bummer, you know, because my party lost,'" explains political scientist Lilliana Mason. "Instead, it's like, 'Well, my party lost, so that means my racial group and my religious group and my cultural group, and all the people that I know and all the people that I watch on TV, everything that I know, everything that makes up who I think I am, it's all gone. I lost it all.

---

* At least, not that you could trace to social science research! But our world's changing fast, and I've heard stories. One "blue" I know sold his and his wife's vacation home and left a rural area because he overheard neighbors at a barbecue spouting what he saw as vile rumors about the Clintons. And sentiments like this one, from a "red" I'm connected to, are hardly rare: "I will self-segregate as soon as I can. I definitely don't want all my neighbors to be white, but I don't want *any* of them to be blue."

I have nothing left inside of my sense of who I am . . . The more things that get involved in each election, the more vulnerable our self-esteem is.'"

In other words, if what just happened is that your side lost an election, and what it *feels* like just happened is that you lost big meaningful chunks of your*self*, it's going to affect the way you look at things. Or rather, how things look to you. And they are going to look *really* bad.

But wait, Moni, you might be thinking. *Haven't things like ideology, religion, and race* always *lined up behind one political party or another?*

Not quite. Especially not all grouped together like this.

Republicans are so overwhelmingly conservative and Democrats so overwhelmingly liberal that we use those labels interchangeably these days. But as recently as the 1970s, there were plenty of liberal Republicans and conservative Democrats.* Between 1972 and 2000, as Mason illustrates in her book *Uncivil Agreement*, identification between Democrats and liberals shot up 24 percentage points, and identification between Republicans and conservatives went up 35 percentage points. Our party and ideological affiliations have joined forces ever since.

The same kind of thing happened with religion and with race. In 1972, the religious divide between Democrats and Republicans, such as it was, hinged on the question of whether you identified as Catholic (leans Democratic) or Protestant (leans Republican). By 2012, when 14 percentage points divided Republicans and Democrats on the question of whether they attended religious services each week, it was whether you were religious at all. As for race, in 2012, Republicans were on average 30 percentage points more white, Mason charts, and Democrats were 21 percentage points more Black.

---

* Just to be clear on terms here, I'm thinking of a "liberal" as someone who puts a high value on promoting social opportunity and equality, protecting civil and human rights, and empowering government to do what it can to take care of its citizens, and of a "conservative" as someone who puts a high value on promoting personal responsibility, free markets, a mighty national defense, and a limited government that stays out of the way so people have space to take care of themselves.

So what sparked the stacking? A crisis of confidence. Back in the 1960s and '70s, as the political scientist Robert Putnam famously laid out in his classic book *Bowling Alone*, people's trust in government, political parties, and all kinds of institutions took a nosedive. They grew isolated from the civic organizations that shaped their lives. So they detached from them and looked for what any of us look for when we need to find our people—sameness.

The giant house party of our nation did its work. People started settling into more demographically homogenous communities. And like the raucous, bonded groups in the kitchen or out on the deck, the strongest cultures of place become beacons for whoever else would get a kick out of joining them.

Which brings us to the present day and our increasingly digital world, where the story of sorting arrives at its challenging twist: you can get up close to *all kinds* of people online, no matter where they are in the physical world, and spend loads more time with them digitally than you could in meatspace.

It adds up to an easier life. And a more easily warped view of the world around you.

Social media platforms give us way, way more freedom to curate our social lives than we get in the real world. Unlike those pesky *real* neighborhoods where we can't control who we're going to run into or when, we can curate our social media "neighborhoods" to include whoever we want. No matter where they are in the physical world, they're a click away in the digital one. It's like attracts like, without the expensive moving trucks or the long-term commitments. It's personalized. It's portable. It's sorting at its most efficient.

And we spend a good bit of time taking advantage of that.

As of 2021, 72 percent of US adults used at least one social media platform. On the most popular platform, Facebook, nearly three-quarters of users log in at least once a day. Those of you who use social media regularly know it's not a quick five minutes. If you're like me, you can get so lost in them—against your own will, even—that you lose any sense of time itself.

And no wonder. The platforms use the "birds of a feather" phenomenon to keep our attention as long as possible. They rely on our love of sameness (and our suspicion of others . . . more on that later) to predict what we want based on who we are. And every post we like, group we join, and profile feature we edit help them recommend more voices like the ones we already follow, more groups like the ones we're already in.

The algorithms' choices seem so useful and so natural—*it feels good to find our people, dang it!*—we start to think that chasing sameness is the best way to live.

But if we want to see the world how it really is, and not how our sorted lives make it *feel*, it can't be.

WHEN SORTING GOES TOO FAR: CANCELLED COLLISIONS

My all-time least favorite sorting story stars a guy named Newt Gingrich.

I'd turn on CNN Headline News after finishing my homework in junior high and see the former Speaker of the House rage against something, usually the Democrats. It was like the World Wrestling Federation matches my brother would watch on lazy Saturdays. Bad-mouth the opponent to the cameras. Talk up the game. Exaggerate with abandon. Except the wrestlers were bulky actors in spandex and Gingrich was a public servant in a suit. He's supposed to be working with his fellow legislators, following the civic script I learned in school, not giving them Hulk Hogan's Atomic Leg Drop. Right?

Whether you admire Gingrich or can't stand him, you have to admit he did something pretty amazing back in 1994. He helped Republicans win control of Congress for the first time in *forty years*. This "Republican Revolution" was a big deal. For decades, Republican legislators could do little *but* compromise with Democrats. Now here was their chance to change the game—and change it they did. Led by Gingrich, Republicans banded together, sharing talking points for the cameras and finding new and sharper opportunities to attack their opposition—who, of course, found their own new opportunities to attack back. It made all American politics that followed more showy, intense, high-octane stuff. It did to DC what the movie *Jaws* did to Hollywood: usher in the blockbuster.

But it cost us. Gingrich hoped Republicans wouldn't squander the advantage they had finally won, and he rushed to fortify the party. At the same time, he doubled down on a widespread and growing sentiment that it was a bad idea for lawmakers to live full-time where they worked—in Washington, DC.

The argument made sense. The DC political scene seemed slimy and out of touch to a lot of Americans—all back rooms and shady deals, with little connection to their real lives and concerns. So Gingrich made one of the most consequential changes to the culture of Congress in the institution's history. He changed its workweek from five days to three in 1995, encouraging his Republican Congresspeople to stay in their home states and *not* relocate with their families to the capital. Instead, the members would commute to DC weekly for three crammed days of federal business. Staying in their home states kept them closer to their constituents, which was noble in its own right and very handy both for fundraising and for fending off every ambitious legislator's worst nightmare—a primary challenge from a homegrown candidate who might seem more "in touch." But it greatly reduced the chance to build personal relationships with their colleagues in the opposition—Democratic legislators in DC.

There was a partisan perk in all this: The separation helped both parties build their own muscle and power. It made it easier for legislators to talk tough about the other party and build more loyalty within their own. They could go across the aisle like pro wrestlers enter the ring: ready for a fight. But it also made the idea of working with the other side—or even really listening to them—a lot less appealing.

Almost thirty years later, hardly any members of Congress—Republican or Democrat—live in the DC area full-time. Think about that: in the nation's capital, where just about half of any legislator's colleagues might be members of the other party, most legislators fly in, speed through a packed schedule, then fly home. Some legislators *do* carve out time for cross-partisan networking, so I don't want to overstate this. But before the change to the congressional workweek, there was a community around Capitol Hill that crossed party lines—made up of legislators and their families—and today there is not. There were dinners, carpools to their kids' baseball practice, and friendships that supported the working relationships our elected officials need to get creative on our behalf. Former Democratic representative David Skaggs of Colorado and former Republican representative Bob Livingston of Louisiana had a "good working relationship" on the House Appropriations Committee not because they agreed a bunch—they didn't—but because their spouses were good friends.

You can't bump into people if you're rarely around them. Now, spontaneous cross-partisan socializing in Congress, though not extinct, is largely a thing of the past. Our supposedly deliberative government sorted itself out of one of the baseline ingredients to good deliberation: spending time with people who don't think the same way you do. And even, yes, disagree.

Why is it so important to be around people we don't agree with? There's a famous story in the business world about Alfred P. Sloan, the CEO of General Motors. "I take it we're all in complete agreement on the decision here," Sloan once said, looking around a conference table at the members of one of his top committees. Everyone looked back and nodded. "Then I propose we postpone further discussion of this matter until our next meeting," he continued, "to give ourselves time to develop disagreement and perhaps gain understanding of what the decision is all about."

This is one of those stories that—as soon as I heard it—made me pine for a chance to reenact it just because it's so damn smart. In asking his staff to "develop disagreement," Sloan wasn't asking them to find things to fight about. He was asking them to look longer and harder at something they weren't really seeing. That's what happens when you're surrounded by people who share your gut instincts: You end up sharing your blind spots, too. And when the whole group has the same blind spots? You'll amp up each other's ignorance and make bad decisions even more spectacularly together than each of you would have apart.

Now imagine what happens when fewer and fewer Americans find themselves in politically "disagreeable" company. 'Cause presidential election data by county shows us that's exactly what's been going on.

There are 3,143 counties (or county-equivalent areas)—as distinguished from electoral districts—in the United States. A "landslide county," to election data nerds, is a county where the winner topped the vote by at least 20 percentage points *more* than the overall national tally. Meaning, the vote split in a landslide county was 20 points more split than in the nation overall.

In the 1980 presidential election, there were 391 landslide counties. So about 12 percent of US counties broke for the winning candidate by more than 20 points over the national result. In the 2000 election, 600 counties met that bar.

Then by 2020, that number had nearly *tripled* to a whopping 1,726 landslide counties. That's 55 percent of all the counties in the United States where politics leans way far in one party's direction.

2000

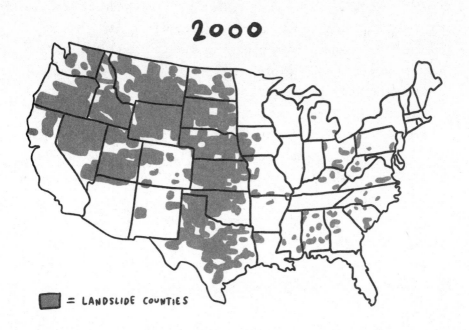

= LANDSLIDE COUNTIES

2020

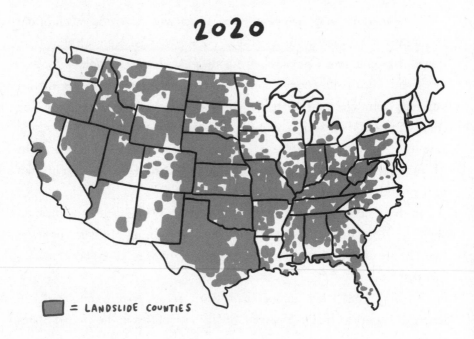

☐ = LANDSLIDE COUNTIES

But counties, schmounties, right? Sixty-five of our least populous counties have less than one person living there per square mile. So how many people are we talking about here? What percentage of US voters actually live in all these counties where politics has ended up being so one-sided?

The answer—for the 2020 election—was 35 percent. Up from just 4 percent in the 1980 election.

"If it feels like Republicans and Democrats are living in different worlds, it's because they are," the *Wall Street Journal* concluded. "There are few places left in America where one tribe of voters is likely to encounter the other. Predominantly white, rural areas are solid Republican; urban areas are dominated by Democrats."

When you're surrounded by people who reflect the same basic set of perspectives, you'll find it harder to grasp any others. Not because you're incapable of grasping them. But just because you're less likely to be given the chance.

Sorting goes too far when the people around us shape so much of our thinking—it stops being thinking at all. And when we stop colliding with people who disagree, even in casual ways, we miss opportunities to see a different angle on something, get a complex picture of a complex problem, or simply turn the volume down—even just for a clarifying minute—on whatever is stressing us out.

Of course, sorting into groups of like-minded people is only one of the things that keeps us from seeing the world clearly. We leap into our groups, happy and agreeable.

And then we turn our attention to those *other* people.

And things get a little dark.

2

Othering

Can there be an *us* without a *them*?

Though it's a natural enough question to ask, the first time I heard it was from my friend Brian Stout, the founding curator of a group of community connectors I'm part of called Building Belonging. It's been bouncing around my head ever since.

Every action has an equal and opposite reaction—so says Newton's third law of motion. Does it apply here, too? Every time we unite around what's similar, do we end up uniting against what's different?

Sorting is the complex, almost invisible process by which we end up close to people who are like us. When we push off from people who are *not* like us in some way that matters, disparaging them as a result, that's "othering."

Othering is about opposition. Wariness. Suspicion. It ranges from relatively harmless othering—drawing group boundaries, if you will—to hateful and deadly. From real subtle, like giving the side-eye to the group of loudmouths at the house party, to real explicit: xenophobia, genocide, all the biggest sins of humanity.

As with sorting, though, othering rarely goes that far, and hey, there are upsides! It feels *good* to bond against an opponent—to fight, win, and

even connect across unrelated differences so we don't have to face the enemy alone. Countless righteous wars and movements have proved it, over and over. Not to mention our most popular high-stakes fiction. You know the 1996 movie *Independence Day*, when the whole world forgets its squabbles and works together to bring down a *fleet of killer aliens bent on our destruction?*[*] The story's super fake, but the lesson is all too real: othering can save the day when it rallies us against a shared threat.

And boy do we feel threatened. By politics? Sure. More than half of Americans felt at least somewhat anxious about "the impact of politics on my daily life" in 2018, and a month before the 2020 election, nine out of ten registered voters, from both parties, thought a win by the other side would do "lasting harm" to our country. Living in politically sorted spaces around people who are all worried about the same things didn't exactly calm us down.

Not to say there hasn't been plenty to worry about—with our democracy, our health, our future, the works! One mental health service provider found that in 2020—the year that the global coronavirus pandemic and that hella stressful election raised the stakes on so much for so many—one in six

---

* All hail '90s blockbusters!

people had entered therapy for the first time. We're on edge, it shows, and it helps to think that *they* keep making it all so much worse.

But here's the thing: Too often, othering makes monsters of good people. It makes hate easier and reasonableness harder. As we'll see, it takes very little to spark. Almost nothing, really. And it twists our senses so we can't see what's really in front of us, so everything is colored by the need to win.

Once we have an *us*, we're pretty hardwired to find a *them*—and we suspend our goodwill and even our good sense in the process.

Two famous old social psychology studies get cited lots for everything they taught us about how we *other*: one by Muzafer Sherif in the 1950s and the other by Henri Tajfel in the early 1970s.

OTHERING IS EASY

Sherif's study, the Robbers Cave experiment, has since become a classic of what's called "realistic conflict theory." In 1954, social psychologist Sherif and his team recruited their test subjects—twenty-two fifth-grade boys from Oklahoma City—and told each of them (with their parents' permission!) that they were off to summer camp. The researchers then split the boys into two similar groups and moved them onto a campground at Robbers Cave State Park, playing the role of camp counselors and taking care to keep the two groups apart at first, so neither group knew about the other.

During the first week, the researchers mostly let camp be camp. The boys in each group spent time swimming, hiking, just getting to know each other. This was a key part of the experiment: The researchers wanted the boys in each group to bond, and they even designed camp activities to help them forge an "in-group" identity. Within days, each group had not only built its own culture (cursing was encouraged in one group and discouraged in the other), but also picked names. One group dubbed itself the Rattlers. The other, the Eagles.

Things got real on day seven, when the researchers let the two groups' worlds collide. They got the Rattlers to "wander within hearing distance" of the campground's baseball diamond where the Eagles happened to be playing—and vice versa. That kicked off stage two of the experiment. How would the groups of boys react to discovering rivals on their turf? How would the "in-group" respond to the "out-group"?

Before the two groups had even met, their language said it all. "The boys revealed a consciousness of the other group by frequent reference to 'our baseball diamond,' 'our Upper Camp,' 'our Stone Corral,'" the researchers wrote. When some tourists walked near the camp, one boy was sure "'those guys' were down at 'our diamond' again."

Which brings us to one of the most chilling lines in the study—and evidence that othering comes way, way easier than we like to think.

Like good social scientists, the Robbers Cave researchers picked their subjects to be demographically similar, so hidden variables wouldn't muddle up their findings. (Like *old-school* social scientists, the researchers didn't include girls, so . . . big grain of salt on that one.)

The subjects were all white, Protestant, middle-class boys around eleven years old from two-parent households. But that didn't stop each group from holding itself superior to the other. It didn't stop one boy, in particular, from tapping into a bigger, uglier racial hate—all, again, before the two sides even met. When the Eagles were playing baseball and heard the other campers nearby, one of the boys used a racial epithet to describe the other group. It's a word I won't reproduce here, but the study printed it in full. When I read it, it felt like a slap.

Othering had the boys in its grip.

Next came flag burning. Fistfights. Stuffing rocks in socks to fling at rivals for the next camp raid. In one of those intriguing coincidences, William Golding's now-classic novel *Lord of the Flies* would be published the very same year.

Tellingly, the boys in the Robbers Cave experiment had most of a week to build a meaningful bond with their group before they knew about their rivals. That raises the question: What does it take, exactly, for one group to feel different *enough* from another group to want to treat them worse? For an *us* to push against a *them*? For *othering* to find a grip on our psyche?

Does the *us* need to be meaningful?

In another foundational study, this time in the 1970s, Henri Tajfel found the answer.

Tajfel, a pioneering social psychologist, wanted to understand discrimination—what it takes for one kind of person to decide another kind of person was worth treating like dirt. This wasn't a casual interest. Tajfel only survived five years in prisoner of war camps during World War II by keeping his own group identity a secret: the Germans who captured him never found out that he was a Jew. The rest of his family was not so lucky. After he stepped off a train in Paris in 1945 with hundreds of other POWs, he wrote, "I soon discovered that hardly anyone I knew in 1939—including my family—was left alive." The Nazis killed them all in the Holocaust, and Tajfel was haunted by the hate.

So he dedicated himself to the study of what caused it. Years later, in academia, Tajfel made a key distinction between interpersonal behavior and intergroup behavior—how we get along one-on-one versus how we get along based on the groups we're in and how we think they ought to relate.

Tajfel knew from his experience deceiving German guards about his Jewish heritage that the difference can be life or death. So what does it take to form a *new* social category membership, he wondered, and have it be strong enough to discriminate against an out-group?

In one experiment, Tajfel showed various clusters of dots on a screen and had each of his subjects—again, all boys (*groan*), though college age this time—guess how many dots there were. Then, he split them into two groups. He *told* them one group had dot overestimators and the other had dot underestimators. But actually, the split was completely random.

Why? At the time, social scientists assumed that in order for people to discriminate against each other, they needed some tense history or relationship, some *reason* to think *those other people* are worse. Tajfel made his groups meaningless—there's no case to be made that over- or underestimating the dots makes you smarter or better—precisely because he wanted to test that assumption.

With the groups set, Tajfel had each of his subjects choose how much real money they wanted to give one of their fellow subjects, knowing only one thing about him: whether he was in their in-group or their out-group. Tajfel was in for the long haul on these experiments and figured that in this first go-round, his subjects might treat everyone, in-group and out-group, pretty equally. The groups were meaningless, after all, and he'd probably have to step up that meaning to see an *us* put down a *them*.

With everything I've told you so far, you can probably see where this is going. But Tajfel, at the time, was stunned. Having no good reason to prefer their own group, his subjects *still* gave more money to people in their own group.

Tajfel had his answer. The *us* does *not* need to be meaningful to push off against a *them*. Then he asked another question: Would an *us* push against a *them* even when it makes no rational sense?

In a modified follow-up study, Tajfel asked the subjects in his meaningless groups to choose one of three ways to dole out money to fellow subjects. They could (a) give the same, largest possible amount of money to *both* a member of their in-group and to a member of their out-group, (b) give a member of their in-group the largest possible amount of money regardless of how much a member of the out-group would get, or (c) give *less* than the largest possible amount of money to a member of their in-group, but ensure that a member of their out-group gets *even less*.

Guess which most of them picked? If you said "c," congrats! You're getting the hang not just of how easily we *other*, but of how fully othering warps our minds.

These two studies are just among the earliest to show how nasty we can be to people who we feel are different from us. More recent research, with larger sample sizes (and yes—sigh—*women*) supports the main findings: we discriminate against others when we belong to different groups, and even when the differences between the groups don't seem to matter.

So what happens in the real world, when the differences definitely *do* matter? When they're charged with high-stakes identities, legacies, and loyalties, and we smile and nod and give the right-of-way to various people around us but are quietly *othering them into oblivion?*

You know what? This is a good time to pause and take a break. Get up and stretch, maybe. Drink a glass of water. Take a few calming breaths.

I'm not going to lie: It gets depressing to dive into division. To poke around at *us* versus *them* and how it makes us forget ourselves. If you're not careful, you apply this dreary reality to the messiness of the world and reach a very un-fun conclusion: *We're doomed!*

But we're not!

Like most humans, I blurt out a sneaky linguistic device in the heat of an argument when I'm sure that I'm right and that no one else is listening: the superlative. *But this is the biggest threat! The worst example! The clearest danger!* It doesn't matter if any of that's *true*, I tell myself, so long as it makes my point louder.

Sound familiar?

Take equally dramatic liberties with time, and your arguments about politics get an even bigger boost. People read the news, after all, not history, and your point needs height! Who's going to call you out with any authority if you claim this immigration policy has *never* been floated before? That Congress has *never* been this dysfunctional? That the country's *never* been this divided?

If you're lucky, a historian.

"To know what has come before is to be armed against despair," historian and presidential biographer Jon Meacham wrote in *The Soul of America*. And thank goodness. Nothing turns an overwhelming challenge into a doable one like perspective, and he and other historians have piped up in recent years to remind us that our situation is not as unique as we think.

Just in the last century, America has pulled through some seriously divisive periods. Like the turbulent civil rights and antiwar movements in the 1960s, McCarthyism and the Red Scare in the 1950s, and the rise of the second Ku Klux Klan in the 1920s, when the hate group's membership included—believe it or not—eleven US governors and sixteen US senators.

Further back than that, of course, is the biggest wound of all, when an estimated 750,000 Americans died when our country went to war with itself.

To be clear: America *is* more divided than it was a generation ago. Ronald Reagan won forty-nine of fifty states to get reelected in 1984, which . . . I mean, wow.

But the story of American conflict is not just a story about how we fight, scare, and hurt each other. It's also about how we learn how to do right by each other, even when we think we've got *each other* all figured out.

"The dogmas of the quiet past are inadequate to the stormy present," Abraham Lincoln told Congress on December 1, 1862. It was the first year of the Civil War, and one month before the official emancipation of enslaved Americans. "As our case is new, so we must think anew, and act anew."

And *see* anew, too.

WHEN OTHERING GOES TOO FAR: WRONG IDEAS

No *us* can see a *them* clearly. And the more *we* vilify *them*, the more distorted the world between us becomes.

One example of how that happens is back at summer camp. In the third week of Sherif's Robbers Cave experiment, after the rivalry between the Rattlers and Eagles heated up to boiling, the researchers got all the boys together to do something kind of silly: count beans.

They made it a team competition: Each boy had a set amount of time to collect as many scattered beans as he could in a jar. To see who won, the covert researchers collected all the boys' jars from both teams and, one by one, projected an image of each jar to *all* the boys, asking each boy to jot down how many beans they thought were in each one.

That was the official story, anyway. In reality, those sneaky researchers only ever projected *one* jar to the boys—the same jar, with exactly thirty-five beans. To show a "new" jar, they swished the beans around so they looked different for each showing.

Their findings? The boys couldn't see straight. They consistently estimated that their teammates collected more beans than the boys on the other team, even though each time they looked at what they thought was a different jar, it had exactly thirty-five beans. The boys set out to judge reality and ended up seeing their group's superiority—sometimes, with a little flair. "When the beans supposedly collected by the leader of the Rattlers were projected," the researchers wrote, "a member of his group whistled appreciatively."

Now, these are eleven-year-olds at camp. Grown-ups know better. Don't we?

After the 2018 midterms, a group of researchers took a snapshot of 2,100 Republicans' and Democrats' political views (of all genders!), then asked them to estimate what proportion of folks from the other party concurred with several political statements. So for a Republican taking the survey, one question read, "What percentage of Democrats think that: The US should have completely open borders?"

To sum up their findings: When we look at the other side, we don't see reality. We see an exaggerated fiction that distorts people's actual beliefs. When this Perception Gap study was released in 2019, it found that, on average, Democrats are off by 19 percentage points when estimating Republicans' views, and Republicans are off by 27 percentage points when estimating Democrats' views.

What does that mean, exactly? Let's draw this out using the immigration question, where both sides were awful judges of each other's positions. The Republicans surveyed thought that 38 percent of Democrats reject open borders, when in reality, 71 percent of Democrats do. That's a 33 percentage point gap.

Democrats did no better. They thought just half of Republicans believed that "properly controlled immigration can be good for the country," when actually, 85 percent of Republicans agreed with that statement. A 35 percentage point gap.

A 2020 study called America's Divided Mind dubbed this the "disagreement divide" and came to a similar conclusion: On both sides of the aisle, Americans think we're more divided by our political beliefs than we really are. We're also really, really bad at correcting stereotypes about who's in which party. In a 2018 study that made my jaw hit the floor, Americans thought that a third of Democrats were gay, lesbian, or bisexual *when just 6 percent are*, and that four out of ten Republicans earn more than $250,000 in a year (that's a quarter-million dollars, folks!) when *only 2 percent actually do*. If this sounds extreme, that's because it is—and so is the othering that flows from it. Researchers out of Stanford and Princeton found as far back as 2014 that people discriminate against members of the opposing political party "to a degree that exceeds discrimination based on race."

Researchers who study political division talk about three kinds of polarization. The first is ideological polarization, due to actual policy disagreements between people. The second is affective polarization, due to growing animosity between people in either party. And the third is "perceived" or "false" polarization, the "degree to which partisans overestimate the ideological division between their side and their opponents."

Ideological polarization is based on reason. Affective polarization is based on feelings. But false polarization? That's just based on a lie.

Seeing how all those wrong ideas about what the other side thinks were tearing the country apart, a group of researchers asked a slightly different question: How good are we at guessing what the other side thinks *of us*?

Still terrible. While Democrats and Republicans think equally little of each other, the researchers found in their 2020 study, each side thinks the other despises them about twice as much as they actually do.*

This is how othering blinds us. We believe the other side is worse, so we make them out to be worse. Not just in how they see the world, but in how they treat good and decent people—*us*. As a result, we don't approach people on the other side as they really are but as they appear to us through a thick layer of our own misperceptions.

No wonder it's tough to *talk* across the political divide. We can't even *see* across it.

---

* And the further someone is to the left or right politically, the bigger their exaggerations are likely to be.

Remember Leo from the Introduction, the man who'd emailed me from Montana saying his conservative son didn't want him in his life anymore? Hoping I could help, I got on a Zoom call with him and asked how many other liberals his son knew in town. Leo thought about it and came up empty. "So wait a minute," I said. "You're the only liberal in your son's life?" Leo nodded, realizing, for the first time, that his son's anger toward him wasn't really about him, but his *group*.

The way we're sorted into groups does its dividing, blinding work all around us. It's a simple formula: What's underrepresented in your communities will be underrepresented in your life and overrepresented in your imagination. It's harder to interact generously with people who hold perspectives that concern you, so it'll be way easier to *other* them.

Seattle's blue beacon shined bright when I moved here in 2007. I'd never set foot in the liberal hub when I convinced my city-hopping newspaper fellowship program to send me here at the age of twenty-four. But coming from fellowship stops in Houston, Texas, with its big trucks and big highways, and Midland, Michigan, "the City of Beautiful Churches," something about that chill Seattle vibe—the coffee shops, the lakes and trees everywhere, the counterculture hustle, the "you be you" mood—just told me I belonged. Not because I was scanning for signals of progressive politics. I wasn't, at all. But because it felt like a culture that echoed my own.

I love my city. It's given me everything. But with the world so strained and stressed, and after fifteen years covering my home and its communities, I'm seeing the cost of sameness.

How blue is Seattle? For starters, we're in a mega-landslide county. Hillary Clinton beat Donald Trump here by 49 percentage points in 2016, and Joe Biden topped Trump in 2020 by a wacky 53-point spread. It's so rare to run into an openly conservative voice in Seattle, one *Seattle Times* columnist dubbed a regular guy named Tod Steward "Seattle's Only Trump Voter™" for being the only one who'd go on record to him with his views.

These conservative perspectives that I and other Seattle liberals rarely collide with? Sometimes I think we've twisted them into something heinous. Take Seattle's conversation about homelessness around 2019, the fourth year of a declared homelessness emergency in the city. The city's progressive culture leans hard toward making compassionate policies around homelessness, and rightly so, in my view. Folks who find themselves without a stable place to live need more empathy and consideration than most anyone else. But when more moderate or conservative home or business owners complained that they felt unsafe near homeless encampments, or got frustrated about garbage strewn around streets and parks, I heard some figures on the left present what I read as genuine concerns as proof of hidden hate. Sometimes I'd catch myself going along with that projection. Then I'd snap out of it. It can take hanging out with my parents or private conversations with my more moderate friends to vent some hot air out of the big blue bubble floating around in my head.

And the assumption that everyone here is a political blue—it makes us forget who we are. I don't know how many times I've seen it now: A local leader welcomes everyone to an event, then cracks a joke that demeans conservatives to a burst of nods and laughter, and I cringe in my seat. It lets off steam and bonds anxious blues together. I get that. But it also chips away at three things I love about my city: its openness, its thoughtfulness, and its compassion. *We're too smart to forget that there are other, valid perspectives out there that we can barely understand*, I'll sit there and think. *Aren't we?*

Social media has made it simple to draw circles around what we do and don't want to hear. Or, more accurately, who we do and don't want to hear from.

"Unfollow if you disagree." The phrase is everywhere on social media, directing people to unsubscribe from the author's posts if they don't endorse what those posts are saying. I usually see the phrase tacked on to a belief that's critical to the author: unwavering support for the Second Amendment, or for the Black Lives Matter movement, or just a personal condemnation of something or someone. "[My least favorite politician] is a criminal. Unfollow if you disagree." It's about defiance in the face of social pressure. Making space for your own opinions, then protecting that space. "Unfollow if you disagree with my ideals because they're not changing!" reads one post. It's about getting closer to your groups, too: "Unfollow if you disagree" is another way of saying, "Follow me enthusiastically if you *do* agree!"

It's also about making distance. On the things that matter most to you, the things that draw the boundary for you between good and bad, you don't want to be challenged. Especially not by the online swarms most likely to poke at you, the invisible, angry voices who you're sure are looking for fights—not good-faith conversations—and give our culture wars their nastiness. And that makes sense.

But here's the thing: When you shove away the hostile, you push away the curious. The people who were learning from you, from whom you might have learned something yourself.

"Unfollow if you disagree" is more efficient othering. And it carries over to real life.

The week before the 2020 election, a prominent anchor on CNN, Don Lemon, told his viewers that he "had to get rid of" friends who would reelect the Republican president "because they're too far gone." He'd be friends with them again, he said, if "they want to live in reality."

Some months later, in a virtual workshop about depolarizing families, I met a woman in Indiana we'll call Lucy. I beamed in from the guest room in my mother-in-law's house while she set her device on her kitchen counter, where I watched her make deviled eggs for her grandkids as we talked. She got this huge smile on her face—we're paired up *perfectly*, she told me—as she heard about my blue politics and red parents. Lucy was raised blue herself, I learned, became a "walk-away" to the red side, and struggles to keep good relationships with the two blues in her family: her eldest daughter, who can't seem to help picking political fights on phone calls (she told me with a chuckle), and her sister. Her face fell then. She brought up what Don Lemon had said back in October, and how two days later, her sister had unfriended her on Facebook. "I kinda think that he gave the approval," she says, "that it's OK to give up on people that you love."

Can there be an *us* without a *them*? There are reasons to believe that the divisions pulling us apart are too big, too charged, too justified to step out of, even for a moment.

But if we stay with these divisions and the distance they create, we're that much more vulnerable to the excesses of othering. The vilification. The blindness. The kind of abject, cold dismissal that makes people hide who they really are just to make it, the way Tajfel hid that he was Jewish just to survive. Othering goes too far when it tricks us into shrinking our world instead of expanding it. When we focus so much on the righteousness of our side, we stop thinking straight, we stop seeing straight, and we lose the ability to truly *consider* what's different.

The way to tame othering isn't to turn down the complexity of what divides us. We can't pretend we're all the same when we're not, or pretend we all agree when we don't. It's to turn up the complexity of what makes us who we are. That takes stepping outside of the *us* versus *them*.

And scrambling out of the holes we sink into when we're surrounded not just by people who are like us but by all the stories they tell.

Our silos.

3

Siloing

What happens when we sort ourselves into groups of like-minded people, *other* people who aren't like us, then add, you know, time? We carve out a space that in turn sculpts our thinking. Habits are set. Patterns repeated. Voices we love elevated and others lost.

Some think of this space as a bubble. But you can pop a bubble pretty easily. And bubbles don't get stronger over time. Others call this an echo chamber. That's closer: messages bounce around, seeming more substantial than they really are to your ears, more representative and meaningful.

But both of these analogies miss some key things: the longer you spend in this carved-out space, the deeper you sink into it, the harder it is to climb out, and the more isolated you become—not just from other groups and their chatter, but from a broad, expansive view of an urgently complicated world.

You end up in a hole that grows deeper and deeper. A hole where it's easy to hear others in there with you, their messages echoing off the walls, and hard to make out anything else.

That hole is what I call your silo.

If you imagine a silo, you might picture an aboveground bin for storing grain, one of those tall cylindrical towers made of steel or concrete you might see stacked near crop fields and agricultural areas. But traditional grain silos weren't towers. They were pits, dug down.

If sorting is about the people you see and othering is about the people you don't see, siloing is about the *stories* you see and don't see as a result.

The ideas in our silos seem wiser and more worthy. So when it comes to the people you other, it's *these* voices—the ones who don't really know what they're talking about—that have the upper hand in telling you what to make of the outsiders.

It'd be one thing if this were purely a real-world scenario. Our silos would grow deeper at the slow pace of stories we hear in real-life conversation. But just as with sorting and othering, our digital worlds make siloing efficient. Information streams toward us in never-ending feeds we sculpt with our preferences. We can tune in from anywhere. The bus. Our beds. The bathroom. The voices are always talking. Echoing. Sinking us in.

If sorting makes our groups, and othering forms the nasty relationships between them, siloing digs the trench, perpetuating vicious cycles where we sink deeper into habits of thought and scope that dazzle and blind us.

How? By pulling us in, intensifying our beliefs, and deposing us as the rulers of our own attention.

SILOS PULL

In some ways, a silo is like a black hole. You're not just in it. You're *pulled* into it, sometimes farther than you meant to go.

On the bus ride home from work one day, I was staring at my phone, scrolling through tweets. At that time—it was November 2011—I tweeted often enough to be known for it. The Poynter Institute named me one of thirty-five social media influencers in all of journalism, *Seattle Business* magazine put me and my smartphone on its cover, and *Seattle Met* dressed me in a Lieutenant Uhura *Star Trek* uniform for a photo shoot to go with its profile of me. Social media felt like the future.

I got off the bus as the sky dimmed that evening. It was dark by the time I slumped on my couch, kept tapping my phone screen, and saw something gorgeous: the photos people were posting of that night's sunset. Seattle's sky is a wet, gray blanket most of the fall, but when it isn't, the low-angle sun catches loads of filtering atmosphere and puts on quite a show.

I scrolled through one photo after another, dropping likes. *Man, I wish I'd seen that*, I thought. And that's when I realized: *I could have*. I'd walked to the bus stop from work, boarded the bus, and walked home. The sun and clouds and atmosphere were doing their dance that whole time, right above me.

I stopped scrolling, right then, to think about this. I looked at my phone. I looked at my apps, my inboxes, this whole custom thing I spent hours and hours on each day. It had kept me from seeing the world around me. Its pull was too strong. What made it so strong? Or rather, *who*?

When I thought about it for another second, the answer was obvious: I did. *I* picked the apps that went on my home screen. *I* decided which ones could alert me to new activity, and when, and how. *I* curated the feeds inside each flowing stream of novelty and stimulation to include people I like, topics I like, things that get me going or keep me amused.

I'd created a custom world to serve my every need. How could the world around me possibly compete with it?

Fast-forward a decade and we're still there, caught between the world we create and the world around us. It's obvious which one wins—and why.

We're craving amusement. Fun. Productivity. And our richer-than-most-countries tech companies have done their damnedest to provide. So each of us is never more than a tap away from dropping into our own silo and being delighted or provoked by whatever we find there.

One reason this happens is due to something that developmental molecular biologist John Medina calls "dopamine lollipops." Dopamine is a neurotransmitter that plays a part in how we feel pleasure, reward, and motivation. That old analog lift you feel when you get a letter (that isn't a bill or junk!) in the mail? That's dopamine. Except that in our digital silos, with their endless streams of information and the umpteen "mailboxes" they flow into, dopamine hits are always a tap or click away. Pretty soon, we're hooked, checking our phones over and over and over again without really meaning to. Ever excuse yourself to go to the bathroom just so you can check some feed or email? Or look up, drowsy, from your phone in bed to find out it's three o'clock in the morning and you're still up? Lollipops!

The custom digital worlds we create exert a powerful pull on us. I used to think they were our portals to the world. Later I realized: they've become our world.

SILOS INTENSIFY

Maybe you already sense what happens to our opinions when we share them only with people who agree with us.

They get more extreme.

In a groundbreaking 1999 study, Harvard scholar Cass Sunstein found that on issues as diverse as gun control, the minimum wage, and environmental policy, people who talk to folks who share their positions both intensify those positions and want to take bigger, bolder steps to address them. He found similar results in later studies, including a 2005 experiment where liberals and conservatives in Colorado became more set and extreme in their views about climate change and same-sex marriage after talking about them in ideologically sorted groups.

There are three reasons this happens, Sunstein says. First, when everyone in a group is already leaning toward a certain position, their arguments start to pile on and push further in that same direction.

Second, it's easier to be liked by others around you when you agree with them—basic fact of human nature—so just about everyone is willing to tweak their positions just a smidge if it helps them align a bit more with the group of people around them. It seems harmless enough in the moment, and it's not like anyone can read your mind to tell that you've changed something.

And finally, when people around you agree with you, you get more confident that whatever you stand for is the right thing to believe. You're getting validation. It feels good, and it builds momentum. So it's just a matter of time, really, before you take another rhetorical step in the direction you're already leaning. Then another. Then, aw hell, we're all friends here, why not take one more?

Add the easy sorting of the digital world, run by algorithms designed to give you what'll keep you around, and you can find thousands of like-minded people to hang with without getting out of bed. Twitter sculpts its "For you" trending topics list based on what it knows you're into, and Facebook suggests groups for people to join based on what its algorithm guesses about their interests. Until it stopped the practice ahead of the 2020 election,* Facebook even suggested political groups.

Do we calm down when we discuss tense stuff with like-minded people? Hell no! The same thing that happens to our opinions happens to our emotions. We turn up the heat. "One of the characteristic features of feuds," Sunstein wrote, "is that members of feuding groups tend to talk only to one another, or at least listen only to one another, fueling and amplifying their outrage."

---

* Or said it would, at least. The Markup, a nonprofit newsroom that pays a panel of thousands of Facebook users to help keep an eye on the platform, reported that users on the panel had received hundreds of recommendations for groups promoting political organizations from February to June 2021.

SILOS DEPOSE

If you used social media platforms in the early days, you might remember the "Load more posts" link. You'd find it on Twitter or Facebook—the dominant platforms of the time—when you reached the bottom of your feed, the chunk of it that the platform had downloaded to present to you when you first opened the app. Click on that link, and more, chronologically older posts would appear, giving you more material to scroll through.

One day, the "Load more posts" link was gone. The platforms had removed it, each on its own time, and replaced it with an automatic loading mechanism. Reach the bottom of your posts, *et voilà*—more would appear, just like that.

This minor change in the design of the platform was a step toward what techies called a "frictionless" user experience. Connecting and sharing with friends on social media should be as easy as possible, went the thinking, so that more people would do it and reap the beautiful benefits.

Tristan Harris didn't see it that way.

Harris, the star of the 2020 documentary *The Social Dilemma* and the cofounder of the Center for Humane Technology, was noticing how tech platforms influence our behavior way before it was cool. For him, that early change didn't just remove a link. It removed user choice. What for? Retention. When some people reached the end of their feed and saw the "Load more posts" link, they didn't click it. They decided at that moment that they didn't need to see more posts just now, and maybe it was time to do something else. To platforms obsessed with keeping their users as long as they could, that was a problem. By removing the prompt altogether, they erased the exit. They took away that opportunity for people to think about what they were doing, which ended up keeping more people on the platform for longer—pretty much without their knowledge.

I wouldn't have noticed this change if Harris, whom I've chatted with a few times on the tech and media conference circuit, hadn't pointed this out at one such conference years ago. At first I was fascinated. And then I was mad.

Here's my point: Your silos are not neutral pits of preferred information. Online, they are structured by platforms that want you to consume that information as long as possible.

The problem, though, is that information consumes *us*, too.

Nobel laureate economist Herbert A. Simon figured this out back in 1971. "What information consumes is rather obvious: it consumes the attention of its recipients," he wrote. "Hence a wealth of information creates a poverty of attention, and a need to allocate that attention efficiently among the overabundance of information sources that might consume it."

So your silos don't just pull you in and intensify what you hear. They depose you as the ruler of your own attention.

Back in 2016, I was lucky enough to take a seminar class at the Massachusetts Institute of Technology with Sherry Turkle, a visionary psychologist who, like Harris, has a gift for paying attention where others don't. One day, she brought up that three-dot ellipsis that appears in most text messaging apps—the one that pops up when the person you're texting with is writing something they haven't sent you yet. When that person stops writing, the ellipsis disappears, and you're left to wonder: Why did they stop writing? What were they going to say?

Our devices are packed with notifications, alerts, buzzes from the digital worlds we create. Our digital inboxes are stuffed with new messages, new posts, new feeds, all of it tugging at our attention.

"Our brains are most productive when there is no demand that they be reactive," Turkle wrote in her book *Reclaiming Conversation*. So, when there are too many demands that our brains be reactive . . . can we be productive at all?

Even when we mean to perform a specific task, we're redirected. As soon as you respond to one notification, you'll see another. And another. More times than I can count I have opened a social media or news app for something like sixty seconds, wanting only to pass the time while I wait for soup to warm up in the microwave or for a friend to grab a glass of water. I will scroll down, who knows, maybe ten posts. And then my food is ready or my friend gets back, and I'll suddenly feel sad and anxious. And I won't know why.

WHEN SILOING GOES TOO FAR: INHUMAN HUMANS

Now that we understand more about how our silos manipulate us, pulling us in with the force of our preferences, intensifying our ideas and emotions, and deposing us as rulers of our attention, let's come back to the findings of that Perception Gap study. The one that showed us that we are really, really bad at knowing what the other side—the *othered* side—really thinks.

You might think that the gap that's grown in our knowledge and understanding of each other can all get figured out if we just stay informed. Well, brace yourself, 'cause the study didn't stop at measuring our flawed view across the political divide. It also checked up on the things we assume can fix it—like getting more news.

We get our news increasingly from within our silos, from the voices and spaces that make up our preferred sources of information. And the more time we spend on the news, it turns out, the more distorted our view of the other side becomes.

This is correlation, not causation, so the researchers can't say that watching more news *causes* greater misperceptions. Only that "people who said they read the news 'most of the time' were nearly three times more distorted in their perceptions than those who said they read the news 'only now and then.'" This goes for both political blues and reds, by the way, with roughly 5-point perception gaps turning up both for people who read the *New York Times* and for people who watch Fox News.*

I know. It's wacky. But if you see it through this lens of siloing, it makes sense. Everything about how we see the world comes from the stories we tell ourselves about it, and our news media make up society's core social

---

* And gaps twice as large turning up for left-leaning sites like Slate and Buzzfeed as well as right-leaning programs like the *Sean Hannity Show*.

storytelling institution. Thanks to the economics of the industry, media outlets are pressured to tell stories that speak not to *everyone*, but to the slices
of folks who are most likely to become their most loyal readers and biggest
fans. News organizations reflect their audiences, which leads them to drop
into their audiences' silos, which leads them to get sucked into the concerns,
assumptions, and exaggerations echoing around inside.

That tendency in our media does two awful but useful things. It makes
each silo's pull on us even stronger, as media outlets crank out stories that
draw us in; and it helps ensure that even when your favorite news outlet
intends to explore *all* sides, it'll get quicker rewards—clicks, loyalty, all that
fun stuff—by appealing to yours.

Sorting, othering, and siloing won't just screw up our judgment and make
valid ideas look awful. The anger and resentment tied into all this make it
easier—way easier—to do something we do our darnedest to avoid: hate.

When I think about hate, my thoughts immediately turn to empathy,
expecting such a kind-sounding virtue to keep us from going too far. But
there's evidence that the way we each marshal our empathy—like seemingly
everything else!—is *itself* biased toward our own groups and away from that
scary *other*. One 2020 study looking at empathy across the political divide
found that people who are more empathetic are more likely to feel angry at
people in the opposite party—and *enjoy it when they suffer.*

I can't help but wonder if that explains something pretty discouraging
about what it takes, in these dangerously divided times, to make a social
media post soar. In a 2020 Northwestern University study of posts from politicians and news outlets, researchers found that posts that were about the
other—about Republicans if the author was a Democrat or about Democrats
if the author was a Republican—traveled further on social media platforms
than posts that had a bunch of emotional language (the old standby for
virality). It gets worse. The researchers also found that with each additional

word that's about the *other*—words like "liberal" and "Biden" in a post by a Republican, for example—the likelihood that the post would be shared by its audience jumped a whopping 67 percent.*

In the early months of the COVID-19 pandemic, thousands of people took to the streets to protest the economic shutdowns, which were saving lives and costing livelihoods all across the country. One day on Facebook I saw a distant acquaintance post an NBC News story topped by a photo of a group of angry people—some of the one hundred protesters who were calling for an end to the lockdowns outside the Ohio Statehouse. The photo, taken from inside that government building, where Ohio governor Mike DeWine was giving reporters an update, caught the protesters midshout on the other side of the glass doors. They were pressed up against those doors, they were mad, and they looked it.

My acquaintance compared them to zombies in her post, calling up an apocalyptic horror movie you've probably heard of. It started a pile on. "These people should be so ashamed," read one comment. "They are brainwashed, crazy cult members," went another. One person simply wrote "Darwin," and that caught on. To the folks on this thread, the maskless protesters risked catching COVID at the peak of a global pandemic and certainly didn't seem like they had survival as a priority. "I guess that's what we hope at this point," one person said, to two laugh reactions. Their meaning: *Maybe the demise of people too stupid to wear masks in a pandemic wouldn't be such a bad thing.* "Darwinism can't happen quick enough," said another, to a like. I felt sick.

This wasn't a popular Facebook post. It had twenty-one reactions total. It didn't go viral. It didn't go far. But we ignore the small exchanges. We

---

* Politicians do know that this is an enormous problem, by the way, particularly the twelve US House representatives who sit on the Select Committee on the Modernization of Congress—the most important small group of legislators most Americans have never heard of. Vice chair Rep. William Timmons of South Carolina put the high stakes of solving the body's dysfunctional polarization to me this way: "If Congress doesn't get it together, we're not going to have a country in a few decades."

dismiss the ones that don't result in some massive shaming or gawking or headline or whatever as just the way it is. But these everyday posts say so much. They say everything.

Now, I have no doubt that if you're on social media, you've seen this and much more vile, dismissive stuff coming from all over. Particularly, you might be thinking, from the side you're *not* on, which you're likely to believe is much worse.

When the COVID-19 pandemic hit, I supported the economic shutdowns as a sucky but worthwhile sacrifice to the overall priority of safeguarding public health. But I saw the passion in people who lived way different lives than me, and I was curious.

Around the same time I stumbled on that Facebook post comparing conservative protesters to zombies, I also happened upon on a *New York Times* story about the protests against the economic shutdowns. Far down in the story, one quote changed the way the whole dilemma looked to me. It worked on me so hard, in fact, bubbling up again and again in my mind, that I would end up bringing it up in a podcast discussion about the pandemic and in countless breathless conversations we had in those days, trying to make sense of a world that was falling apart.

The quote was spoken by a man named Phillip Campbell, a thirty-nine-year-old dad from southern Michigan who drove to Lansing to be one of three or four thousand people protesting the shutdowns that day—mostly from inside their cars. "Mr. Campbell said he knew the virus was dangerous. He had friends who worked in health care. But he wanted to feel confident that the sacrifices he was making were being taken seriously," the journalists wrote. "Mr. Campbell said the situation for many people he knew was dire. He estimated that about one-third of the people in his life were in free fall, without money for rent or food."

Then came the view-changing quote: "It's like I've got my mom hanging from a cliff and my child hanging from the other side and I'm being told to save one," he said, using a metaphor to reflect the clashing risks to people's health and to their finances. "What am I supposed to do? I have the right to be frustrated with the choice."

In the moment I read that quote, Campbell's dilemma made sense to me, and it began to shift the way I perceived this dilemma writ larger, this awful trade-off between economic well-being and public health. Isn't economic well-being also a factor in public health? Whose calculations look different, way different from mine, and how should I account for that difference in my position on this issue?

I found myself wishing that the group mocking those folks could have been in a state of mind to hear Campbell's point or even be exposed to it. But if they were so sure these folks were worthless stupid zombies, would they have scrolled that far down, to hear the voices of the protesters themselves? Would they have read the article? Would they have seen this headline—"Why These Protesters Aren't Staying Home for Coronavirus Orders"—and thought of gross, brain-eating zombies, and moved on?

Siloing goes too far when the stories we tell about each other are not only wrong but demeaning. When we spend so much time in spaces that intensify our basest judgments that we believe the other side is barely human at all.

BRIDGING

In her book *The Happiness Hack*, my friend and neuroscience educator Ellen Petry Leanse explains what happens to your brain when you spend a lot of time with folks who reflect your own beliefs back to you. Basically, you stop thinking about those beliefs at all.

Your brain likes to stay efficient. Take shortcuts. Save cognitive power. So as you become entrenched in your beliefs, your brain moves them to a part of itself that's good at automatic, reactive thinking, and away from the part that reasons things out, 'cause who has the time? As a result, you react to competing beliefs the way you'd react to anything that seems totally unnatural or wrong: with disgust and repulsion.

"Our life experience is shaped by our assumptions, biases, and blind spots," Ellen told me. "We think it's reality, yet it is only the conditioned perception we have been taught is truth."

This is great news for groups that are battling it out over their beliefs. Nobody wants soldiers to question if a threat is a threat. They want them in the fray, sure enough of the cause to hit fast and hard at every opportunity.

But if you stop considering other points of view, if even your *brain* wants you locked in where you're comfortable, how can you be sure that the group battles you're waging are justified? How do you know that what you think—if it's what everyone around you thinks—is *really* what you think?

The people who share your beliefs don't tend to encourage these kinds of questions. Neither do the media, politicos, and other storytellers who count on your loyalty. That's not because they're evil, or because they want you in angry mob mode all the time. I've talked to loads of fellow journalists and politicians about this and trust me—*no one* likes how divided we are! It's just that bad incentives are so baked into the business models and strategies that determine who lives and dies in these industries that they're damn hard to challenge without succumbing to the worst fate of all—irrelevance. Don't get me wrong. People are working on this. *I'm* working on this. But in the meantime, you and I need to stare an ugly reality right in the face: the more predictable your beliefs are to the institutions that crave your attention, the more reliably they can tell you stories that keep you hooked—and keep the institutions breathing.

～ェ～

Understanding people who hold opposing political beliefs is hard enough when you rarely meet anyone like that (sorting), harder when they're a *them* to your *us* (othering), and harder still when the stories that surround you give you little if any reason to take even small, slow steps in their direction (siloing).

Add in the tension stirring up society right now, and stepping out of our silos to get a clearer, truer picture of our world and its people can feel not only risky, but reckless.

When the people I talk to get nervous about crossing the political divide, it's usually because they fear or loathe what they expect to find there and don't want it to hurt them, stain them, or send bad signals about their goodness, intelligence, or desired impact on their world.

When one person turned down my invitation to join a political *other* in a public conversation, he told me he was afraid it would validate what he considered to be dangerous views. "I hope you understand," he said. When someone who'd joined me in a cross-partisan workshop let me know years later that he'd lost interest in the exercise, he said he'd rather spend his energy advocating for the policies on his side. "I have to help the people who've been hurt," he said. When a brilliant and perceptive conservative woman in my circle declined to join a liberal in a private conversation, she told me she was too scared the liberal would "cancel" her for her views on social media. "I just can't take that chance," she said. And when a liberal community organizer told me she supported my work but could never do it herself, she pointed to her experience seeing her family members deported during the last administration. "I can't do your job," she told me, "because I can't see myself getting close to people near Trump."

I told you at the beginning of this book that I'm here to help you cross the divides you want to and not the ones you don't. Choosing where to try to span these gulfs, and *when*, and *how*, is an entirely personal decision that no one other than you can touch. You should know, though, that this clear, practical truth is tough for me to admit. That's because, to be totally frank with you (and if it isn't already obvious), one of my deepest personal convictions in life is that understanding the people who confound us is always, always worth it.

Don't worry; you don't need to agree with me on this!* But what I hope you *can* agree with me on, or at least consider, is that these gulfs between us—these big divides we've been agonizing over together for going on three chapters—are neither as big nor as dangerous as we think.

The evidence is strewn throughout these pages, telling a story we rarely hear. Believing what you see across the political divide is like believing

---

* Or anything else, really.

what you see in a fun-house mirror: *everything's* warped—including the divide itself. Our ideas about the other side's ideas? Wrong. Our ideas about the other side's hostility toward ours? Distorted. Our ability to learn the truth about the other side from within our hyperactive silos? Totally, totally busted.

And what of the sense that these divides are too long and too treacherous to bother spanning?

Considering the track record here, I, at least, would be skeptical.

At his many talks and conferences, john powell,* the head of the Othering and Belonging Institute at UC Berkeley, likes to tell the story of a pastor who, hearing that he ought to build bridges with people who are very different from him, asked powell a tricky question. "john, are you saying I should bridge with the devil?" powell's response to the pastor always gets a laugh or two: "Maybe don't start there."

Then powell goes on, making a distinction between building what he calls short bridges and long bridges that I find handy as heck. "Build short bridges and become more practiced, become more skilled at building bridges," he says. "And then, at some point, you may need to re-question, 'Who are you calling the devil?'"

Bridging is the answer to sorting, othering, and siloing. It's what we do when we step out of our silos and try to see things from a different point of view. It can take patience, humility, and a good heap of courage. But it works.

Research keeps showing us that the more you mingle with people in your "otherized" out-groups, the less prejudice you'll feel against them. In fact, a study of 515 *other* studies found that chatting in person with someone from an out-group cut down prejudice 94 percent of the time. But it's

---

* powell doesn't capitalize his name, he told the *Berkeley News*, because he believes that people should be "part of the universe, not over it, as capitals signify."

not just about prejudice. Bridging fights back against your out-group biases to sharpen your judgment—even when it's your job to stay impartial. In one study of how federal judges make their calls in the courtroom, liberal judges' opinions moved to the left when they worked with other liberal judges, and conservative judges' opinions moved to the right when they worked with other conservative judges. But when liberal and conservative judges worked together, that dampened their ideological tendencies. In both cases, what made the difference wasn't exposure to information or education, but people.

We don't *interact* with ideas, causes, or beliefs. I picture all of these proxies peeling off us like invisible, skintight masks and just floating away, leaving us, *all* of us—the only ones who make and unmake this world we live in—rubbing our eyes and blinking.

The way I see it, we interact only with each other. We sort into our groups, push off our *others*, and settle in, too often and too deeply, to silos that keep us from seeing each other for who we really are.

No *us* can see a *them* clearly without opening our eyes wider than we're used to and building bridges to span divides we fear are too big to cross. You know what? They might be. But the most important thing about a bridge isn't that it's crossed, but that it's *there*. That it exists and is maintained so that one day, when someone who's been nervous is ready, it can hold their weight, carry their truth, and expand their world.

SOS is a call for help. There's so much we're not seeing.

It's time to find out what.

Part II

Curiosity

If there's one question I want to persuade you to ask more often, it's "What am I missing?"

"What am I missing?" is not just any question. It's *the* question. It's the doorstop to put down in the hallways of your mind, pathway after pathway, to keep open possibilities from slamming into harmful assumptions.

Answering it is not easy. For starters, we can't look it up. There's no textbook to consult to tell us just the things we don't see. It's not in our phones, and Google can't run the search for us. There's no algorithm, either, to make it all "frictionless." When you're going with the flow of a divided world, you can't get a clear picture of what's around you. What you do make out is too warped to trust, transformed by the echoes in our silos and the shared animosity we feel toward groups of people on the other side of countless issues—groups that merge into one big enemy we fight. Sorting, othering, and siloing narrow what we see while convincing us we see enough.

So . . . yeah. We're missing *a lot*.

It's not for lack of interest, though! And that's where I see hope. I see it in the growing number of people who sense our shared blindness and are done accepting it, done waiting for this dangerously divided world to undivide itself. I see it in how we're looking inward, to the patterns of our thinking and the rhythms of our relationships. And I see it—from sea to shining sea—in the quickening drumbeat of posts and op-eds from people who are waking up to their own place in this toxic equation and helping the rest of us find our power to change it. Or, at least, our resolve. "I'm as guilty as the next person, but I have vowed to open my mind, stop yelling at my television set, and start becoming a better listener," wrote liberal David Weinstein in California's *Laguna Beach Independent*. "These are challenging times, but that is when patriots show up to do the tough work to make our country stronger," wrote conservative Lenny Mirra in the *Valley Patriot* in Massachusetts. "You have nothing to lose but your mistrust!"

To keep our minds open when so much pushes them closed we're going to have to kick it old-school. We're going to have to talk—*really* talk—with actual different people. This is the work. The resistance. This is how we push back against the patterns of SOS, inviting fresh insights to crack the walls of our silos and flood in.

It feels good to confirm our impressions, sharpen our wit, tighten our bonds. Specialize but not broaden. Not challenge. But it feels even better, I *insist*, to find but not be *con*fined to our groups, to invite a truer world in—fear, discomfort, and dopamine lollipops be damned. And bonus: it really can be easier and even more fun than you think.

The work begins by following a signal. Something to watch for and track to make sure you're hauling yourself out of your silo once in a while and taking a clarifying look around.

I found that signal when I caught my brain in the act. When I realized that seeing things from another point of view has an obvious name—and its own unmistakable feeling. In Part II, I'm going to tell you what this signal is, what it means, and why it matters. First, by getting real about how each of us sees the world. Then, by getting to know the drive to learn that's been nick-named our "knowledge emotion." And finally, by breaking down the most powerful tool for understanding other people that any of us will ever have.

Let's start with a big, beautiful mess: everyone else's perspectives.

4

Perspective

How you see the world determines how you want to talk about it.

One model that does a decent job of explaining this is known as Hallin's Spheres. Picture two concentric circles in a big open space. The inner circle is the Sphere of Consensus. It has all the beliefs that a society, for the most part, agrees with. The earth is round, killing is bad, look both ways before crossing the street—that sort of thing. The outer circle is the Sphere of Legitimate Discourse. It has all the issues people would reasonably debate. Dogs versus cats, whether this candidate's better than that candidate, ditching daylight saving time, you get the idea. And then there's the big open space outside these circles. This is called the Sphere of Deviance. Out here is where you toss the belief that the earth is flat, that one race is better than another race, that you could soar into the air by jumping off your roof and flapping your arms just right, crap like that.

What happens as we get more politically divided? The Sphere of Consensus shrinks, I think, and the border between the Sphere of Legitimate Discourse and the Sphere of Deviance heaves, buckles, and breaks.

You know when people say we lack a shared reality? The fact that we can live in the same world, marked by the same set of events, and have such

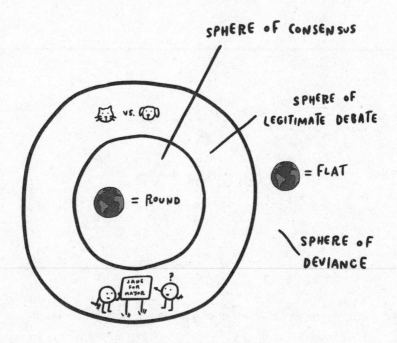

different views of what it all means is astounding, frustrating, and just real life. Which drives home a critical point: What happens in the world matters, but our *interpretation* of what happens in the world matters more.

That doesn't mean we should pay any less attention to facts. It means we should pay more attention to perspectives.

BEYOND YOUR KEN

People tend to think of "perspectives" as different views on the same thing. That's always seemed a bit detached to me. *People* do the viewing, right? Unique people walking unique paths that led them to those views? We don't see with our eyes, after all, but with our whole biographies. It's time our sense of perspective took that into account.

The Scots have a word related to the bounds of our knowledge that I find super wise. It's a "fossil word," which means (fun fact!) that it's essentially dead to language except for its use in one surviving phrase. The word is "ken," and the phrase is "beyond one's ken." The whole concept was born on the high seas.

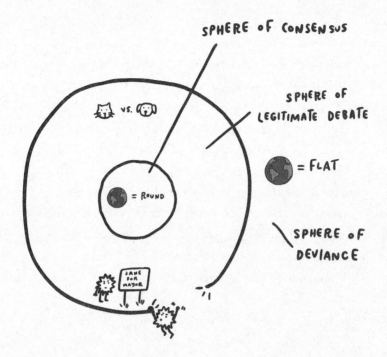

When Scottish sailors first talked about their "ken" in the 1500s, they were talking about how far they could see to the horizon out on the water.* Then writers began to use "ken" to refer first to the range of your vision—at sea or not—and then, to the range of your knowledge or understanding. To what your *mind* can see, and not just your eyes. "One's range of knowledge or sight," goes the dictionary definition of ken. If something is "beyond my ken," it's beyond my understanding. I don't *see* it, so I can't know it. It's beyond my horizon. It's beyond me.

What I love about this word is that it draws our knowledge with obvious bounds and limits. It's finite. Proximate. Something we can reach the end of. "Ken" reminds us of something important: you can't *know* what you aren't close to.

Look beyond your ken, and you won't see anything clearly. Sometimes you won't see certain things at all. I'll never forget what happened to Seattle when I sailed into motherhood. Seemingly overnight, it transformed from a

---

* Which, if you're curious, is about three miles in clear conditions.

city of bars and restaurants to a city packed with parks and playgrounds I'd never seen before in my life.

Other times, you'll see the barest hints of shapes out there beyond your ken. Shapes that'll seem neutral, interesting, or threatening. When they seem neutral, you'll shrug 'em off. When they seem interesting, you'll look a couple times, and maybe move closer to get a better look. When those distant shapes seem threatening, though, you won't want to move closer or move on. You'll want to run away, fortify, or even attack.

It's weird to do anything drastic when you can barely make out the thing that's scaring you. So you'll do something to resolve that: You'll manufacture certainty. You'll convince yourself that the shape you see beyond your ken fits the description of that sea monster everyone in your silo's been buzzing about. And you'll fight, flee, or rage accordingly.

When you fill in those gaps in your perception, you're motivated by what scientists call NFC—your need for closure. And you want to reach what's called "cognitive closure," the "desire for a firm answer to a question and an aversion toward ambiguity." You can't see everything, so you'll tell yourself you've seen enough.

What to do about this? It would make sense to shrug and say to yourself, *Well, it's not like I can step outside my own perspective.* But you can.

Asking "What am I missing?" is the first step. It's that doorstop against cognitive closure that comes too early, that hasn't gotten close enough to know enough at all.

So then, who do you ask? What expert should you consult to understand other people's perspectives? Well, let's turn that around for a minute: What expert should *I* consult to understand *yours*?

Authors, researchers, and credentialed thinkers and doers of all kinds connect the dots for the rest of us on a lot of things that matter. They speak with confidence about what they know, but are they any less vulnerable to the blinding effects of sorting, othering, and siloing? Do *they* ask "What am I missing" often enough? When it comes to the patterns of people, particularly in anxious, whirlwind times like these, there's just no substitute for primary sources. I'm not saying we ignore all the thoughtful frameworks and narratives that teach us something about how people work. As long as they open our minds, they help!* I am saying: Let's not turn to the experts, then turn away from each other. Let's do our own exploring, too. Let's put our perspective next to someone else's with no middleman, meaningfully and frequently enough that what we observe becomes a check on what everyone's going on about.

Only some people have the time and resources to research, theorize, communicate, promote. So someone is better at writing; are they better at living? Let's kill that idea once and for all. You, me, each of us has expertise

---

* Besides, I've got a bunch of good new ones for you right here in this book!

as unique as our paths through the world—a ken built over a lifetime as undeniable as any other.

The story of the world feels like it's the experts' to tell. It's not. It's all of ours.

The trick, then, is to scoop it up and add it up. To leave our harbor and learn *from* each other *about* each other for each other's own sake.

INTOIT MOMENTS

Which brings us back to that signal I mentioned. The way you know that you're stepping outside your silo and taking a good, *productive* look beyond your own perspective. To show you how it works, let me tell you about the night I finally started to fall for Seattle.

I'd been here all of nine months, and though I loved the city's culture, its weather was another story. I was twenty-four, struggling to develop my new tech beat at the *Seattle Post-Intelligencer*, and winter was coming—a mix of wet and gray that kept my head down, my days short, my shoes soaked, and my new life much harder to adjust to than I'd thought.

It's so cliché for newcomers to resent the rain. But I *hated* it.

One night at a bar called the Crescent Lounge, I got to chatting with a guy named Loren who'd grown up here. He learned I was new in town, and, inevitably, he asked what I thought about the weather. I told him, bracing for the usual "You'll get used to it" platitudes. He paused, glancing up from the karaoke binder we were flipping through. When he hears the rain on the roof of his car, Loren told me, he does something unusual. He'll have turned off the engine by then, having arrived wherever he was going. But before he raises the hood of his jacket, opens the door, and steps out, he sits back in the driver's seat, closes his eyes, and listens.

As he told this story I could sense it. The warmth of the car. The crinkling of his jacket. The drumming of the rain. It's soft, the rain in Seattle—persistent but gentle. When it makes itself heard, it's actually pretty rare. I imagined turning off the engine of my puny silver Hyundai Accent and finding a rhythm in the steady downpour.

"Rain has an aural beauty," he said. "That's why I love it."

Then *boom*. Just like that, the idea that rain is awful—the weight of it in my head, at least—was gone. I felt this sense of space, a lightness that caught me off guard, like someone had opened a door in a stuffy room, but I didn't know the door was there, and I hadn't realized the room was stuffy. Passages in my mind appeared out of nowhere and I wanted to revisit things I thought I knew and are now . . . different. *Is* the rain so awful? It's kind of nice to have green grass all year long, and all these cozy coffee shops. The gray sky is whiter, really, and bright, and it shimmers. And that sound? Like music.

I looked out the window to the headlights climbing up Olive Way. Rain streaked the glass, and I caught myself wishing this wasn't a loud bar so I could hear it. My eyes were wide. This all happened in an instant.

I looked right at Loren, my mind still racing. I would see him again, here and there for another couple years. But even after we lost touch, I still remembered him for this game-changing meeting of perspectives.

"I never thought of it that way," I said.

〜〜〜

That's what I call the signal: an **"I never thought of it that way" moment**, or an INTOIT moment.* That phrase describes something amazing. Catch yourself thinking or saying it, and it's the clearest sign you get that a new insight has spanned the distance between someone else's perspective and your own.

Some INTOIT moments start to work on you instantly, like this one did for me, leading to big swings in your take on things. Others are slower or more subtle, etching you without changing you, like pockmarks on the moon.

---

* Pronounced "into it" for short. (Sorry, *W*!)

We say that new insights "hit" us. That exciting new knowledge "blows our minds." Big or small, INTOIT moments come when you collide with a new idea and the boom is big enough to notice.

INTOIT moments can strike anywhere—in conversation, while reading an article or book, even way after the idea first crashed into your brain, after you've had time to process. Regardless of the source, you can sort INTOIT moments into two groups by asking a question: Did the moment *strengthen* my idea or *challenge* it?

Just for fun, I asked several of my more curious friends to tune their internal radar for when "I never thought of it that way" moments had come to them. It took a little explaining at first. *You want me to do what now?* But they agreed, and together we collected dozens of INTOIT moments, intersections between perspectives where meaning was made for each of them in a kind of mental chemical reaction.

My writing buddy Danny went on a hike with a friend who told him the original, indigenous name of the peak they were climbing. He was impressed. "I never thought to home in on the destinations that I go to and get to know them from indigenous names. And I thought, *I totally should do that.*" Danny was already interested in learning more about indigenous cultures. This INTOIT moment strengthened an idea he liked and gave him a way to bring it out in his life. Most of the moments my friends shared with me were similar.

INTOIT moments that challenge our ideas, *bridging* us to a perspective we were not already leaning toward, are rarer. They're surprising—and sometimes uncomfortable.

My former colleague Kathie heard a conversation among some folks at a business about how they had to restock the toilet paper in the bathroom slowly—a few rolls at a time—because people kept stealing it. "A bunch of ladies chatted about how pathetic it would be to steal toilet paper," she told me. "Then one lady remarked that no one would steal toilet paper—big, bulky, cheap—unless they really, really needed it." Everyone got quiet thinking about that, Kathie included. "It was true," she said.

My former neighbor Tana had a challenging INTOIT moment when she watched a scene in the film *Mary of Nazareth*. When the shepherds come to see the newborn baby Jesus, Mary hides and Joseph reaches for his knife. Tana, a devout Catholic, never pictured the figures in the Nativity as anything but gentle and peaceful. Their going into "papa/mama bear mode" initially stunned her. "But after thinking about it, that would make sense," she said.

My friend Traca—who's made it a point for years to have three "curious conversations" a day—kept thinking about INTOIT moments long after I first described the concept to her. "It gives me a way to explore my own beliefs," she told me. "And through that process, sometimes, I end up holding those beliefs a bit looser than before."

Hearing that brought me back to a night that those of us who lived through it are unlikely to forget—the night of the 2016 presidential election. I was slumped on the beige carpet of my basement rec room, the TV on the wall tuned to CNN, the reality of the result weighing down everything. My side had lost. That was ordinary enough in an election, but this president-elect seemed like a bug in the system. He was the kind of guy, I was sure of it, who could take the centuries-old norms and principles that have brought us this far and burn them all to ashes. I felt like something failed. Like democracy had broken. On a reflex, I called my mom.

When she answered, I couldn't help it. I choked up. *"Mami, qué pasó?"* I asked her. *What happened?*

"Pues, ganó," she said. *Well, he won.* I heard her excitement. She was happy, of course she was—*Why was I even calling?*—and she was doing her best to hold it in, hear me out, and calm me down.

I told her my fears about leadership. About character. I spilled a stream of worries about this country we'd adopted and cherished and loved. *This is the worst thing that could happen to it,* I thought. I was certain.

Mom let a beat hang between us when I finished. Then she spoke. Growing up in Mexico, she was used to democratic elections being a big game of pretend. The person who became president was whoever the Partido Revolucionario Institucional, the ruling party for decades, wanted to become president.

As I listened to Mom's memories, I recalled one of my own. I was a kid, seven or eight years old, walking down the sidewalk with my grandmother on a hot, dry day in her neighborhood—Fuentes del Valle, San Pedro—so she could cast her vote for the candidate from Partido Acción Nacional, the opposition party that never won.* Abuelita knew it wouldn't make a difference. *The real votes are never counted,* she bent down and whispered to me as we entered the air-conditioned polling place. I didn't have time to object—*Entonces por qué viniste? So why did you come?*—before she'd led me to a painted wooden bench by the wall. That's where I sat and waited, rocking my sandaled feet, as I watched her grab a ballot, go behind a little curtain, shift her spider-veined ankles once or twice in her black pumps, and step out again. She handed her filled-out ballot to a staffer, wrapped my hand in her warm and bony one, and led me back out into the heat. When I brought my attention back to my mother, it was as if I'd carried it back from another world.

"*La democracia jaló, Mónica. Yo voté, y jaló.*" Mom was telling me about Trump, about the election, about our country. *Democracy worked, Mónica. I voted, and it worked.*

I blinked. Bringing my hand to my face, I held my phone in silence. Democracy had broken that night. I knew this. I *knew* it. But then again, democracy had worked the way it was supposed to, hadn't it? The contradiction and truth of that shook me and hurt me and pissed me the hell off. *Dammit. I'd never thought of it that way.*

So after I trudged upstairs from the rec room, loaded the dishwasher with the stemless wine glasses we'd only poured half a bottle into, brushed my teeth, and slipped into our queen-sized bed next to my sleeping husband, I made a promise to myself. A promise that one way or another, no matter how tempting it would be to dismiss and vilify and even hate whoever didn't see things the way I knew them to be, that I would do everything in my power to remain stupidly, insistently, ferociously curious.

---

* This would all change on July 2, 2000, when democratic reforms in Mexico led Vicente Fox, the candidate from PAN, to win the presidency after seventy-one years of single-party rule.

5

Friction

When you ask "What am I missing?" INTOIT moments can be your answers.

That's because "I never thought of it that way" moments are entirely and exclusively about *you*. What surprises *you*, what challenges *you*, what changes or freshens *your* thinking. Each one is a mental reflex and a total surprise. You can't predict when you'll have them or what you'll have them about any more than you could draw the comprehensive map of your mind at any given moment, with all its trillions of shifting features.

All you can do is observe your INTOIT moments when they light up your mind—and seek them out like our civic health depends on it.

But how do you do this, exactly? How do you spark the kinds of insights that have any hope of building bridges in a divided world? First, you find some friction. You put yourself in spaces where you can interact with people from outside your silos—spaces where it's possible to explore the boundary between their perspectives and your own.

And then, you get curious.

I don't mean that in a cute, "things I learned in kindergarten" way. Curiosity is a serious thing, and it's past time we get serious about it. What we learn relies first and foremost on how open we are to learning, what room we make in our minds and conversations. When we treat curiosity as a passive state that turns on or off on its own, we're missing an opportunity to *own* this wild and wacky virtue of ours by priming our minds to receive curiosity, then pointing it where we want it to take us.

What do we need to know about curiosity to direct it at the things we're missing? And how can we use it to extract new insights and understanding about a tense, messy world—even across big divides?

Sit back and relax, 'cause I've got your curiosity starter kit right here, broken down into four steps I've picked up from fifteen years of being curious for a living, mostly on behalf of the people who've sent me on my favorite adventures: the lovely, zany, and endlessly complicated friends and

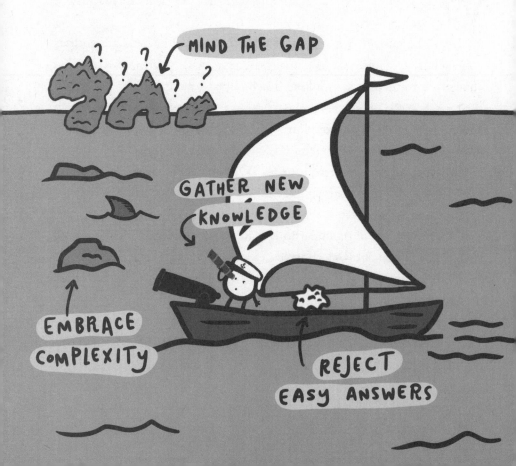

neighbors I've been honored to (imperfectly!) serve as a journalist right here in Seattle:

1. Mind the gap
2. Collect knowledge
3. Reject easy answers
4. Embrace complexity

You ready? Let's go.

STEP 1: MIND THE GAP

Curiosity is one of the urges and drives of life. When you're hungry, you need to eat. When you're thirsty, you need to drink. When you're curious, you need to *know*.

What do you need to know, exactly? Whatever you just realized you're missing. Curiosity flips on when you see a gap—any gap—between what you know and what you *want* to know. But unlike hunger or thirst, it requires your attention. Get distracted by something else, and *poof*—your curiosity's gone. But mind the gap—keep your attention trained on the mystery, and that might set you off on a little adventure.

For a fun illustration of how this works, imagine, if you will, that you're driving past North 80th Street and Aurora Avenue in Seattle. You let your eyes wander past the road and notice something really weird about the small, vacant, fenced-in, grassy lot behind the dental office.

It's covered in stuffed animals.

The first time you drive past it, you wonder what the heck, then put your eyes back on the road. You've got things to do. Places to be. By the time you've turned west, your curiosity's vanished.

The second time you drive past, you notice it's not just stuffed animals scattered on this lot. You could've sworn you spotted fake flowers there, too. But you were halfway through another thought about how you're going to respond to the ten-paragraph email your colleague sent about that project you're leading. You train your attention back on that. Interest gone.

The third time you drive past the lot, you keep your attention on that gap in your knowledge. *Who the hell covered that lot in stuffed animals—and why?* you wonder. You're gonna hit the gas but no, you're running early to work and this is too wacky. You pull over, get out, and take a picture of the lot. At home, you post the pic on social media with a question much like the one a neighbor posted on the message-board site Reddit: "Does anyone know the deal with the empty lot on 80th and 99?"

That empty lot and the speculation it inspired among Seattleites who passed by it sent a former colleague, journalist Anika Anand, searching for her own answer to this very strange, very real puzzle. "The first time I [Anika] drove by the lot, I did a double take, and then craned my neck closer to the passenger side window and squinted until a car behind me honked," she wrote in the Seattle newsletter she and I cofounded in late 2016—*The Evergrey.*

Curiosity at its core is an urge to close a gap in your knowledge. Mind the gap, and you'll fuel your curiosity, which, in turn, will fuel *you.*

This process sounds simple, but it's actually the aggregate of a bunch of ideas from various researchers, which were summed up nicely by George Loewenstein, a professor of economics and psychology at Carnegie Mellon University, in 1994. That's when he consolidated modern curiosity research into a popular framework known as "information-gap theory." Overlay some principles of that theory onto our little neighborhood mystery, and they go something like this:

- **You notice a gap in your knowledge.** Anika knew that vacant lot looked like some kids' menagerie. What she didn't know was why.

- **You want to close the gap.** Anika asked the owner of a nearby auto repair shop if he knew anything. "He laughed in a way that made me sure he knew but wasn't going to tell me," she wrote.

- **The closer you feel you are to closing the gap, the more intense your curiosity will get.** Anika went down rabbit holes on the inter-net until she found some quotes from a woman "who was *particularly* upset" that the city was selling vacant plots of land to developers instead of making them into parks. She gave the woman a call.

- **The more pleasure you get from learning, the less it matters if the learning is hard.** The call led to a confession, an interview, and an invitation. Anika joined community activist Cass Turnbull—who *The Evergrey* dubbed "the guerrilla gardener"—to document her upkeep of the lot-turned-menagerie in silent, personal protest of new development in the neighborhood. "It's a goofy way to point out the changes happening in the city," Turnbull said. Anika documented all this in a story that solved this mystery once and for all.

When you keep your mind on the gap between what you know and what you don't, it tends to get both bigger and smaller. The gap gets bigger because the longer you ponder a puzzle, the more puzzling it gets. The gap gets smaller because of the second step to curiosity, which tends to overlap a good bit with the first.

Set your mind on the hunt for new knowledge, and you're bound—bit by bit—to turn it up.

STEP 2: COLLECT KNOWLEDGE

What are your burning questions about structural rehabilitation design? What keeps you up at night about Viking rune stones? Why am I asking you this?

To prove a point. (Unless, of course, you're a seismic retrofit engineer or the curator of a Nordic museum.) If you don't know *anything* about something, you can't possibly know what to ask about it.

Which brings us to the second key step to channeling your curiosity: before you can see a gap between your existing knowledge and the knowledge you want, you have to have some, well, *existing knowledge.*

That's why, from the early days of *The Evergrey*, we turned to the locals in our community not only for all the best ideas on how to connect to the city, but for all the best questions to help everyone understand it. It became a habit with most of our projects, including our series of neighborhood guides. You've got to know stuff to ask stuff, and there's *way* more curiosity-fueling knowledge in the lives and perspectives of our thousands of readers than in those of our tiny team.

To put our collective curiosity to work, we followed a pretty foolproof process: announce the topic we're exploring in the newsletter, ask for people's deep-down questions about it, send the strongest questions back to our readers for a vote—*Which question are you most curious about? Which one should we report on next?*—then write up a story on the winning question that fills the gaps only our community can know they've got.

It's how Beth Anderson got us thinking about earthquakes in Pioneer Square, knowing it's packed with historic landmarks the Big One could turn to dust: "What's being done to protect this historic neighborhood, particularly from earthquakes? Have there been any efforts to retrofit all the old brick buildings?"

And it's how Ian King had us dig into the history of one of our most vibrant neighborhoods, knowing it's packed with restaurants and shops that offer Scandinavian fare like aquavit and lutefisk: "Why did Ballard become identified with Scandinavian residents? What brought them to Ballard in the first place?"

The broader your baseline knowledge about something, the more curious you will get about it. Up to a point, anyway. According to the information-gap theory, your curiosity is most intense not when you know too little about something, or too much, but *just enough* to make it tug at you. Here's an example: Picture a leading seismic retrofit engineer getting pulled into a conversation about basic earthquake upgrades to buildings in historic neighborhoods. She'll answer questions about why those buildings are at risk politely enough, but she won't ask any of her own. She knows too much already. But spot that same engineer at that weekend's summit on advanced structural rehabilitation, and you'll see her wide-eyed and taking notes about the latest developments in prestressed structures and seismic vibration control, pushing the frontiers of her knowledge. A staffer at the National Nordic Museum in Ballard won't sit on the edge of his seat next time someone reviews the neighborhood's Scandinavian history. But if someone's dishing on the various styles of Viking rune stones—a feature of their exhibit—he'll probably join in.

Picture the people in your life who you think of as super curious. Unless they're kiddos, firing questions at anyone who'll answer, they probably know a little bit about a lot. Enough to keep them asking questions in a virtuous cycle that checks the vicious one spun up by sorting, othering, and siloing.

Want to prime your mind for curiosity? Expose yourself to something new once in a while. The more knowledge you get, the more questions it sparks. Those questions pull in more knowledge, which sparks more questions, and on and on and on.

STEP 3: REJECT EASY ANSWERS

Most of the time, complexity ain't sexy. We're too busy or tired for it. Prone to reaction, not reflection. Swimming in our silos because who has the time? So we sidle right up to curiosity's archnemesis (*shakes fist in the air*): certainty.

The reason why is simple: If you think you know, you won't think to ask. The voices in your silos have all the answers anyway. Easy answers that surround you, that jibe with your perspective, that promise that this or that issue "really just comes down to *this*."

That's why the next step to channeling your curiosity—as you mind information gaps and collect baseline knowledge—is in some ways the most important. It's to reject more easy answers about your world so you can ask more of the questions that will help you explore it.

In 2018, Seattle's King County had the third-largest homeless population in the country and was in its third year of a declared homelessness state of emergency. Tents had shown up on sidewalks, along highways, and in city parks. The most recent one-night count found 12,112 of our neighbors living homeless across the county.

It was about as big and complicated an issue as our city had. At *The Evergrey* we weren't sure how to tackle it, but we knew that locals' questions were a good place to start. And the more questions we could collect—and answer—the better.

But we had some serious limits. It was just me and our one reporter then, Ana Sofia Knauf, with a daily newsletter that reached 12,000 locals. To take on this beast, we needed help. So I started making calls. First to Monica Nickelsburg at GeekWire, a news site for the city's booming tech industry. Would she partner with us on this? Then to Stephanie Snyder at Hearken, the platform that made it easy for us to poll our readers for questions. Would they allow us to collect questions from several publications in one big digital bucket?

They *would*, and then some. So while Monica Nickelsburg and I ran a pilot call for questions for our respective audiences, I made more calls. To Cambria Roth and Mason Bryan at Crosscut, a regional news site that had done loads to unify the city's coverage of homelessness under its #SeaHomeless initiative; to Jill Jackson at KUOW, our public radio station; to Ashley Archibald at *Real Change*, our city's street paper that serves and employs our homeless neighbors; to Daniel DeMay at Seattlepi.com, a general news site for the city; to Neal McNamara at community site Patch, who'd asked to join after seeing the pilot; and to Beth Kramer at *ParentMap*, a magazine for local families.

Together, we asked our communities for their deep-down honest questions about homelessness, got *more than four hundred of them*, and sent the best back to our respective audiences for a vote in bunches matching each newsroom's expertise (questions about business and tech's role went to GeekWire; questions about homeless families went to *ParentMap*). In the end, we reported a total of ten deeply researched stories that summer answering our community's most popular questions about homelessness. Questions like:

What are other cities doing that works and why aren't we as effective?

Who is doing what to reduce new entrants to the homeless population?

How do the unhoused think we should address our housing challenges? What would they tell homeowners? Renters? Politicians? Businesses?

The questions weren't simple, the stories weren't either, and that was the point. In asking locals to come up with the questions themselves, we were pushing them to ask, "What am I missing?" To pay attention to gaps in *their* understanding based on the imperfect knowledge *they'd* collected. We got questions from all kinds of folks, including several readers who were currently or formerly homeless themselves.

In some of the best questions, you could see the easy answers people rejected to ask them. Like with the first of two reader questions Ana Sofía reported on for *The Evergrey*, asked by local Craig Danz: "Does Seattle get an influx of homeless people from outside areas attracted to better services?"

Twenty-seven people in our initial callout asked a version of this question—one that rejected a popular notion about homelessness in the area in order to ask if it's really true.

It's not, as we shared in our story.

Although, of course, it's complicated.

STEP 4: EMBRACE COMPLEXITY

Confusion is such a killjoy. I can't tell you how many good story ideas died on my desk as soon as I realized I had no idea where to start. It's the flip side of a principle from the information-gap theory. If it feels like you're close to an answer, your curiosity will pick up. But if it feels like the answer is far away—perched on the summit of a distant, difficult mountain—your curiosity will slow down.

You know what the key word is in all that, though? "Feels."

Big, tough questions are big, tough questions. You'll want to take short-cuts. Close doors. Simplify. But there is no simplifying tough issues while still getting them right. You need the friction. As the legendary broadcast journalist Edward R. Murrow once quipped, "Anyone who isn't confused doesn't really understand the situation."

To be curious, you'll have to resist. You'll have to ask, "What am I missing?" and hover in uncertainty a while. Whether that *feels* like a slog or not is all about how you see it, and there's a better way to see it.

It's not confusion; it's complexity.

And complexity, it turns out, is not a curiosity killer at all.

Take the evidence dug up at one of the most fascinating research facilities in the country—the Difficult Conversations Lab at Columbia University. In one of the lab's studies, researchers had pairs of people who disagreed on a polarizing issue (say, gun regulations) do three things: read an article about the issue, talk about the issue, then evaluate how their difficult one-on-one conversations went.

In one experimental condition, the participants read an article that made the case for and against the polarizing issue "like a lawyer's opening statement," wrote journalist Amanda Ripley. In the other condition, they read an article that was more complex and nuanced, describing different points of view on the issue with compassion, "more like an anthropologist's field notes."

The lab's findings? What the pairs of people read before they talked made a big difference. The people who read the simple article tended to get bogged down in negativity. The people who read the more complex article got more curious and were happier with their chats. "They don't solve the debate," lab director Peter T. Coleman told Ripley, "but they do have a more nuanced understanding and more willingness to continue the conversation."

If you're confused, you're overwhelmed. You're looking for the exits in the search for understanding. If things are just getting complicated, though, isn't it another way of saying they're just getting interesting? You've dug up lots more gaps your curiosity can rush to fill. It's a challenge. A dare.

In a lot of ways, confusion is just complexity before you put curiosity to work.

༆

Is his first book of essays, the French philosopher Michel de Montaigne gets all excited about travel.* He talks about how healthy it is for our minds to see

---

* Yes, I just jumped from present-day Seattle to the French Renaissance. Curiosity knows no bounds, amirite?

different things and check out different customs. Not just so we can know, like, how many steps are in the old Pantheon in Rome, he says. But also to "rub and polish our brains against those of others."

Rub and polish our brains against those of others. Now, I wasn't going to pass on much of any of the loads of centuries-old quotes and quips people have collected about learning and curiosity and all that. But for Michel here, I had to make an exception, because this idea that our brains need polish and that the polish is other brains . . . *Merci beaucoup*, Michel. You nailed it.

To bridge divides, we need friction. To make sure that friction sparks the kinds of insights that serve as a check on the warped, narrow view from our silos, we need to put our curiosity to work—minding the gaps between what we know and what we don't, collecting knowledge that inspires different questions, charging ahead on the most complicated issues, and not letting lazy, easy answers suffice.

But first, we need another polishing brain to talk to.

And, ideally, some clue of what the heck to say.

6

Conversation

My favorite word in Spanish has no translation in English. It's the word "*sobremesa*." It refers to the conversation that follows a meal while everyone's still sitting at the table ("*sobre*" = over; "*mesa*" = table). And it always makes me think of my grandmother's giant, round wooden dining table and one of the biggest mysteries of my childhood:

Why do grown-ups think that sitting around and talking is *fun*?

That table seemed ginormous when I was little. It had eight big chairs that made a loud *squonk* on the marble floors when you moved them. "*Ay, siéntate, Mamá!*" one of my aunts would say—*Oh, sit down, Mom!*—when my grandmother would get up at the slightest hint of anyone needing anything from the kitchen.

The midday meal is a big deal in Mexico. My aunts Martha and Lety and my uncle Beto would leave work to eat at my grandmother's. She never fixed the low flames on her gas stove and spent half the morning cooking the multi-dish feast she'd arrange on the table's lazy Susan. At eight or nine years old, I'd have to stand at my seat to spin the tray and reach the rice with tomatoes, the chicken mole, the refried beans, the *milanesa de res*—breaded skirt steak with a squeeze of the Mexican limes that grew in her garden.

We'd drink Coke or apple-flavored Joya, or, for the adults, Carta Blanca beer made right there in Monterrey, everyone spinning and spinning looking for the bottle opener that hid among the serving dishes.

After cleaning my plate I'd get something from the candy jar shaped like a monkey's head—dulce de leche lollipops or Gansitos Marinela snack cakes—then push through the room's swinging door to go watch cartoons or play.

The adults would trade their plates for ashtrays, their Cokes for Nescafé instant coffees. That's when their conversation *grew*. It turned to work, current events, everyone's lives, occasionally to my parents and how the hell it's going, raising me and my little brother, Bernardo, in the States.

All I'd hear from the rec room at the back of the house was the occasional roar of laughter. They never turned on the little TV in that room, I thought, so what the heck was so funny? Passing by on my way to the yard, I heard deep voices and loud voices. Sharpness. An argument. Uh-oh. But then, laughter again. Almost immediately. *How?*

An hour would go by. Two. Lunch started at 2:30 PM and the *sobremesa* would finally be done—tablecloth up, everyone gone, my grandfather, who'd sneaked off when no one noticed, awake from his siesta—at 6 PM, dang close to dinnertime in the US.

～⁀ᔕ

If I'm being honest (and I always try!), it's *still* a huge mystery to me, how powerful it is when people come together just to talk.

It puts our minds into contact. Our thoughts and questions and nagging worries all show up. Whatever we're trying to hide . . . something's bound to come out. So no wonder it's easier to look for insights in places that don't involve us—books and articles and the like.

But there is no question that the most valuable opportunity to put our curiosity to work is *precisely* in that vulnerable place where perspectives meet in all their raw complexity, ready to push and bend, to reveal and be revealed. Working through the friction requires some edge. Some risk.

It requires, in other words, conversation.

Conversation is by far the most powerful tool for understanding people across divides. Why is it so great? For starters, it is way, *way* more than just people *talking*. Now, granted: Very few of the bajillion conversations you'll have in your life are going to live up to the full potential of this everyday art. Most of them will be necessarily short, simple, and forgettable.

But when you *do* choose to make the most of what conversation is capable of, finding yourself in exchanges with their own energy and momentum, what begins as a passing meeting of minds can grow into something transformative and unstoppable. Something that, even quietly and subtly, can build, maintain, or cross bridges that span the gulfs between us all.

In my lifelong love affair with what I call **bridging conversations**—the kind that help us understand each other by letting us explore the spaces between our perspectives—I've zeroed in on two superpowers of conversation that help our exchanges reach that level, two characteristics I missed when I puzzled over the *sobremesa* around my grandmother's table, but that I now keep an eye on in all my exchanges. These are conversation's power to fuel itself and bond its participants.

CONVERSATION IS SELF-FUELING

When you break it all down, a conversation only needs two things to get it going: willing minds and a little time. Given that, it can often generate the fuel it needs to go in the direction it's meant to—if those willing minds know to let it.

I hadn't learned to trust this conversational superpower when I looked up from my notebook during a summer journalism workshop, years ago, totally confused by something that its instructor, Pulitzer Prize winner Jacqui Banaszynski, had just said.

It was the summer after my college graduation, two months before I was set to kick off my first journalism gig as a cops reporter at the *Houston Chronicle*. The prospect had me terrified, but Jacqui had me rapt. Her writing was exquisite, her teaching clear, sharp, and serious. I'd watch Jacqui's loose white hair sway as she paced the circle of tables where we, her acolytes, had arrayed ourselves, hooked on her every word. And I knew that until the day I could carry myself with that much confidence, I wanted to do everything this woman told me to do, and do it to the very best of my ability.

When I looked up from my notebook, Jacqui had just finished explaining the follow-up questions exercise we were about to try: (1) Turn to a partner and ask a question. (2) Ask a follow-up question based solely on what they said in response to your first one. (3) Ask your *next* question based only on *that* response, and so on, not breaking the pattern, 'til they say stop.

No, Jacqui, I thought. *That won't work at all.* Back then I showed up to interviews for my journalism internships at New Hampshire Public Radio and my hometown newspaper, *Foster's Daily Democrat,* with long lists of questions I spent tons of time preparing. The day of an interview, I'd check to make sure I had that list when I left the office, when I got into my car, when I got *out* of my car, when I stepped into the building the interview would be at, when I waited for the elevator, when I stepped *out* of the elevator, just everywhere, all the time, because without that list I wouldn't know what to say, and my interviewee would look at me funny, and the conversation and maybe my career would all be *over.* The only way I was going to ask *my* questions, Jacqui and her genius and this workshop be damned, was by asking my first question, taking notes, asking my second question, taking notes, and so on down the list. *It never fails,* I thought.

Except that it always did, for one key reason: Every time I did my interviews this way, I refused to let them develop as conversations. I refused to let them generate the fuel they would need to go deeper and deeper. I refused to let them *grow.*

Jacqui didn't put it this way in her workshop, but one of the things she was teaching us with this exercise was to really, truly mind the gaps. To trust that discussions between humans always turn up great material, so long as we are engaged enough to listen to ourselves and each other and let our curiosity do its work.

I tried Jacqui's exercise that day and barely knew what I was doing. But I sensed that the faith she put in curiosity was right, and that if I could tap my curiosity, and encourage whoever I interviewed to do the same, it would power our conversations. It would give them their fuel.

Eventually, I learned not only that I *could* trust each interview to take us where we needed to go but that I *should*, because that takes the conversation in surprising new directions, leaves more room for the people I talk with to share deeper stories, and makes the stories I produce truer and better. I began to write down fewer questions on those lists before my interviews and eventually none—preferring to let them play in my mind on the way and emerge on their own, *if* the conversation calls for them.

Like all good journalism skills, this one's not just for journalists: *All* conversations benefit from the freedom to wander where they will, and the close attention of participants to lead them there. And when a *bridging* conversation succeeds in leaving room for our questions, it addresses our tensions, too, which levels everything up by making it easier to get curious. Why? Because rejecting easy answers to explore more complicated ones isn't so hard when it isn't so stressful. Then the rest of the job of getting curious comes down to a repeating cycle of minding gaps and collecting

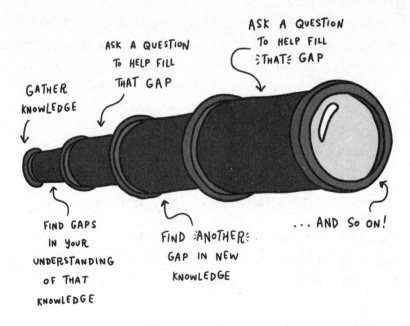

ASK A QUESTION
To HELP FILL
THAT GAP

ASK A QUESTION
To HELP FILL
⸭THAT⸭ GAP

GATHER
KNOWLEDGE

FIND GAPS
IN YOUR
UNDERSTANDING
OF THAT
KNOWLEDGE

FIND ⸭ANOTHER⸭
GAP IN NEW
KNOWLEDGE

... AND So ON!

knowledge (knowledge → gap → more knowledge → more gaps), each one getting you a closer and closer look at something you want to see clearly.

The more of these cycles you run in your conversation, the more you'll learn, the deeper you'll go, and the more chances you'll have to spark "I never thought of it that way" moments that pump *even more* fuel into the whole experience. You've been there, in conversation, when a story you share from your life reminds someone of a related one from their own. They share that story, adding to the pool of knowledge collecting between you. You ask a question, seeing a gap open up between what you know and what you want to know. Their answer releases an INTOIT moment for you—a new insight. It fills you with energy. You're pumped. And now this flood of questions streams into your mind, and the first one to answer is: *Where do I start?*

I let conversations generate so much fuel now, it gets me into trouble. But it's trouble I'd earn all over again: the urgent phone calls I didn't pick up because someone was in the middle of an amazing story. The checks I wrote to the municipal court of Seattle because I'd rather get a parking ticket than pump the brakes on this awesome, spontaneous debate. The flurry of apologies to someone I left waiting because that last conversation made nothing else matter, including the time.

When people come open and engaged to conversation, there's always something to spin up. "You had to be there," people say when they try and fail to convey not just what happened in some memorable somewhere, but the energy everyone felt as a result. They're more right than they know.

When we're *in* conversation, we're somewhere we've never been before. We're meeting particular minds in particular states at some particular moment. You had to be there because there's nowhere else like it in the world.

CONVERSATION IS BONDING

As conversations generate fuel, they also spin up something else: a connection. If two people are talking, they are in a relationship that has the potential to grow deeper. Always. You never know when a hi at the grocery store, your order at the drive-thru, or the comment on your social media page might be the first of many exchanges you'll have with someone you're grateful to know. Even a small bit of connection goes a long way, as the knowledge you share and the gaps you fill reveal points of commonality that stitch you together. What's *so effing cool* to me is that this happens to us all the time—all the time!—without our consciously knowing it, or even working that hard to make it happen. Like the time I said hello to a woman I'd never seen before at yoga after she'd told our instructor that she couldn't speak English very well. I offered Mandi a ride home and in the car learned she had two kids the same age as mine. Or the time my husband, Jason, got to talking with the man sitting next to him on a flight from California. They geeked out big when they realized they both loved video games and became fast friends.

The connections we generate in conversation help us build trust with each other, which helps us release deeper stories, revealing more gaps in our collected knowledge. But it also gives us courage, helping us to ask the questions we really want to ask and give the answers we really mean. When there's more trust, there's less fear, and taking risks in bridging conversations becomes easier. The bonds we make in conversation help us talk about harder things.

A journalist who's used this conversational superpower to help people talk better about tough issues is nationally syndicated columnist Connie Schultz. Schultz is a Pulitzer Prize winner from Ohio, and through her social media she hosts some of the most thoughtful cross-partisan digital dialogues I've ever seen. Thousands of people come to her Facebook page for real talk about tough political topics. Everything from same-sex marriage to race issues is on the agenda, whatever people in Ohio and beyond are mulling about at home. You'd expect people to scream at each other, but to a surprising degree, they don't. They listen and reflect. I was scrolling through her page some years ago, wondering how she managed to do this so well on such a big scale, when I landed on a photo of her dog, Franklin.

I remember one thing people used to say when they railed against social media in the early days: "No one wants to know what you had for breakfast!"

The funny thing is, seemingly little things like knowing what you had for breakfast, along with whether you watched that show last night, or how you felt about the traffic this morning, help people relate. Everyone has breakfast. Hearing about yours makes me think about mine, and though it isn't breaking news or anything, knowing that I have Multi Grain Cheerios with almond milk every morning tells you something about me, even if it's a little, tiny something.

It also helps remind those of us trading words on screens online that there are human beings behind them.

When Schultz shared that photo of Franklin, she invited her Facebook followers to share photos of their own pets. Dozens of dog and cat photos flowed in, along with loads of likes and laughs.

Posts like this are not meant to distract contributors from serious issues, Schultz told me, but to help them build the bonds that help them tackle tough issues well. The prompts are practice: they get people into friendly interactions, regardless of their views on other things, building up the camaraderie that can help them muscle through the tricky stuff.

FROM IDEAS TO PEOPLE

Conversation's two superpowers help us span divides by making it easier to be curious, generating fuel that helps us take close looks with less stress, and creating bonds that build trust, so we can approach tougher topics, let our guard down, and be honest.

But there's one more thing worth mentioning here.

Think about your favorite long conversations of all time. The ones that felt fun, productive, and kind of challenging. Maybe one was on a road trip. The *sobremesa* after a meal. Or at some bar where you closed the place down without even meaning to.

Chances are, these conversations were driven by more than just cycles of gaps and knowledge. You wanted to know not just what each person thought, but *why* and *how*. You started talking about some piece of a perspective but crept from what you think to why you think it. You were interested in ideas and became more interested in each other—on what their ideas say about *them* and what your ideas say about *you*.

At some point, if you let it, curiosity about ideas morphs into curiosity about people.

This is important for two reasons. One: minding these kinds of gaps and questions gets you exploring right there at the border between your perspectives, releasing one INTOIT moment after another. Individual people are the world's foremost experts in only one thing, after all—themselves.

And two: getting interested in people opens a bottomless supply of questions and the best kind of drive to explore them.

Psychology researcher Jordan Litman has identified two types of curiosity—which, in the broadest sense, is just a thirst for knowledge. But whether we are thirsty because our throat is parched or because there's this delicious-sounding new drink and our mouth waters at the thought of it are two very different things. Litman calls the parched type "deprivation-based curiosity," or "D-curiosity," and the mouth-watering type "interest-based curiosity," or "I-curiosity."

D-curiosity begins with that icky feeling of not having knowledge you really want to know and sets out to make the bad feeling go away. It can be as simple as knowing the name of that actor in that show but dammit, it's not coming to you. Or it can be a lot more loaded. The most effective title for an email newsletter I've ever seen is "WTF Just Happened Today?" It was started by a fellow Seattleite named Matt Kiser after the 2016 election, targeted squarely at liberals and others who felt utterly confounded by the Trump administration, and it grew to forty thousand subscribers within a year. That's the power of deprivation curiosity for you.

D-curiosity is careful, specific, and reactive. You're more likely to tiptoe as you learn, dodging anxiety or tension along the way. If you find what you're looking for, then phew! You're done, and you're out of there.

I-curiosity wants none of that. It's adventurous, driven by an *interest* in closing an information gap, rather than the *anxiety* of leaving it open. You've got to build enough trust to pursue that interest all the way, of course, and run enough cycles of gaps and knowledge about each other to keep the conversation well fueled. But then you get proactive. You explore, and together, you help each other learn.

Over time, you might realize what I came to appreciate many years and many hundreds of interviews after Jacqui Banaszynski's workshop. I began to see that all my little questions about someone's ideas or opinions or contributions always danced around a bigger one. And that training my mind on that one driving question, once I could see it and name it, makes every interview not only fluid and fascinating, but productive. *What made this woman drop everything to pursue such an audacious project that's turning heads? Why do millions of people think this man's unusual ideas are so exciting? Why does this new tax idea make these people really happy but these other people really mad?*

Be D-curious about ideas, and you may hit a stopping point. Be I-curious about the people around you, and you could go on forever.

Unless, of course, your conversations lose their grip.

7

Traction

OK. So I've given you the lowdown on how divided we are and why. You've seen how your curiosity can give you a clearer view of different perspectives—helping you build and cross bridges whenever you want to understand someone else without judgment. This is plenty—and enough!—considering the damage that all these wrong, warped ideas we hold about each other do to our world. I've let you know why you want to be *in* conversation to let curiosity work its magic.

But I haven't shown you how you know the moment is right. What kinds of conversational setups are good for suddenly asking someone for their take on gun control or trustworthy elections? When is the right time or place to bring up why in the world that person you know believes that thing they believe—the one that makes you wonder if they're really just terrible and you should do your best to dominate, humiliate, or avoid them?

Is texting OK for that? Email? How about a back-and-forth on social media? Do bridging conversations hold up better over Zoom or over coffee? Should *some* good, strong drink be nearby, no matter what?

I don't have yes or no answers on this. Instead, I offer you dials. Here. *I hand you your very own portable conversation console, complete with five clearly*

labeled dials that jump to life, their needles shaking back and forth. Bring this to your next conversation or prospective conversation, and these dials—time, attention, parity, containment, and embodiment—will help you figure out if you can bridge divides *productively.*

What are these dials, exactly? Here's the 101:

To start with the obvious, conversations need **time** to develop knowledge that reveals gaps, form bonds that build trust and depth, and find their fuel and direction to let people explore the boundary between their perspectives. Over three days in February 2016, profoundly curious about how conversation showed up in my life, I tracked every single in-person exchange I had with every single human being—from a seconds-long "Hi" with a colleague to an hours-long dinner conversation with friends. Out of 169 total exchanges, 79 percent clocked in at five minutes or less, and just 4 percent went on for an hour or more.[*] For each exchange, several of which rose to the level of a bridging conversation, I rated how much I learned through it, and how much I enjoyed it. I made charts and everything, folks. And surprise, surprise: the longer the conversations lasted, the more I got out of them.

---

[*] I told you I'm obsessed! And 4 percent of these going for an hour or more, by the way, is a *lot*. I was doing an academic fellowship at the time—the Nieman Foundation fellowship at Harvard. Everywhere I turned, someone was talking. In all, I spent an average of six and a half hours per day in in-person conversation!

The second dial on your console is **attention**. We are a generation of shameless multitaskers, so it's always worth asking: How much of your attention is on the conversation you're having, versus the email you're drafting, the social media feed you're scrolling, the browser window you've tucked behind your videoconference pane, or the umpteen unrelated problems and preoccupations floating through your head? Whether you're remote or in person, it's possible for your conversations to find fuel, depth, and direction without your mind being fully engaged in them. But it'll come in fits and starts. Especially if the person you're talking to can tell you're not fully with them and decides they may as well not be fully with you.

Next up is **parity**. When you read this book, my ideas interact with your ideas, but your ideas have no way of interacting with mine. When you ask questions at a panel discussion or leave comments on a thread in social media, you can have a say but a limited one; you're cast in the role of a responder rather than co-creator, and someone might shut off your mic or delete your comment. You have to be on level ground with others in a conversation for it to do meaningful work for *all* of you, sharing equal status and at least a chance at equal speaking time. Tracking or enforcing either of these things would be hella awkward, so parity is an imperfect science and the toughest of our five dials to measure or interpret. But the reason it matters comes down to this: If the context you're in values one voice over another, the conversation will value one voice over another, too. And it may not be yours.

The fourth dial is **containment**, and it's the one I wish more of us would give a damn about. When digital platforms display our conversations to huge groups of people, those conversations become as much or more about performing our perspectives than exploring them. That can really clobber curiosity, and I can't stress this enough. We're so accustomed now to speaking to a massive arena of potential listeners on social media that we never stop to think how effing weird that is—to say something into the world and have no clue who's hearing it. These huge and often invisible audiences of ours become a messy wildcard in conversation, tugging at our ego and anxiety in ways that warp our search for knowledge, gaps, bonds, and direction—even when we pretend they don't. What will your digital friends and followers think if they took what you're saying in a different way than you meant it? What hostile, vengeful listener might be out there, ready to twist your words against you? Would you say more of what you want to say if you didn't have to worry?

Finally, we have **embodiment**. That includes your gestures, your facial expressions, your volume, pace and tone, everything biology synced up with your mind to help you get your meaning into the world. There is one and only one context where human beings can use 100 percent of our embodiment to (try to!) make ourselves understood, and that's in-person interaction. Every other means of communication—speaking by phone or videoconference, through writing, texting, social media, and so on— denies you *some* access to that full complement of human expression. Not to rag too much on technology, though, because the trade-offs—where we accept them—are pretty great. Who doesn't appreciate being able to talk to someone when they're way far away from you (access), doing lots of things at once while you talk (multitasking), reaching lots of people at once when you talk (scale), tinkering with what you say before you say it (editing), adding tone and sass with emojis and GIFs (visuals), and dropping in and out of ongoing conversations anytime you want (asynchronicity)? To be clear: You don't need full embodiment to have good bridging conversations. But it helps!

Obviously, there's no actual portable conversation console. Luckily, it doesn't matter. So long as you take a moment to ask *yourself* what these dials might show, you can make smarter choices about whether to spark or join exchanges. Ask:

- What kind of time do people have to let this conversation grow?

- How much attention can we practically commit to it?

- How possible is it for everyone who's talking to meet on level ground, so we can ask and answer questions evenhandedly?

- To what degree is this conversation contained to only us? If we have an audience, how likely is it that we will want to perform at the expense of connecting with each other?

- How much of our full, embodied complement of communication tools can we bring to help us get our meaning across?

Let's look at two different scenarios to see how this translates to real life and to give you a chance at reading those conversation console dials yourself.

These scenarios star a pair of cousins—a conservative woman and a liberal man.* Considering the turbulence of the last couple presidential races, they each carry some strong opinions about how well America's elections are living up to the ideal.

We'll play out scenario 1 from the perspective of the liberal man, and scenario 2 from the perspective of the conservative woman.

Scenario 1: The Social Media Post

You (a liberal man) are scrolling through a social media site on your smartphone as you wait for a friend to meet you for lunch. You stop scrolling when you see something your conservative cousin published this morning—a link

---

* My apologies, centrist readers; I haven't forgotten you!

to an article arguing that the Left wants to relax election security to an alarming degree. Alongside the article, she added her take that this would mean the end of democracy as we know it. Your pulse quickens. *This is absurd*, you think, *not to mention harmful*. You tap the button to add a comment on her post. You've known for a while that your cousin thinks like this, and though you've rolled your eyes at her when politics comes up at gatherings, you've never really asked her why she thinks voter fraud is a concern when to you it's clearly not. Maybe now's as good a time as any to find out.

Now it's *your* turn, dear reader: Our protagonist is wondering if he should kick off a bridging conversation here or not. Where would you put the needle on each of our dials? *(Psst! I'm actually asking! Before you go on, walk yourself through the dials. In this scenario, would they each register as high, medium, or low?)*

- **Time:** *Low.* The man's friend is due at the restaurant any minute, and he can't exactly ask him to wait. If he manages to post a comment now, he won't see any response until way later.

- **Attention:** *Low.* See above. Plus, his cousin posted this hours ago. Who knows what her attention is on now, and whether she'd put it squarely on his comment when she sees it?

- **Parity:** *Low.* This is his cousin's online territory. A few other people have commented, all in approval of her take so far. His comment might really irritate her. If she wanted to block him, she could.

- **Containment:** *Low.* This is a public post. The cousins have plenty of mutual friends on this social media site. Who knows how they'd react—or who the heck else is listening?

- **Embodiment:** *Low.* It's just words and text. As bare bones as it gets. Well, and maybe the thinking emoji, so she knows he's just trying to be curious?

With all the dials on low, leaving a comment on his cousin's post—I think you'd agree—is not the best idea.

Now to be clear: It could work out just fine. So much depends on how the cousins choose to navigate whatever develops, and our dials can't see the future. But with the conversation so ill equipped to grow and channel their curiosity meaningfully, is it likely that the man's comment might spin up understanding between them and release an INTOIT moment or two? Probably not.

Scenario 2: The Phone Call

You (a conservative woman) are on a phone call with your liberal cousin to square up on logistics around a big family barbecue this weekend. You've both signed up to bring food and the like, and you've set aside a little time this evening to chat it all through. With the conversation wrapping up, your mind turns to a moment from the last time you saw your cousin— at a mutual friend's birthday party—that really bothered you. You'd over-heard him go on and on with your mutual friend, who's also liberal, about a massive Republican assault on voting access across the country, and how it would spell the end of democracy as we know it. Maybe you could try changing the subject from beer and bratwurst and ask him why he thinks voting access is the issue when security around elections seems to you to be the more pressing problem.

Hey there, reader! Quiz time again. Where do *you* read the dials here?

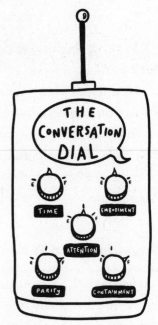

- **Time:** *Medium*. The woman's cousin hasn't said he needs to go any-time soon, and it's already evening—past time for dinner or work meetings. Then again, she's not there, and he might have things he'd rather do than talk politics.

- **Attention:** *Medium*. Except for a couple moments where she had to repeat herself because he'd gotten distracted by his dog and then, later, when the signal dropped, both cousins seem to be generally tuned in to each other.

- **Parity:** *High*. If things get hairy, both of them can hang up.

- **Containment:** *High*. With no one else around, this discussion stays just between the cousins.

- **Embodiment:** *Medium*. Her cousin has a way of being sarcastic some-times, and it'd be nice if she could see his face when he talks about this stuff. Still, both cousins say a lot with the tone and cadence of their voice.

This scenario presents a very different picture from the first. With containment high, there's little chance that either cousin would put on a show with their opinions. No one else is watching, except maybe the dog. It's hard to say how much time they'd really have to get into things, and it is easy with a phone call to sneak out of an uncomfortable conversation you're not pumped to get into. *You know, I should probably go. Early day tomorrow . . .*

Still, if the woman can ask her questions in a way that helps her cousin unpack his views genuinely and honestly,* a good bridging conversation has a chance, at least, of really happening.

⌒⌒⌒

We could test our conversation console on a bunch of other potential interactions. Maybe one of the cousins considers asking the other their questions in person, a few paces away from family, at the barbecue (embodiment = high, containment = medium). Or maybe they both find themselves on opposite sides of the same group text where someone *else* raises the topic and a bunch of folks step out of their physical lives to go all in for an action-packed half hour (time = medium, attention = high, parity = high).

Point is: All the dials reading low is no guarantee of a bad bridging conversation, and all the dials reading high is no guarantee of a good one, either. But keeping an eye on the time, attention, parity, containment, and embodiment available to any conversation is a good first step to making it a bridging one.

And speaking of making conversations, the actions you can take as a result of tracking these dials don't just boil down to engaging or not engaging with a conversation as it is. You can also *turn up* the dials to make a conversation better. Did someone who disagrees with you leave a charged comment on your social media post? Dial up parity and containment by moving things to a private message thread. Is your friend pulling you into a text thread that's spiraling into something fraught and emotional? Dial up time and embodiment by giving them a call.

Your curiosity—and your nerves—will thank you.

---

* More—much more!—on how to ask great bridging questions is coming later in this book.

THE TRACTION LOOP

The British philosopher Michael Oakeshott was on to something when he called conversation an "unrehearsed intellectual adventure." I take only one issue with the idea: Conversation isn't just intellectual. It's also emotional, about the heart as much as the head.

So when a conversation cowers at the foot of the next big challenge—emotional or intellectual—the unrehearsed adventure stalls, along with our attempt to see what we're missing. When our conversations get stuck, we get stuck, too.

But what if we figure out how to take on those challenges? Could we just reach up and try?

Well . . . on the one hand, we don't want to fall. We don't want to burden ourselves with conversations that stress us out or scare us. On the other hand, we can't just avoid each other all the time, or treat every exchange with someone who doesn't see things our way like some high-stakes showdown.

All that just blinds us, reducing our world to whatever's contained in the solid walls of our silos. So as we start to reach, we need to find some purchase with each other's perspectives. We need to get a grip.

Isaac Asimov called conversations where people connect and learn together "cerebrations" (yes, just one letter off from "celebrations"). The bridging conversations I'm talking about don't *party*, exactly. They *work*. But it can be fun work! Especially if you can develop another quality that's going to help you climb toward the kinds of insights and understanding that keep your world from shrinking.

You're going to need balance.

Bridging conversations where we learn something new (**reach**), connect to each other (**grip**), and respect what each other has to offer (**balance**), I've learned, build up something that's crucial to staying curious in dangerously divided times. It's something you need, and need to keep, to spin up those cycles of knowledge sharing and gap spotting that help you curiously scout the boundaries between your perspectives. Something I like to call **traction**.

Every bridging conversation begins with just the *possibility* of traction. You're sharing a space—physical, auditory, or digital—where you *could* talk. Or maybe you're already talking, but about lighthearted things, nothing tricky. You've read the conversation dials—time, attention, parity, containment, and embodiment—and decided the foundation is solid enough under you to bring up a risky topic. But what if the conversation can't handle it?

You'd think it'd be impossible to quantify what separates a resilient conversation from a weaker one. But researchers at the Difficult Conversations Lab at Columbia University managed to do it. They found out that if a conversation has three moments of positivity for every moment of negativity, it's less likely to succumb to an emotional or intellectual "collapse."

What positivity and negativity look like will vary from person to person, but it begins with glue. What binds you together? This is why talking at a party about the weather or the pretzels is so cliché. It's that important to find *something* in common to connect on. Positivity also comes from making each other smile or laugh. But while connection and amusement make any conversation a pleasant use of time, the real test of a potential bridging conversation is to see if it can wade into something more substantive. Can you ask tough questions? Learn from each other? Explore something meaningful and *still* find points of connection and reasons to smile?

A friend of mine, Boting Zhang, came up with a handy way to think about how to show up to a bridging conversation after she brought ten Trump voters and ten Clinton voters together for a series of in-depth digital discussions after the 2016 election. "I think of the analogy of being a winding river," she said. "You don't want to be a stagnant pond, which is in my mind people being stuck and not wanting to talk or engage. But you don't want to be a rushing current, emotions [spewing] forth unchecked."

You can tell you've built up the traction a bridging conversation craves when people get comfortable with the uncomfortable. When someone in the group that's debating major controversies in the headlines says, "Should we sit down?" When the person you're direct messaging on social media about racism starts sending his replies right after you've sent yours, and you scroll back through two hours later to realize you've spun gold together.

One of the most beautiful things in the world is when people change their plans for each other. And they will do it for a great conversation. I see it all the time. It'll become too engrossing, too productive, and yes—too *fun* to step away. So people will give it what it needs to grow stronger. They'll *dial up* their time, attention, parity, containment, and embodiment of human expression.

Building traction in a conversation is an imprecise art. But if you practice four conversational skills with the goal of finding reach, grip, and balance, your unrehearsed adventure will take you further than you thought you could go. Together, these four skills form what I call the Traction LOOP. I'll be reaching for this loop as I share tips to guide your bridging conversations in all the following chapters in this book. And they are:

- Listen for
- Observe
- Offer
- Pull

Listen for

There's a cute little quip about how you have two ears and one mouth, so you should listen at least twice as much as you speak. Too often what people hear in that concept of "listening," though, is a proxy for silence. They hear

that listening is just hanging back and letting someone else have a turn. But that's not what it is at all.

Good listening is not silent waiting. It is more thoughtful than the gestures of hearing—nodding your head, saying "OK," appearing to take the logic of words. We have an innate ability to see through each other's put-on postures, and we have only so much patience for being with people who aren't present.

Listening, the way I see it, is about showing people they matter. To build traction, you have to not just listen, but **listen** *for* the meaning people are trying to share with you, the signals they send about where the adventure could go next. You have to *hang* on their words to find the grips to latch on to, the places to gain traction and climb.

Observe

When we listen, we hear what's being said. But people use their whole embodied selves to say a lot more. Like if they're bored or bothered, if they're ready for a vulnerable story or question, or if they've just had enough, we'd better pay attention if we want to keep our traction.

A concept that helps me **observe** the people in my conversations for these cues comes from a practice called "adaptive leadership." One of its foundational tips is to switch your attention back and forth once in a while from the equivalent of "the dance floor" to "the balcony" at a large party. On the dance floor, you're in the thick of what's going on. Only from the balcony do you see its rhythms, patterns, problems. That's where you might notice that some people are *not* dancing, or that some misplaced audio equipment is blocking the way out. Sometimes you have to step back from a conversation for a moment to check and see if something is making traction slip. Only then can you try to fix it.

Offer

When we talk with someone, we take turns sharing meaning with each other. But it's not like I pour meaning into your mind and you pour meaning into mine. Instead, we're creating meaning right there between us, together.

When we **offer** something *to* the conversation, it's different than just speaking. Speaking, as we tend to think about it, is self-assured, with its own sometimes hidden purpose. You offer something to a conversation so that whatever it is—a piece of your story, a contrast in what you believe, a point of connection or disagreement, or just a reaction—can add knowledge, point to gaps, and grow the conversation in the direction it needs to go to be meaningful for everyone.

Pull

Detecting curiosity when it rises in you takes a bit of noticing. The sensation, sometimes mixed with urgency, makes me feel like I have to ask a question, and I have to ask it now.

Or do I?

There are lots of ways to **pull** new material in during a conversation—to encourage another person to *offer*. And sometimes all you need is a vacuum, a space for someone else to step into. We interviewers know this from experience: letting a beat of silence hang in the air can be enough to nudge someone to share more of their perspective, adding traction along the way.

Strong conversations, the kind that can change the way we look at our world, seem to happen all on their own. In a way, they do. We're wired already to connect to and learn from each other—and to *enjoy* it, sometimes, even when it's challenging. But these powerful exchanges that seem so organic are anything but. There are patterns we can track and cultivate to make our conversations strong enough to span the gulfs between us.

Now that we have some tools for building traction with other people, it's time for some real talk about people themselves. We need to talk *with* the humans around us to get a fuller picture of our divided world. But before we can listen for meaning, observe how it's received, offer our story, or pull on information that fills gaps in our knowledge, we often get stuck protecting our perspective or attacking another person for theirs.

And that's because of our tendency to do something that blocks our view of people altogether—*assume*.

Part III

People

tried for a while, but I don't think I can sum up the most complicated creatures on the planet.

I hope it's cool, then, if I tell you a story . . .

8

Assumptions

To get from Seattle, Washington, to Sherman County, Oregon, you drive east over Lake Washington, up and over Snoqualmie Pass—where your ears might pop—then south, watching mountains give way to quiet hills and plains. You cross the Columbia River into Oregon, pass Biggs Junction and Wasco, then arrive at Moro, the county seat. Population: 353.

Those 250 miles took about five hours to cover one Saturday morning in March 2017, when a small bus carrying fifteen or so people from the Seattle area (plus about six folks who followed in a caravan in their cars) made its way toward the Oregon State University Extension Office.

Inside that office, sixteen residents of Sherman County were waiting, a bit uneasy, to meet and talk with these urban visitors about the political divisions gripping the country. Most of them had voted for Donald Trump. Inside the bus, people wondered—and worried—about what the day would hold. Most of them had voted for Hillary Clinton.

I sat at the front of that bus with *The Evergrey*'s cofounder, Anika, trying to keep my hands from shaking as we reviewed the schedule for the day. The visit would begin with a brief Sherman County bus tour. Just 1,705 people lived on the county's 851 square miles, and much of that landscape is wheat fields—a bright carpet of beige under the day's sunny sky. By noon, we'd be back at the extension office, chatting over sandwiches and answering this meticulously chosen question: "What would happen here today that would leave you feeling like this was a good investment of your time?"

Behind us on the bus, a young woman with glasses and blue-tipped hair gazed out the window. Her name was Laura Caspi, she was twenty-seven years old, and the closest she could come to describing how she felt after the election was "helpless." She watched people elect someone she found awful, and started to think that those people must be pretty awful, too.

"In my head I dehumanized people who did vote for [Trump] because I couldn't understand it," she told me later.

"How did you know that you were dehumanizing people?" I asked.

The answer, it turned out, is that Laura had calculated her way, step by step, to a powerful assumption some of you might find familiar. It goes:

1. My vote *against* the candidate I despise is a vote *for* things that feel absolutely good and important.
2. A vote *for* the candidate I despise must be a vote *against* these good and important things.
3. Anyone who votes *for* the candidate I despise must be *against* good and important things.
4. Anyone who votes for this candidate must be a bad person.

It could've been a judgment to make and forget, but something nagged at Laura. Her life was so thoroughly sorted that not a single person in it was conservative or Republican. This was a damning assumption she was making about a lot of people. Was it true?

The question made her sign up for this strange event she saw in *The Evergrey* and get up at 5 AM one Saturday to board a bus to another world: "If people are voting opposite me, are they feeling opposite me on all these issues that are important to me?" *Or*, she asked herself, *is there something I'm missing?*

Sitting by herself on the bus, Laura watched the urban landscape give way to rolling hills. She rarely left the city and didn't own a car. She had a

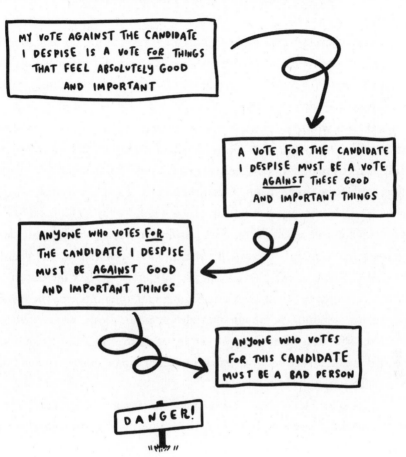

reputation among her friends for being impulsive and curious, but did she really want to have conversations with *these* people? What if she tried and just couldn't?

OUR BIGGEST ASSUMPTION

Just before the 2020 election, the *New York Times* published a fascinating interactive feature—an online quiz called "Can You Tell a 'Trump' Fridge From a 'Biden' Fridge?" It's exactly what it sounds like: a series of pictures of the contents of refrigerators in the homes of Trump voters and Biden voters. You flip through the photos—all unlabeled—and make your guess: *Whose fridge is this?*

I clicked through the quiz and found myself making up little rules. If I saw a lot of mass branded stuff—Coke, Velveeta, Kool-Aid—I'd think, *That's a Trump fridge.* If I saw specialized, "snobby" stuff—almond milk or Greek yogurt—I'd think, *That's a Biden fridge.* I felt clever and correct.

And I was wrong. I did terribly on the refrigerator quiz, and so did everyone else: The *Times* reported that readers had made 176,985 guesses by July 2021, correctly matching refrigerators to a family's chosen candidate a measly 52 percent of the time—barely better than half. "The current scores suggest that as a whole, we can't distinguish people's politics from glances into their fridges much more reliably than if we just flipped a coin," read the article.

It started to make sense when I ran into a distinction raised by author Ian Leslie. People aren't puzzles; they're mysteries. What's the difference? "Puzzles are orderly. They have a beginning and an end. Once the missing information is found, they're not a puzzle anymore," Leslie writes. "Mysteries are murkier, less neat. Progress can be made toward them by gathering knowledge and identifying the most important factors, but they don't offer the satisfaction of definite solutions."

We look for puzzle-piece answers to the mystery of people, but they don't exist. So what we find, instead, are assumptions: guesses that *look* like knowledge, hiding gaps in our understanding and soothing us with certainty while we make the biggest assumption of all: that we can solve a mystery from a distance.

⁓⁓⁓

Anika and I launched *The Evergrey* on October 24, 2016—just two weeks before the presidential election—with five core values: to be curious, honest, useful, bold, and inclusive. I had an internal motto to guide our relationship with readers and its contrast with other media: where others are distant, we are close.

Our weekday newsletter went out to our couple thousand subscribers the day after the November 8 election with the subject line, "Are you OK?" At the top was a photo sent in by one of our readers from an election-watch party in the city. In the foreground, there's a coffee table with a bottle of beer and a can of something. Behind that, on the carpet, a guy is lying on his back in front of the TV, his head in his hands. "This is not the morning most of our city thought it would have," we wrote. "If you want to talk, we're here to listen. Just hit reply."

Our progressive readers didn't hesitate to describe their crushing despair. But as emails from a couple conservative readers reminded us, talking to them as if they were *all* shocked liberals after the election was neither honest nor inclusive. It just . . . assumed. So in the following day's edition, we asked our readers to help us stay curious about everyone's perspectives. Several of them told us how hard that was in practice. They were siloed in Seattle: How do you get curious about other views, they wrote us, when you don't know anyone who holds them?

Then one day, Anika found a fascinating interactive map in the *Washington Post*. Enter the US county you live in, and the map tells you the county closest to yours where people voted exactly opposite in the 2016 presidential election. We typed in our county, King County, where 74 percent of voters had gone for Hillary Clinton, and our "opposite" county popped up—Sherman County, Oregon, where 74 percent of voters had gone for Donald Trump.

That knowledge revealed a gap. So, we asked our readers a pretty bold question: If we could find a way to visit Sherman County and talk to people there about politics, would they want to go? About two dozen of them responded to say they would—which made my whole month—and we got to work.

I found a small local publication online, the *Sherman County E-News*, and reached out to its publisher, asking to jump on a call. The gulf between our worlds felt like it could swallow this entire wacky idea whole, so in my cold email to Sherry Kaseberg I leaned on the only things I had: goodwill and common ground. We both wrote newsletters for communities we loved in a country that was tearing itself apart over divisions no one could understand. Would she hear me out on an idea to help?

To my surprise, she would. My voice shook on the phone as I stammered a proposal. We could organize something, bring some folks from Seattle to visit Sherman County for guided conversations. Not to argue, I said, but to learn. We'd be taking umpteen risks. We'd have to do it together. I held my breath.

"That sounds lovely," she said. *It did?* It did!

Sherry was in her eighties and knew everyone in Sherman County, including the person who would make this wild idea a reality: Alexander "Sandy" Macnab.

Sandy had just retired from a thirty-eight-year career as a beloved Oregon State University county extension agent for Sherman and neighboring Wasco counties. Agricultural agents help solve local problems by bringing research-based know-how from universities to rural farms and fields, then communicating back to campus what issues need addressing.

He was a bridge builder too, and it showed.

My schedule was hectic, but I saved my event planning calls with Sandy until the end of the day so our conversations could go on as long as they had to.* It was Sandy who came up with the event's name: "Melting Mountains: An Urban-Rural Gathering," referring to the snowmelt that runs down the Cascade mountains dividing the eastern and western parts of our states, nourishing the land below. It was Sandy who sparked unrelated but *totally related* discussions on things like abortion that stayed with me for days. And it was Sandy who helped us see where our own bias was showing.

In one of the structured activities Anika and I drafted, people from the two counties would pair off to ask each other any of several questions, including "What do you hope to see happen in our country in the next four

---

* He would pick up and say, "Good morning!" even if it was the afternoon. ("It's more cheerful!" he said.)

years?" and "What concerns do you have about our country in the next four years?"

"Four years, huh?" Sandy said, reviewing our draft. "Are you assuming he won't get reelected? Why not eight?"

I bristled. *How dare he; we worked hard on this.* Then a moment later I realized: *Oh wait, he's right.* We changed "the next four years" to "the next few years," removing the question from the context of presidential terms entirely. The change helped us preserve parity, and I was so grateful: if anything in the event's design put one side's perspective over the other, people wouldn't feel heard, and we would fail.

The fact that he could be honest with us, and us with him, meant everything.

MELTING MOUNTAINS

"What would happen here today that would leave you feeling like this was a good investment of your time?" It was the opening question for the event, and if I'd closed my eyes, I wouldn't have been able to tell which answers came from which county:

"Having a real talk with real people, instead of all that angry yelling on Facebook."

"Getting to know people who don't live like me and who don't think like me."

"Just learning something that helps me understand a bit better why we're all so different, because maybe we're not as different as we think."

Then we were off. First up was a series of questions people moved to different corners of the room to answer. Among them: "Do you live within fifty miles of where you were raised?" "Does at least one local official know you by name?" And the zinger: "In the 2016 elections, for whom did you vote for president?"

But the main event was the one-on-one exchanges. People from different counties paired off to ask each other questions and listen, without interruption, to the answers. I loved the first question—"What's your favorite childhood memory?"—because it made sure that they saw a person before they saw an opponent.* Then, we teed up the pairs for the rest of their discussions with three additional questions:

- What's one national issue you feel divides our nation currently? How do you feel about it and what in your experience has shaped your position?
- What concerns do you have about our country in the next few years?
- What do you hope to see happen in our country in the next few years?

After several rounds of pairings—the room buzzing with tense energy— we brought the big group back together to share their thoughts on what they'd learned. I'll never forget when Darren Padget stood up—all six feet, nine inches of him.

Darren is a fourth-generation wheat farmer at a time when the average American is four generations removed from anything approaching that lifestyle. He took a deep breath and gazed at the bits of sandwich crust scattered on the conference room tables from lunch.

"If you knew," he said in a deep, gruff voice, "what it took to get that simple sandwich on your plate . . ."

There were several beats of silence. After that moment I began to hear something different in the comments from folks in Sherman County. The news is about cities. Their rural kids go to college in cities. Just about every TV show and movie is in a city. Many of their family members move to cities because the economics of farming don't allow them to remain on the farm. The price of grain is pennies ahead of what it sold for in 1980, anyway, so it's no surprise that "small American farmers are nearing extinction," as *Time* magazine declared in 2019.

---

* We borrowed the question, by the way, from Michael Hebb, the Seattle-based designer of an infamously illuminating set of conversations called Death Over Dinner.

The political power of rural America was the talk of the nation after the 2016 election, but the economics of politics mean candidates for elected office rarely make the time to go there. Sherman County is reliable Republican territory with fewer than two thousand people in it. Why bother making the trip? About 99 percent of all American job and population growth between 2008 and 2017 happened in metropolitan areas with cities of at least fifty thousand people. So from the perspective of the folks in Sherman County, at least, the power is concentrated in cities, not in their home, where the population has slowly declined.

"We just don't have the people," Darren would tell me later. "I get it."

Watching Darren and others talk about what it was like to welcome us—to welcome *anyone at all* from a major American metropolitan area—I began to understand that the nervous energy here wasn't just about political differences. It was about the chance to be seen.

Another Sherman County resident who drove that point home was Ron Holmes. Ron's aunt was a nurse, he told me later with a chuckle, who "delivered half the babies in this county." He worries less about the growing political divide between people than the growing divide between people, period. Rural living means you *know* each other—whether you like it or not, in some cases.

"You've come down here to Sherman County today, and you've never been here, and maybe you'll never come back," Ron shared with the group, glancing at the folks from King County. "But us, we go to the cities all the time. We know how they work. We need to."

Despite all my supposed bridge-building cred, I realized right then that I'd come into this trip believing that it was people in rural areas who had more to learn from people in the city than the other way around. What a strange, self-serving assumption. It was an instant INTOIT moment for me, and—by the slow nods and murmurs I heard around me—a few others. Who do we think we are? Who do we think *they* are? How are we so sure?

Economic reasons, Darren told folks at the event, led him to vote for Trump. His health-care costs had jumped 426 percent in the last few years, and regulations like the Waters of the United States rule were threatening his business.

"That's right," another farmer said. People from Sherman County nodded their heads while people from King County leaned in, puzzled but curious. *The Waters of the United States rule? What the heck is that?*

Turns out, the rule defines what bodies of water fall under federal regulation, and it's a big deal. Farmers for years have been nervous about how the rule could be interpreted to cover small, seasonal, rain-made ponds in their large chunks of farmland, or even furrows—the tiny mounds of dirt that separate lines of wheat plants and protect them from drying or freezing winds. Losing control of their land is a nightmare for a farmer, for whom every acre counts. The regulations are complex and confusing, and many of them didn't trust the Obama administration to address their concerns. They might trust Republicans, though—and the businessman America had elected president.

That detail was an INTOIT moment for Laura Caspi. Learning about that policy and other details she heard about people's lives here checked two of her biggest assumptions. The first was the idea that any vote *for* Trump must be a vote *against* the things that drove her own vote.

"It didn't enter my consciousness that they voted that way for reasons I hadn't even considered, or for reasons that didn't matter to me," she said. "Our lives are so different . . . We're not even playing the same game at the end of the day."

Laura's second checked assumption was about the conversation itself. Anika took several photos during the visit, and my favorite was of Laura and one of the Sherman County residents she was paired with, a farmer named Fred. In the photo, they're giving each other a high-five at the end of their conversation—Laura with blue-tipped hair, Fred with a cowboy hat. She had been afraid that it would be tough to make this bridge to people who looked at the world so differently, even for a short couple hours. The topics *were* difficult and tense. But it wasn't hard to talk. And that gave her some hope.

"I felt like his granddaughter," she said.

When our time together was over, nobody wanted to leave. People kept chatting in the conference room, the hallways by the reception desk, and outside under a big sky in a bit of March sun. People traded contact information. We took a "nice" group picture outside and a goofy one. Back on the bus, the conversation was so loud on the way back to Seattle, I could barely hear myself wonder why I'd ever doubted that this could happen, that it could work. We're all just people, aren't we?

Many good things would follow Melting Mountains. A few participants from across the counties would stay in touch, continuing their conversations over email. Liberals and conservatives from around the country would reach out to me, Anika, and Sandy about doing something like Melting Mountains in their states. Journalists, too, took notice. The trip would be featured in case studies, conferences, and articles. At *The Evergrey*, we stretched our runway for bold projects to unleash curiosity. But before all that would happen, I sat next to Anika on the bus home, tired, relieved, and a little baffled. What had felt like so much now seemed like so little.

And later . . . like not enough.

People from King County didn't get a chance to ask hard questions about big issues. It would break my heart to learn, later, that Jordan Goldwarg, who came down with his husband from King County, heard something about same-sex marriage from one Sherman County resident he was paired with that stung. The Sherman County resident didn't know Jordan was gay, but the exercise went by quickly, and Jordan never got a chance to say so. Though he took plenty away from the trip, Jordan carried with him the missed opportunity to tell that resident who he really was.

Sick at the thought that our instructions not to interrupt each other during the one-on-one conversations might have kept Jordan from being himself, I finally asked him, years later, what he would've said if he'd felt he could. "I probably would've said, 'I appreciate your viewpoint on that, but I do want to let you know, I'm gay; that's my husband over there; I'm curious if you can tell me a little bit more about why you feel that way, 'cause it's really difficult for me to hear that you don't think people like us should be married,'" he told me.

People from Sherman County also wondered, in their own way, if they'd been seen for who they are.

When I caught up with him in 2020, Darren had some great stories about the times he's hosted folks from places like Tokyo and Singapore at his seven-thousand acre farm.[*] "When we have visitors out here, they've never seen a horizon with no buildings on it. They've never drank water out of a garden hose," he said. So he shows them. He walks them to a corner of his yard near the well, turns on his hose, takes a drink, and invites them to try. "They look at me like I'm nuts," he said, which gives him his opening. From there he shares how he tries to run his farm as both a businessman *and* a steward of the land. I imagine his guests can hear the pride in his voice as clearly as I can, what it means to him to show off a lifestyle where he can drink the same water as his crops.

Darren deeply appreciated the effort we made at Melting Mountains and struggled to articulate what bothered him. I encouraged him to try. "You came down for an afternoon. You came into a little town. You drove through the hills, but nobody was there explaining to you what you were seeing,"[†] he said, taking a breath. "There was a lot of things you could have seen, but I had to tell myself and back up and go, look, this was a limited deal. We can't tell it all, like, 'OK, we've got a captive audience!' If I was a king, I'd have made a few modifications, but you know what? Nobody's done it before or since, so kudos to you guys for looking out. And nobody got physical or violent or argued or anything like that—it isn't the way it needs to be. I can't say it's always that way with my in-laws."

He chuckled at that. Hell, so did I.

---

[*] In July 2020, Darren would be named chairman of US Wheat Associates—the international marketing arm for the wheat industry—representing 105,000 farmers nationwide.

[†] Sandy did a bus tour to start the visit, but we arrived late, and it was short!

On our conversation console for powerful bridging conversations, Melting Mountains had undivided attention, our best attempt at parity, total containment (what I share here I share with permission), and full embodiment that made all the difference. What we didn't have enough of was time.

But if there was a mountain of assumptions to melt between our two counties, we showed we could at least get started.

⌢⌢⌢

One of the King County residents at Sherman County was a young woman named Leah Greenbaum. At the time, Leah was a graduate student at the University of Washington's Evans School of Public Policy and Governance. I called her the day after the trip as I prepared a story about it for *The Evergrey*.

The trip, it turned out, revealed an assumption Leah had been living by: she had been relying on her class materials, policy papers, and media articles to explain communities of people she didn't have any contact with at all.

After sitting in the room that day, she realized that those expert sources couldn't explain as much as she'd thought. "I want to get out there and talk to primary sources from now on," she told me. "I love the media, my best friends are journalists . . . but I'm not going to look for easy answers anymore."

I was taught this in middle school: secondary sources are *never as good* as primary sources. So why do we accept the answers they give us about who other people are and how they think? The enduring lesson of Melting Mountains is this: If in one short interaction you find reason to question the assumptions you've received from your silos, what other assumptions in your life are you totally wrong about?

It's impossible to check *every* assumption about other people before it lodges itself in our brain. Some gut checks will save your life, like assuming that someone who points a gun at you can kill you. Others are just a flat view of the world sneaking into yours. You read one confident thought piece about a group of people, and hey! Puzzle solved. Gap filled. Time to move on.

That's the danger of easy answers beckoning to us from everywhere, baiting us with dopamine lollipops and coaxing us to not only judge each other *more*, but engage each other *less*.

The problem isn't the partial answers we're always collecting from a variety of sources in our busy lives. It's the questions we stop asking because we think we've learned enough.

ASSUMPTIONS AS QUESTIONS

Three years after the trip to Sherman County, I attended a workshop about assumptions. It was run by my friend Julie Pham, an innovator in organizational development, who has the distinction in my life of being one of the most curious people I know.* This doesn't stem from a particular talent at being curious, I've realized. We all have that capacity. It's more that when natural barriers to curiosity crop up—fear, risk, vulnerability—Julie takes the time to find a tactful, thoughtful way to leap over them. She once asked a friend why he hadn't invited her to a party—and got a considerate, satisfying answer. She just can't stand open gaps. Besides, she said, "I want to feel like I can continue to surprise myself."

In one of the first exercises in her workshop, Julie asked us to close our eyes and visualize a fictional scene she littered with tacit invitations to make assumptions about people. At one point, she had us imagine that we had met someone "in the construction industry." Being mostly white-collar big-city folks, all of us pictured a construction worker—the kind of person you see in a hard hat near construction zones—except one woman who imagined a construction manager. How did she think past the stereotype? Because she had a friend who worked as a construction manager. It demonstrated a truth about our assumptions: they are only as good as our experiences.

Later, Julie paired us off in private virtual breakout rooms to talk about the assumptions we were making about *each other*. I looked at my own little Zoom window while the man I was paired up with confessed his assumptions,

---

* And, before we were close friends, she was one of the people from King County who joined *The Evergrey* at Melting Mountains.

newly conscious of the signals I send into the world just based on what I look like. He assumed I was far left mostly because of my short, asymmetrical hair. I'm more moderate left in my politics. He also assumed—to our mutual delight—that I was a cat person. "I hate cats!" I told him.

When assumptions aren't so silly, they lead to some awful, destructive biases. So it was significant when, to close the workshop, Julie hammered in a key point: We can't *not* make assumptions about people. Assumptions are how we navigate a complicated world where we don't know and *can't* know everything about everyone. All we can do is notice the assumptions we're making and ask why.

Fail to notice your assumptions and they might harden into lies. Turn them into questions and they'll get you closer to truth.

PLANTED SEEDS

In November 2020, I drove back down US Route 97 to Sherman County with plenty on my mind. The last time I'd gone this route, we'd brought a small gift on the bus with us to Melting Mountains: a pretty potted orchid for the desk at the extension office and a card to thank the Sherman County folks for hosting, showing up, preparing the meal, all of it.

This trip I had a box of Seattle smoked salmon, a growler of Rachel's Ginger Beer, and a package of MarketSpice cinnamon-orange tea—my favorite. Sandy had offered to let me stay at his place, since I planned to catch up with a handful of folks who'd joined us four years earlier. I heard Darren's voice in my head as I crossed a quiet stretch of the Columbia River into Oregon: "*You drove through the hills, but nobody was there explaining to you what you were seeing.*"

Every chance I get, as a journalist, I talk to people in their own places— their homes, their offices, the coffee shops where they're one of the regulars. Pieces of people get reflected in the spaces they make and love, so there's no better way to get curious about them *with* them. Sandy grew up on the banks of the Deschutes River in a family that's been in Sherman County since the 1800s. After he retired in 2016, a grateful community installed a beautiful iron bench bearing his name right by the front door of the extension office.

Once I arrived, Sandy was going to take me on a *real* tour of Sherman County.

"You hungry?" he asked when we met in a voice I missed: matter-of-fact and with that lilt at the end so words like "Sun*day*" sound like "Sun*dee*." A half hour later we were sitting on the outdoor deck at Big Jim's Drive-In in The Dalles—the biggest town near Sherman County—looking quite the pair: Sandy, a big guy with a flat mat of gray, mussy hair, sipping water through a straw while I stuffed my face with what Sandy told me was their specialty, the Big Jim Burger.

Sandy was one hell of a tour guide. Riding shotgun in his Subaru, I learned how to spot sagebrush and cheat grass; how to tell the difference between a seeded field of wheat in November and one lying fallow for next year's crop; and how acres of spinning wind turbines, when you stand among them, really do sound like passing jets.

We hadn't talked at all about Melting Mountains when Sandy said he'd been thinking about it lately, and a line from the theme to the show *Cheers* kept coming to his mind. Not the one about people knowing your name, but a less famous lyric that comes after, about how all our struggles are largely the same.

I thought back to the assumptions workshop. Some of mine about Sandy were dumb and off by a mile—expecting he'd drive a pickup truck and listen to country instead of the '70s station I loved and hummed along to.

Following the lines of the hills outside the car window, I kicked myself for one assumption I had only just noticed: the assumption that Sandy wouldn't be curious. "Us liberals are always asking *all* the questions," a fellow bridge builder told me on a Zoom call once. A journalist who'd moved to a rural area some years ago shared the same sentiment. The conservatives whose views she asked about "never ask questions about *my* beliefs," she said.

So there I was, surprised when Sandy wanted to know all about my family and chuckled at the wacky details. We'd just followed each other on Facebook and he'd seen a post I'd shared marking twenty years of being an American citizen with the story of my mother's naturalization ceremony in New Hampshire. Sandy had been waiting for the chance to ask me more about that. He *asked* if he could ask first, ever courteous. Then follow-up after follow-up, he pulled on the thread, releasing my story and my thoughts on immigration, his curiosity as alive as anyone's.

I told Sandy about the workshop, about the assumptions people make of each other, about the assumptions I'd made of *him*, and how it felt liberating, even fun, to reveal those secrets.

"Did you make any assumptions about me?" I asked him. He laughed.

"For starters," he said—glancing at the petite, five-foot-two, liberal Seattleite in his passenger seat—"I didn't think you'd take such huge bites of a Big Jim Burger."

When I arrived at Sandy's home that night in tiny Dufur, Oregon, I put the big box of Seattle smoked salmon on his counter and the growler of Rachel's Ginger Beer in his fridge.

As I went to swing the refrigerator door closed, I stopped. *Would someone guess this is a Biden fridge now?* I wondered, remembering the online quiz and scrutinizing how the growler sat in Sandy's fridge near the butter, the eggs, the milk. Would this one piece of indie urban-ness—one friend's gift to another—ruin the puzzle for thousands? *Maybe so*, I thought.

Then I closed the fridge, started the kettle, and joined Sandy with a mug of MarketSpice tea.

ASSUMPTION ASSISTANT

Our assumptions tag along with us to every interaction. I imagine an invisible assistant whispering introductions to people I don't know at all as if she does, in fact, know everything about them. Yours is there with you, too, waiting for a chance to be useful.

ASSUMPTION ASSISTANT

"Nice to meet you," a conservative woman says to a young man with a pierced nose and a tattoo on his arm. *He is a far-left liberal who will publicly share whatever you say that he finds offensive*, her assistant whispers.

"Nice to meet you too," the liberal man says to the woman with a cross around her neck. *She is a far-right religious zealot who thinks people like you are destroying America*, his assistant warns.

You can't fire your Assumption Assistant. You can't even give them the day off. They're a part of you, and hey—a lot of times, you need them. But you can choose not to pay too much attention to what they say. Or rather, to the *certainty* of what they say. Treat their assumptions as questions, and your assistant will get quiet while you get curious.

People are mysteries, not puzzles. This means we can never be sure about them. But we can *always* be curious.

Conversation, in all its messiness, helps us explore where our perspectives meet, digging up insights that help us see the people around us more clearly.

But why are the conversations we have so often so unproductive? Why, when we talk, do we end up talking *past* each other?

It's because we get stuck. First, on our assumptions—these false answers to questions we never stopped to ask. And then on something else. Something we tend to treat like nothing can come above it: reason.

9

Reason

Exploring where different perspectives meet gets tricky when we're devoted to our own. This makes sense: it's the one we're attached to every day of our lives! But if we're going to get out of our silos and take a good look around, we have to see when we're getting in our own way and do something about it.

The first thing to keep an eye on is our assumptions.

The second? The unreasonable ways we reason.

INSISTING

Maybe you've heard the old story of the blind people and the elephant. In Buddhist scripture, several monks approach the Buddha and tell him about the vicious arguments tearing up their community—that "wanderers of various sects" who held "differing views" on deep questions "kept on arguing, quarreling, & disputing, wounding one another with weapons of the mouth," always saying of their own beliefs, "Only this is true; anything otherwise is worthless."

In response, the Buddha tells the monks about a king who summoned all the people in his community who'd been born blind, then asked one of his servants to show them an elephant. To some of the blind people the servant showed the elephant's ear, to others the trunk, to others the tail, and so on, always saying to each group, "This, blind people, is what an elephant is like."

When the servant had finished, the king asked all the blind people, together, to tell him what an elephant is like. The people who were shown the ear said an elephant is "just like a winnowing basket," the people who were shown the trunk said it's "just like the pole of a plow," the people who were shown the tail said it's "just like a pestle," and so on, always saying, "The elephant is like this, it's not like that." The blind people then got so angry hearing each other's insistent, diverging beliefs, they "struck one another with their fists."*

After recounting this story, the Buddha turns back to the monks worried about the arguments in their own community. "In the same way," he tells them, "the wanderers of other sects are blind & eyeless." They don't *really* see the full answers to deep questions, the Buddha tells them, even though they pretend to. He tells the monks:

> With regard to these things
> they're attached—
> some contemplatives & brahmans.
> They quarrel & fight—
>   people seeing one side.

In the story, each of the groups of blind people has a piece of a larger truth. Pitting one piece against another doesn't do any good. A better *seeing* of this new creature would come from their working to understand each other's perspectives and adding them up into the reality before them. It would take trust. It would take struggle. And more than anything, it would

---

* The scripture notes that this infighting "gratified the king," which . . . ew.

take rejecting the certainty that any one of them has all the information they need.

We think of perspectives as interpretations of information. But when it comes to the things that divide us, perspectives *are* information. And gathering more perspectives gets us closer to a bigger, more complicated truth. You won't resolve the debate over abortion by listening closely to a woman who believes abortion murders human beings and another who believes abortion grants women the freedom to live full and free lives. But you will get a clearer picture of what's at stake for different people, and why the issue is so challenging in the first place.

One way we get stuck on reason is when we insist on our own perspectives *to* each other instead of letting them inform and enrich one other. That's not conversation but competition, and no one wins. Even if someone appears to win because she's good with rhetoric and argument, she misses the opportunity to learn about an opposing view that could make her thinking wiser and her arguments stronger. Insist to a Sherman County farmer that the right vote is for a Democrat without seeing his perspective on federal land management, and all you'll really insist on is the stereotypes you already hold about each other. Your best reasoning skills will get you kudos in your own silos and not much else.

One place I've seen a lot of this is on unmoderated or poorly moderated news website comment boards. Different people with different perspectives come together around a topic and *insist* on their own perspectives *to* each other, rarely asking about or considering how different people there might see things. Many of them come as blind as the people in the parable, jumping into the comments without reading the story, reacting to rather than reflecting on whatever is being discussed.

No wonder my newsroom colleagues didn't want to read or learn from these comments. Even if some were great, most were terrible! And with such little time, attention, parity, containment, and embodiment to help the exchanges become conversations, saving these forums was only possible with a lot of listening and investment. Sometimes, it would take too much, leading some outlets to give up on them entirely. For instance, one community newspaper in Washington, the *Issaquah Reporter*, has lately added a disclaimer beneath all its articles online: "In consideration of how we voice our opinions in the modern world, we've closed comments on our websites."

Buddhists sensed it 2,500 years ago as clearly as we sense it now: when we insist on our own perspective, we leave no room for others, believing that the framework we put around things is the only valid one there is.

PUSHING

Another way we get stuck on reason is when we can't see past it to our intuition. To explain why, oddly enough, I'm going to need another elephant. This one stars in a handy analogy developed by social psychologist Jonathan Haidt.

Haidt marshals decades of research to show that when we make judgments about our world, we use both our reasoning mind and our intuitive mind. In his analogy, the intuitive mind is like a big, strong elephant, and the reasoning mind is like its tiny human rider. The rider may have a clear idea of where he wants to go, just as you might have a heap of logical evidence for where you ought to lean in any given judgment. But at the end of the day, you're going to go where your elephant wants to go because, well, it's an elephant.

Let's say you're a parent wondering if you should let your eleven-year-old daughter walk alone to school. Very few kids have ever been abducted from their neighborhoods. Yours knows her way around just fine, so you know she won't get lost. The area is almost crime free, and you yourself walked to school alone at that age no problem. On its own, your rider might compute that it's fine to let your daughter run off to school alone every morning. But it doesn't matter. Your elephant is terrified that something might happen to her. How could you live with yourself? So you don't let her go to school alone, and when she asks why, your rider helps you insist on all sorts of reasons. Including the infamous "Because I say so."

We like to think that we are "reasonable" people, and that our reason is in charge of our decision-making. But it's not. Our intuition directs our reason, and not the other way around. Not only that: our reasoning mind evolved not to marshal evidence on one side or another and examine it objectively, but to explain our intuition to our fellow humans with whatever evidence is required. So our elephant's rider, as Haidt points out, acts more like its press secretary—explaining its agenda and covering for its actions.

Why is this relevant to conversations across the divide? Two reasons.

First: Every time we approach someone who holds an opposing view expecting they'll have no good reasons to back it up—reasons that make sense, at least—we will be disappointed and rather stupidly surprised. We say people must have lost their minds for thinking this or that thing we find absurd or terrible. But for any popular divisive issue, reason shows up strong on both sides—if you know where to look. This doesn't mean that both sides are morally equivalent, or that one side isn't ultimately more right. All it means is that people don't tend to hang their convictions on utter nonsense. So if you think the other side is devoid of logic, "facts," or good faith argument, you *might* be right: some beliefs are just plain deviant and some believers are just plain trolls. But it's far, far more likely, I've found, that you're buried a little too deep in your silo to see why their arguments, from their perspective, do at least *make sense*.

I thought of this when I caught up with a liberal friend of mine who told me about a long exchange he'd had with an aunt of his who'd voted for Trump. They were together during a holiday visit, which presented a rare opportunity for him: There was enough time, attention, parity, containment, and embodiment for the two of them to plumb the depths where their perspectives conflict. He figured his reasoning would easily win her over. But nope. "She had a lot of rational-seeming rebuttals to my Trump complaints," he told me. "And I realized, 'Oh, your arguments are coherent. They're wrong,* but they're coherent.'"

---

* Just his opinion!

That was a big "I never thought of it that way" moment for him. One that I've had countless times now, too, with my parents and loads of people I've met whose convictions initially confounded me. As much as we'd like to believe it, the people who disagree with us are not idiots. Human intuition may not hinge on reason, but it does hinge on something more significant—a lived life. Who's right or wrong is a separate question. But most *all* of our arguments, if we can articulate them, are coherent.

Now here's the second, bigger reason we need to be aware of this interplay between our intuitive mind and our reasoning mind. Because we are all equipped to explain our perspectives to each other, trading our reasoning back and forth stops being productive much sooner than you'd think.

Play it out with me. You begin a conversation about gun violence by sharing your take—that owning guns is protected by the Constitution, a free citizenry *must* stay adequately armed against a government that could at any point turn tyrannical, and the recent spate of mass shootings are due to problems with people, not guns.

The person you're talking to then shares their position: the government needs to keep citizens safe, we can restrict guns to that end without infringing on people's right to own them, and guns make acts of violence far more deadly.

Once you both lay out your positions, you push back on them with challenging questions: What about the fact that many people support more gun regulation? What about the fact that our mental health system is failing families and communities who need it? Hoping for a concession with each challenge, all each of you gets from the other is *more reasoning*. Once you've covered all the ground you can think of, you do that thing that kills traction. You *insist*. You repeat your points, creep closer to judgments on theirs ("I mean, really? How could you *believe* that?"), and cross your arms, feeling more defensive and less curious by the minute. And that's the second way we get stuck on reason: when we push our reasons at each other without getting curious about the intuitive hopes, fears, and concerns behind them.

Can a conversation like this build back to traction? Sure it can. But it needs a pause for your exhausted reasoning riders and some direct

engagement with those mighty, intuitive elephants all that reasoning is trying to cover for.

Why? Well, Haidt and others have deduced a funny little quirk in how
we approach different kinds of ideas. When we encounter ideas that line up
with our existing beliefs, we silently ask ourselves, "Can I believe it?" We
look at the evidence presented to us, consider it on its merits, and see if the
points add up to a belief we can feel good about. When we encounter ideas
that challenge our beliefs, though, we ask ourselves something else: "*Must*
I believe it?" And when we ask "*Must* I believe it?" it means our intuition is
resisting. Our elephant doesn't want to consider this crap. It doesn't like it.
So our rider starts to look for one good reason—just one will do!—to dismiss the entire offending concept.

STOMPING

A lot of our discourse happens on the internet, a nonplace that makes us
into nonpeople. Our words show up, but not our bodies, rarely our faces,
and certainly not our full roster of interactions, expressions, hesitations,
and tone.

It's easy to forget that there is a mind and a heart and a person behind
the ideas we see on the internet. It's easy to read someone's genuine thought
and judge it, scowling, without the person even knowing you were there.
Accountability, consequences, they're all optional here, or doled out with
humiliating, mob-like vengeance. It's easy to dismiss. To hide. To mock—
in groups! To never ask, to never clarify. To put up fake people—bots and
the like—and get away with it. To *other* with ghostly, secret abandon.

This is a third reason we're stuck on reason: We do so much of our
collective "reasoning" in spaces where people disappear. We are reduced to
words and images. Those words and images become signals. Spend some
time online, as most of us do, and you detect patterns in those signals—
patterns that offer easy answers, tempting us with the certainty that we
know everything we need to know about each other's thinking, when we
know very little. We stomp out complexity, crushing curiosity flat.

The sucky thing is how baked in it all feels. Thanks to social media, we can each access thousands of online arguments about similar topics, many of them "trending" on various platforms because they're so provocative, outrageous, costly, or humiliating. You see someone on the other side say something and, time and time again, you see that idea leads to this other awful idea. People's posts blur together into slick attempts to seem genuine and reasonable while actually—you're convinced—they're just promoting some bad agenda. After a while, the retorts and rebuttals begin to look like a script you know the ending of. Turning to your own disagreements, suspicion rules the day. Why give people the benefit of the doubt when they're sure to give the same bad-faith arguments we see over and over again?

"Those of us who've been here for a while know [the] tired choreographies, the moves and countermoves," writes essayist Lili Loofbourow. "We sometimes skip the content of the text itself and reflexively fast-forward to the shitty point we 'know' is coming even if maybe it isn't."

Loofbourow hates that we so often presume the worst of each other's thinking online. But she argues—compellingly and depressingly!—that it's the most rational, reasonable move we've got.

What ends up happening in a lot of these discursive spaces online is something I call chaining. To draw out an example, let's say that you're pretty sharply liberal, and you stumble on a post from a woman you know who says she's sad about the looting of small businesses in her city during a series of recent protests. You've seen people who seem to be against the fight for racial justice—a fight you care a lot about—rage against property damage and looting. So rather than allow that this person might just be sad about the looting of local small businesses, and get curious about that gap in your knowledge, you manufacture some certainty: This woman does not support a more equal world for all races. Not only that, you think, she's probably racist herself. You unfriend her on the spot.

How is this progression chain-like? Let's break it down to one potential mental path: Of all the people who lament rioting and looting during protests, *some* might also be critical of the organizations behind the protests.

Of all those who are critical of the organizations behind the protests, *some* might also be critical of the movement for racial equity. Of all those who are critical of the movement for racial equity, *some* might be resistant to the broader cause of racial equity. Of all those resistant to the broader cause of racial equity, *some* might be motivated by a sense of racial hatred or superiority.

But because you've seen so many loud, awful voices say loud, awful things while raging against looting, and you've seen it repeatedly, you chain all those concepts together, embracing one easy answer after another in an instant until a mild belief is linked directly to a damning one. Not just for this issue, but a dozen. And not just from the left but from the right and all over. For instance, a concern about how a mass shooter got an assault weapon hides a desire to take guns away from law-abiding people. Compassion for immigrants held at the US border covers a conviction that our border should be completely uncontrolled.

Chaining is not just assumptions run amok. It's a learned mistrust of people's signals. When we chain, we don't just flatten the uncertainty of "Some people who believe A believe B, some people who believe B believe C," and so on, into "All of the people who believe A believe Z." We act as if all the people who *express* A *really believe* Z. So it's that much harder to listen to each other—or even want to—across these toxic, warping divides.

In divided times, being curious in online conversation is an act of resistance. Resistance to the idea that people are *probably* manipulating you. *Probably* trolling. *Probably* abusing whatever trust you dare to give. In that sense, staying curious here takes an *un*reasonable act of faith in people. Even if all you see is their outline, their hand waving. Even if you've been burned before and will get burned again. Like writer Angel Eduardo likes to say, "Social media is the boss level of discourse." It *shouldn't* be easy to understand each other's takes on difficult issues with little more than text and memes—and it isn't! Especially in spaces where people think they've seen and heard it all before, where there's next to no time, attention, parity, containment, or access to the embodied tools of human communication to open gaps and help us see each other fully.

These spaces are tricky as hell for deep disagreements in divided times, but they're also where so many of our perspectives naturally collide, and so much kick-ass curiosity is *possible*.

Some people will tell you to avoid tough disagreements online. Most of the time, considering the work, relationships, and mild or severe irritation at stake, and *other things going on in life*, that's probably best.

But when you have your wits about you, the right frame of mind, and a pretty good idea that this person isn't hopelessly hooked to endless point scoring, you can take advantage of the daily miracle the internet gives us: real-time interaction, day and night, with a *parade* of different, flawed, mysterious, and endlessly fascinating humans.

FIVE THINGS TO TRY

We get stuck on reason when we insist on our perspectives at each other instead of letting them inform each other, when we push our reasons at each other instead of examining what's behind them, and when we follow patterns and projections to conclusions that stomp out the complexity of who people really are. What can you do in your next bridging conversation to avoid this and build traction along the way? Here are a few things to try that make use of our Traction LOOP and help you get some reach, grip, and balance:

1. Pry your mind back open
2. Check the links in the chain
3. Name what you keep coming back to
4. Name what *they* keep coming back to
5. Make talking points starting points

Reach

Pry your mind back open

I've heard it described as a "wall coming down"—that moment when you're listening to some idea, and something in your mind decides it's done wanting to entertain it. There'll be times when this is the right thing to do.

Considering the rampant misperceptions we have about each other in divided times, though, there'll be more times when it's just likely to close you off. So if you observe your mind shutting that big barred castle gate to some idea, you can choose to pry it back open with a simple little hack based on the work of Haidt and other social psychologists: Just focus on the idea your mind is resisting and will yourself to ask, "Can I believe it?" I know. It sounds too easy. But as I'll show you in a minute, it actually is enough.

Check the links in the chain

When we don't have all the information about someone's ideas, our minds are happy to fill in the blanks with baloney. So as people share opinions that creep toward something controversial for you, you can listen for the ideas someone's sharing that you're wanting to link to more extreme ones, then observe the chains of beliefs that are forming in your head. Is there a curious question you can pull to see what's really attached to what, so you don't accept an assumption you'll hold against the person for the rest of the conversation?

Even when I'm not in active conversation with somebody, I use both these strategies daily when I read articles and op-eds that stand for things I don't agree with. Take the op-ed I ran into in July 2020 in which a direct descendant of Thomas Jefferson argued that we should take down the Jefferson Memorial in Washington, DC. Assuming absolutely nothing about how any of you would feel about this argument, I'm going to be frank with you about how I felt about it. Not because I have any interest in promoting my particular take (I don't!), but just so I can show you, with a real example, how these strategies work.

　　All it took was seeing the op-ed's headline for my mind's gate to come crashing down—*Ew! That'd be awful!* I thought—and for a reckless chain to develop in my mind: *This person wants a memorial to a founding father taken down? I bet he'd throw away all the good stuff in our history if he had the chance!* I was going to move on when I considered the turbulence around race and history rocking the country that summer and decided, *No. Wait. OK.* I clicked on the headline. I read the piece, willing my mind not only to listen for its points but to stay quiet enough to absorb them, to bring down the threat level, to relax.

After I was done, I still thought it'd be a mistake to remove Jefferson's memorial from its place in DC. But I understood that the author had an enormous respect for American history—he wants more of that history to be told, particularly the stories of enslaved Americans—and that he was arguing not just that the memorial should be taken down, but that it held up a too idealized version of a fascinating, iconic man. He also thought that Monticello—Jefferson's historic Virginia estate where the author played as a kid—would serve as a more fitting and grand memorial anyway. It was an argument I hadn't considered, and I had to admit: it wasn't bad.

Grip

Name what you keep coming back to

When we insist on our own perspective, we leave no room for others, believing that the frame we put around things is the only valid one there is. How can you tell if you're falling into the trap of insisting rather than conversing? One of the biggest tip-offs is repetition. If you observe yourself offering the same point over and over again, then listening for affirmation of that point more than any new knowledge or gaps opening between you, it's a good sign you're losing traction. You can get it back, though, by offering that you're circling around this point and venturing a guess as to why. So in a conversation about abortion, you might say, "I keep coming back to this idea that life is sacred because to me it just comes before everything else, and it's really hard to look at it any differently." You could then follow up by pulling on a related thread, to see if there's something they're dancing around, too: "Does that make sense? Is there any principle you feel that strongly about when it comes to this?"

Name what *they* keep coming back to

The above tip works in reverse, too: If someone you're talking to keeps coming back to a similar point, it's likely there's something they don't feel is coming through yet. Can you help them figure out what it is? Try listening for what their elephant—their intuition—really wants to discuss, then offering it up as a topic to explore beyond the issue itself, but invite them to tell you if you're wrong. You're just guessing, after all. And besides: it might be that this point sounds repetitive to you only because it bothers you. Either way, it's worth a pull. So in a conversation about gun control, you might say, "I hear you coming back to this point that we just need to pass more laws about guns. It sounds like you ultimately trust the government to make some big decisions about how citizens can arm themselves. Is that right?" Then, observe your body language. Are you ready to listen to their answer to this or any other prompt? If you've crossed your arms or frowned or squinted or are stewing inside just looking at the other person, it's your intuition that needs a talking-to.

Still confused by what they're saying? To keep your grip, when you observe a narrow moment of confusion within yourself, offer it into the conversation, then turn your confusion into a question to pull in understanding. Candor is your friend here: "Honestly, I'm having a hard time with how we could have that many more restrictions and still respect the Second Amendment. Can you say a little more about how you view the right the bear arms? What do *you* think it would take to violate it?"

Balance

Make talking points starting points

The less you sound like the talking heads in the media or the talking avatars on social media, the less likely your conversation will follow the same tired scripts to frustration or contempt. So if you find yourself about to echo the meme that got a ton of likes in your silo, ask yourself what you really want to say and what you really want to know. And if that meme or talking point is really going to help you get there (sometimes they do!), make it your starting point. Sharing a meme you like on social media? Offer up why you like it instead of letting it speak for itself (and for you). Bringing a good op-ed, post, or talking point up in conversation? Say what part of it you agree with and pull on others' impressions. Talking points in all their forms tend to stomp complexity out of nuanced issues. What do they think about its assertions, and what do they think it's missing?

Even when you steer clear of the unreasonable ways we use our reason, it's hard to know what to make of that thing you can state, change, defend, but never really disown.

And that's your opinion.

10

Opinion

One evening in 2018, I participated in a panel discussion organized by a group of attorneys in downtown Seattle about how you work through big divisions. I knew everyone else on the large panel except for a thin man with a deep, sure voice sitting across from me. I peeked at the program. His name was David Smith; he's a philosopher and lecturer who teaches ethics courses around Washington State; and when it was his turn to explain his approach to the topic, I leaned forward, extra curious, and heard a claim I'd never heard before.

"We have an assumption that people choose their opinions," he told the audience. But they don't. "Their beliefs form naturally over the course of their lives."

We don't choose our opinions? I repeated to myself. And BOOM. An INTOIT moment burst my mind wide open, gaps appeared like chasms in my thoughts, and all these new questions flowed out. If we don't choose our opinions, why do we spend so much time trying to talk each other out of them? How savagely should we judge each other by them? If our beliefs form naturally over the course of our lives, is it *the course of our lives*, rather than a battle of reasons, that best explains our opinions to others? I had to talk to this David guy, stat.

What if our opinion of opinion is way off?

~⟨⟩~

At one point in his lecture—"Civil Conversation in an Angry Age," it was called—David unpacked a prescription for bridging divides in the form of two questions that peel us apart from our opinions so that we can look at them fresh.

The first is, "Are you willing to believe that you are wrong about something?"

"Is it safe to assume all sixty-three of us are wrong about something right now?" David asked the virtual, pandemic-era class I joined one evening. In Zoom squares on my screen, heads considered, then nodded. "*I* think so, because we've been wrong about so many things before," he continued. But there's a problem: we don't know what we're wrong *about*. "That simple observation, 'I'm wrong, I just don't know what about!' should produce some humility," David said. "Some willingness to listen."

David then asked his second question: "Which do you value more: the truth or your own beliefs?

"'Cause they're not synonymous," he told the class. "If I'm wrong about some things—my beliefs about everything all put together—my beliefs are not synonymous with the truth. If I value my own beliefs more than the truth, I'm going to defend myself to the death. And why would I listen to you?"

To have a chance at really hearing other beliefs, David teaches, you have to value truth more than your own opinion, and you have to come in with a measure of humility. Watching his class, I was amazed at how powerful our own thought can be. With nothing more than these two questions, we can help our minds move from certainty to uncertainty, finding gaps that help our curiosity catch on.

If, that is, we're not preoccupied with winning.

WINNING LOSES

Elizabeth G. Saunders, an author and time-management coach, summed up what often happens when we take our hunger for victory into the noisy discursive battlegrounds of the internet: "When you feel you won online, you've rarely changed anyone's mind," she writes. "Instead, you stand as the triumphant king of a lonely land smoldering with the ashes of people you've decimated with your words who are less likely than ever to ever listen to your side again."

Our focus on ideas and opinions makes wanting to win a natural instinct. As does our craving for those dopamine lollipops that satisfy us just with the feeling of domination, rather than needing evidence that we've actually persuaded the people we're doing battle with beyond the thread.

The effort—more for optics than substance—is a huge drain on our time.

How caught we can feel in that need to "win" reminds me of a famous old web comic: "Are you coming to bed?" asks a voice offscreen in the *xkcd* sketch. "I can't. This is important," responds a person at a computer. "Someone is *wrong* on the internet."

A "victory," online or off, may not be what you think it is—in other words, it's not proof that your idea is better than their idea. Even when you do "win" because your arguments edged out theirs, did they make the best arguments for their position? When someone stands down, was anything learned? Was anyone persuaded? If the exchange was hostile and combative, who would admit to being moved by it? How would you ever know?

Sometimes, what feels like your victory just means they lost steam, or you happened to be better at on-the-spot communication. I was sitting at my kitchen table with my mom one night years ago, talking about the latest political flash point, when I first realized that my more seasoned rhetorical skills had made her tired of our debates before they'd even started. "You're just too good at this, Mónica." At the foot of the next big showdown, I observed her whole body just sink in surrender. *No,* I thought. *That's not the point.* It was another INTOIT moment for me. I've spent my career trying to help people understand each other. In the community-focused projects

I've run and been a part of—*The Evergrey*, the popular Ignite Seattle public speaker series I emceed for three years, countless participatory events around the city—I've put tons of time and energy into helping first-time writers and speakers shape their stories into strong personal essays or compelling public talks. I *know* that everyone's perspective matters. I *work* to elevate perspectives that don't get heard. So why should more practice at articulating ideas put my own perspective above anyone else's?

Point is: you can't get traction with a mind you're trying to outmaneuver or defeat.

That's why, if you're serious about staying curious when you talk to people who think differently from you, it's always better not to try to win. If what you share ends up influencing someone's thinking in a direction you find good, well, *great*, but it's so unlikely to happen in a huge way *right then*, when you'd taste any kind of victory, that pursuing it for that end won't satisfy anyway. It's more likely to make you impatient and irritable, or to push you to manufacture certainty and rush to judgment, all out of a kind of desperation for some acknowledgment of your rightness that's good for . . . what? Making someone else feel bad?

All my journalistic interviews were pretty one-directional, sure; the focus was on the person I was interviewing, not on me. But I can't tell you how satisfying it is, disappearing time and again into someone else's story, letting its rhythms tell my curiosity where to go next, and paying a whole lot of attention because I knew that somehow, some way, I was going to have to translate some fraction of everything this person's story *means* to an audience that wasn't here with me to absorb it. Even when I'm not writing a story about someone, paying attention as if I were keeps my focus on learning, so it doesn't drift too far into winning.

I know I've switched to the bad kind of win/lose mode in a conversation when instead of listening for meaning, or a contrast, or a gap, I'm just hunting for my edge. I scout for something to sabotage: a weakness. A slipup. A contradiction to attack and exploit. I observe myself abusing rhetoric to maneuver and set traps. I zoom closer into one or another detail, getting overly picky about wording and consistency with the person's past statements, pulling for a "gotcha," stomping out the sparks of every good point, and reading way too much into every misstatement.

But there's a good win/lose mode, too! It happens when you go at it in good faith, building enough traction with each other to make the most of the battle—the reach, grip, and balance to enjoy some rounds of good-natured banter and spirited debate. The conditions for this are rare, sure, but *fun*. Conflict and scrutiny can turn up our brains to full strength, which is great. You might even really reach each other. Going back to our intuitive elephant and their reasoning riders, your elephant *can* listen to reason. It *does* consider challenging evidence. It's just way more likely to do it, the research shows us, when it's hanging out, calm and secure, with other elephants. Then suddenly, our intuition to like other people makes us open up, just a little bit, to what they're trying to say.

BRIDGING OPINIONS

We believe opinions to be fixed, fair channels to judgment—both to our judgment of others and to their judgment of us. But what if the deepest issue isn't the content of our opinions but what we assume they represent—about us, about others, and about the ways our perspectives clash to make our world?

David Smith has put me in a philosophical mood, so here, then, is my theory: To be most useful and alive, our opinions—particularly our political opinions—*must* be in curious conversation with each other. When we're divided, politics feels like it's exclusively about stopping the other side. But at its core, politics is about how we coexist *wisely*, how we create and re-create societies that support us in all our different priorities and preferences. They're imperfect experiments—the systems we have in place to do this now. So as we evolve, they should, too. That's why, to keep our society responsive to this mishmash of people, we need to visit and revisit each other's take on how living these days *feels*. Where do our political norms and structures hit or miss the mark for people—for *you*—and why? What concerns you? What gives you hope? This is how our opinions serve us: not by pushing us to defend our point of view to each other at all costs at all times, but by representing it in ongoing negotiations that both honor and transform it.

That's not how we tend to hold out our opinions, though—flexibly. Rather, we guard and fortify them, sharing them as beacons for the like-minded and shields against the skeptical, not so they help us explore each other's perspectives, but so we can insist on ourselves to each other, push for our way of thinking and stomp out the other side. What would it take, then, to help people share their opinions in an adaptive, nuanced, *conversable* world, rather than one where their opinions will be taken as proxies for who they are?

Curiosity requires uncertainty and uncertainty requires flexibility. If truth matters more than our beliefs, then we can choose to enter bridging conversations holding those beliefs more loosely, just for now, just to see what happens. It takes some courage—*What if I'm talked out of a good thing and talked into an awful one?!*—though personally, I find the opposite scarier and more likely: *What if I'm stressing myself out fighting monsters that aren't there?* To be clear, I'm not saying that we let go of our convictions in conversation. Not at all. Only that we let them breathe. We let gaps appear around their edges without, you know, freaking out. Then we build the traction in conversation to present them and explore them, setting out not to prove something, but to learn something.

If we were less afraid to hold our opinions loosely, could we consider new ideas more freely? We're scared that bad ideas would win. OK, but what if the opposite is true? What if the good ideas, the ones that ultimately have the most power, are what would spread further, faster, instead? Isn't that what good ideas, well presented, should do anyway?

When I heard David Smith say that we don't choose our opinions, my mind went immediately to a facet of how we treat each other that we can all recognize—one that renowned political psychologist Shanto Iyengar pointed out bluntly to journalist Ezra Klein in 2015. "Political identity is fair game for hatred," Iyengar told him. "Racial identity is not. Gender identity is not. You cannot express negative sentiments about social groups in this day and age. But political identities are not protected by these constraints."

If our opinions are the natural result of our life's interactions, to what extent *does* someone who is a Republican or a Democrat choose to be Republican and Democrat? I imagine my husband, who's loved *Star Wars* his whole life, just *choosing* to love *Star Trek* more instead.* His dad took him to see the *Star Wars* prequels in the movie theater three times *each* when he was a kid. He memorized the most obscure lines from the movies. The life-size limited-edition Yoda his grandmother got him years ago still stands in our TV room, scaring young children. My husband couldn't just wake up one morning and *choose* to be a *Star Trek* fan. And you couldn't just talk him into it. I mean, you could try, like I have, but . . . no.

Whatever your answer to that conundrum, I bet you could agree that political opinion is fair game for *accountability*. I mean, it has to be. We have to own what our political opinions lean toward and away from, what actions they inspire in the world, and the trade-offs that result for society. But are our opinions fair game for hatred? Hatred goes beyond opinion to the subject of David's class—civility—and that most debated of virtues: respect. For years I've been reflecting on what respect ultimately is, whether we can agree on its basic criteria, and the extent to which it's even possible to disagree passionately, honestly, and firmly, *but also* respectfully.

David's opinion is that respect is not only necessary to bridge-building conversation, but critical. "I think it means I interact with you in ways that recognize your full humanity regardless of your identity or beliefs," he said. Regardless of group, then, too. Of *us* versus *them* opposition. This kind of respect can't start with a judgment. It has to start with people themselves.

Your opinion is not a final answer. It's a snapshot of where your mind is right now. It's not something you have to defend. It's not even something you have to have at all! With every new controversy, social media will demand to know: *What do you think? What do you think?! What do you THINK?!* But

---

* Which I would not mind at all, by the way. Guess which of us lobbied to give our son the middle name "Riker," then dragged our young family to a Seattle *Star Trek* convention in that aforementioned Lieutenant Uhura uniform to get a baby picture with actor Jonathan Frakes?

no, you don't have to know what you think about *everything*. The most you can do to keep your opinions sharp and useful is to expose yourself to the new, the old, the surprising, and the interesting. Especially in this time of constant change and challenge. Everyone has freedom to move, and they will move at their own pace.

Remember earlier when I said that the most important thing about bridges is not to cross them but to keep them? So many times now I've run into people who say they tried. They built a bridge, they reached out to someone on the other side, they started a conversation. But when the other person didn't cross on their terms, on their time, they thought, *Fine then, forget it.* They burned the bridge to the ground and stomped back to their silo, making sure to spread word that this whole bridge-building thing is good for nothing. It's for the naïve and spineless—a total waste. *Trust me,* they say, *I know.*

But they don't. Respecting people, I think, means respecting that the process by which they change, grow, and transform is a mystery as deep as people themselves. That doesn't mean we tiptoe around each other. It doesn't mean we hold back. It just means we don't act as if we can control or predict other people. We can barely control or predict ourselves.

We shouldn't focus on understanding, rather than winning, just because it's smarter. It's also the only approach that values other people as *people* by giving them the space to be who they are. You can't get traction with a mind you're trying to defeat. Uncertainty that searches for truth gets there faster than certainty that asserts it. "We are more intimately bound to one another by our kindred doubts," wrote Seattle-based essayist Charles D'Ambrosio, "than our brave conclusions."

CHANGING MINDS

Have you ever changed one of your most deeply held beliefs? It probably didn't happen in a single step, or over the course of one conversation. In all likelihood, it took a while. Not just because your reasoning and intuitive mind needed all that time to consider the evidence. But also because deeply held beliefs feel like a part of us, and it's hard and strange to peel away from one conception of yourself to grow toward another. There's a lot of resistance.

And, as David Smith knows personally, a lot of pain.

At the panel discussion where I first ran into him, David shared how his philosophy on the ways we form and change our opinions was shaped in a big way by his own yearslong experience shifting from one strong set of beliefs to another. He shared some details, but not enough to close the gaps in my mind that begged me to ask my questions. Finally, months later, I emailed him, asking if he'd be up for a chat. We met at the Pub at Third Place in Seattle's Ravenna neighborhood on a cool summer night, ordered a pair of Old Rasputin stouts, and got to talking.

David grew up in a fundamentalist Christian community that gave him lots of joy and lots of answers. He didn't know any Jews or Muslims or anyone of a different faith, but he believed deep down what he'd picked up from his community: that people of different faiths were morally and spiritually inferior. Then he began graduate work at a religiously diverse university, and things stopped adding up. He met people of other faiths and they did not seem inferior. They seemed impressive. That added friction challenged what he thought he knew. And he realized that his view of things might be wrong.

"My world expanded exponentially 'cause I grew up in such a small world," he told me. "By small I mean just such a narrow world, when you're only interacting with your own and everything outside your world is inferior."

David had grown up driven to do the right thing. He thought he knew what that meant, what beliefs it led to, but now he wasn't so sure. His experiences with people of different faiths planted seeds that grew, slowly, *over fifteen years*, until he made a choice that changed everything. He was on the cusp of reaching tenure at a private Christian university. But to secure it, he would have to affirm a faith in the theology he'd grown up with. Suddenly, he couldn't sleep. He'd worked hard. He'd met all the requirements. But he had to face a hard truth: his beliefs had changed.

So he walked away from the job, the tenure, all of it. He lost relationships with people he cared about. It hurt. But once he'd arrived at a new set of beliefs, he couldn't ignore them.

When new beliefs come, we don't always notice. "They just pop up like dandelions in May in the yard," he said. Not because we willed them to, but because they found fertile ground in our minds.

David stressed to me, though, that he doesn't see himself as having "changed" his mind about his religious beliefs. "The *evidence* changed my mind," he told me. "It was automatic."

But when it comes to life's mysteries, *evidence* can point different people in very different directions.

When I shared David's story with my friend and colleague John Wood Jr., a renowned writer and speaker on racial and political reconciliation, he told me about something that happened soon after he met Triawna, a woman he later married. At the time, John, then twenty, wanted very little to do with organized religion. To him, Christianity was misguided, full of *othering*. He saw too much exclusion and too little community. But in Triawna, who is devoutly Christian, he saw someone who is smart and good and wise. Was she misguided, too?

So one day, many conversations into a long debate about faith, John took her to task. "You're a really smart person," he remembers telling her. "How can you believe in a book full of -*isms*? If God is real, he's got to be about love."

Triawna responded with what, for John, was poetry: "Though I speak with the tongues of men and of angels, and have not charity, I am become as sounding brass, or a tinkling cymbal. And though I have the gift of prophecy, and understand all mysteries, and all knowledge; and though I have all faith, so that I could remove mountains, and have not charity, I am nothing. And though I bestow all my goods to feed the poor, and though I give my body to be burned, and have not charity, it profits me nothing."

"Did you write that?" John asked her in awe.

"No!" Triawna said. "It's from the Bible—1 Corinthians 13: 1-3."

That was an INTOIT moment John wasn't about to forget. He spent the next nine months reading the Bible cover to cover and sharing his thoughts with Triawna. "At the end of that process," he told me, "I considered myself a Christian."

~~~~~

When you hear something that begins to work on your current set of beliefs, when that seed gets planted in your mind, you won't know what it will grow into. It may displace other thoughts in your brain. It may conflict with something you already know, leading to a dilemma you'll have to resolve or process. The seed may get dug out of the soil altogether. As you walk through the world, reading articles, having conversations and arguments, letting thoughts consciously mingle in your mind as you cook or take a shower, something might water any of the millions of seeds planted in your mind. And any day now, any minute, it could grow into something that so fundamentally changes the way you think, it could change your whole life, the way planted seeds eventually changed David's and John's.

We can't predict how our opinions will change, but we can notice when new shoots are growing. We can sense when "I never thought of it that way" moments bloom in our brains and become more aware of the pathways they encounter. And we can give everyone we talk with room to go where they're headed—on their own terms, in their own time—influencing each other with nothing more simple or more powerful than our own stories.

"*Le cœur a ses raisons que la raison ne connaît point*," wrote the French philosopher Blaise Pascal. *The heart has its reasons that reason does not know.* What if we stopped acting as if our opinions alone explain us? What if, when we look past reason and opinion to the bigger mystery of people, we can learn what those reasons are?

In that space we could discover fresher ways of thinking. In that space an INTOIT moment could plant a seed.

Does it all come down to everyone just agreeing on the same set of "facts"? I'm not convinced it's ever that simple. When we talked about all things divisive one day, Bill Adair, the founder of PolitiFact.org—a pioneering and Pulitzer Prize–winning fact-checking site—told me about the commencement speech he'd given the graduating class at Warren Wilson College in the spring of 2019. He advised the graduates to set a reminder on their phones every day called "Understand someone else," to read an article they disagree with every day, and to have a conversation with someone from outside their like-minded networks every week.

"Plant seeds for more understanding and humanity every place you can," he told the students. "You never know where they will sprout."

EIGHT THINGS TO TRY

We get stuck on opinion when we obsess over winning and persuading at the expense of learning, and we treat our opinions as proxies for who we and others are—overguarding and overjudging accordingly. How do you approach opinions flexibly enough to boost your curiosity? Here's another batch of Traction LOOP tips:

1. Share "snapshot" opinions
2. Change the question
3. Listen longer
4. Acknowledge agreement
5. Untie thought knots
6. Hit reset
7. Acknowledge good points
8. Say "I don't know" when you don't know

Reach

Share "snapshot" opinions

If you come into a conversation holding your opinions more loosely, it can make it easier for everyone in it to explore each other's perspectives, rather than take turns presenting and defending them. How do you do that? By offering your opinions as snapshots of what's currently in your mind. Presenting them as changeable and movable from the start gives you room to revisit and rearticulate them as you let them mingle with others' beliefs. It's not to be cagey or to play down your passions, but to stay open, glide into the flow of conversation, and encourage others to loosen up as well. So next time someone asks you what you think about a tricky issue, try kicking off your answer with something like, "Here's where my head's at right now . . ." or "Well, here's what's coming to mind as I think about it. We'll see where it goes . . ." You can use this trick to add some slack to the criticisms you offer, too: "When I hear you say that, all I can think is, 'No way. That can't be right.' Can I tell you why I think I'm reacting that way?"

Change the question

A handy way to switch from being out to prove something to being out to learn something is to change the question you're trained on in conversation. Instead of asking "Whose perspective wins?" ask, "What makes each perspective understandable?"* If you want to be more curious when you talk to people who think differently from you, don't try to win or change minds. It'll distract you from a more interesting and productive conversation that, incidentally, will be much more likely to end up changing minds.

Grip

Listen longer

Your conversation's heating up and you've just asked someone to say more about their opposing opinion. They've started to elaborate, and you can't

---

* Which I've adapted, by the way, from the words of my colleague John Wood Jr., who wrote in a Braver Angels newsletter: "The question for the purposes of our work here is not 'who is right?' but rather 'what makes each view understandable?'"

wait to jump in with your response. It's moments like these, though, where a little restraint goes a long way. I was reminded of the importance of this when my friend Danny told me about a conversation he'd had with his father about vaccines. The coronavirus pandemic was raging, Danny had gotten the shot as soon as he could, and his father wasn't sure he wanted one. Danny tried to stay curious, but they lost their grip on each other, and his father said he didn't want to talk about it anymore. Looking back at what happened, Danny thought he knew why. "I would ask him a question, he'd answer a little bit, and then I'd immediately jump in with my opinion," he told me. "I was too quick!"

Minding the gap for longer—giving people some space to fill it up—is one of the toughest things to do in a bridging conversation. How do you know you've done it enough? Here's a good rule of thumb: When you're really itching to offer a comment on someone's opinion, make yourself pull with one more question first.

Acknowledge agreement

When you're in conversation with someone who disagrees with you, finding something you agree on is like building a base camp partway up a mountain: you can climb higher faster. So if you listen for those points of agreement, then offer them into the conversation, you're likely to give the whole effort a boost. "You know, I totally agree with that," I imagine Danny saying to his father. "I would've preferred we had more time to test the vaccines, too."

Untie "thought knots"

A "thought knot" is what I call the exhausting thing that happens when you've way overthought something, pushing your reasons and opinions so much on each other, you're backed up into corners and nothing makes sense. You'll know you're losing traction this way when you observe the signs of overthinking: exasperated sighs, heads in hands, rolling eyes, that sort of thing. Wherever you think you're going, it's not working. The mistake I constantly make in this situation is to try to untie these knots by thinking more and pushing harder. It's easily the most common way I end up draining traction from a conversation, and it's no good. Don't get me wrong; you *can* wriggle your way out of these. But first you need to hit reset . . .

Balance

Hit reset

Sometimes backing out of dead ends in conversation starts with starting over. If you're in an in-person conversation, take a breath. Readjust how you're sitting. Readjustments are like yawns, I've learned: they catch on. Within moments, whoever you're talking to will also take a breath, sigh, pour themselves another tea or beer, whatever works for them, and suddenly you've got a nice bookend to the previous combative or exhausting thread, and a great opportunity to start semifresh on another one—but with all the momentum and energy you've built up between you ready to stir you up. If you're not in person, try communicating your break explicitly by describing it in your text or direct message. Watch it have the same effect. "Grabbing a glass of water, hang on." "The kids need a check-in, brb." Then, since you've probably leaned on your reasoning mind a bunch, let your intuition kick in. What's coming up as a gap or good point from what you've said so far? Offer it or pull with it and see where it takes you. A reset is like a pit stop. You're not off track. Just tuning up.

Acknowledge good points

Want to turn around a conversation where everyone's just scoring points? Try scoring points . . . for the other side. This is another behavior that, when you model it, can spread. If you catch yourself thinking "That's a good point" or "Sure, that's fair," to *anything* they say (start small if you need to; it builds with practice!)—offer that up before asking your next question or making your next point. This adds that measure of humility, helps balance the conversation with respect, and builds endurance to probe deeper where opposing perspectives meet.

Say "I don't know" when you don't know

It's wacky how rare this is! But nothing blocks the escalation of a bad kind of win/lose mode quite like admitting that no, you don't know everything (and neither does anybody else). A candid "I don't know" is a signal that you're not in it to win it, to seem impressive, or to hold forth. In that sense, I find "I don't know" to be the most critical *honest* answer to a question in a bridging conversation: it keeps gaps open longer, letting more curiosity flow from whoever wants to drop some knowledge.

～

It can take some guts to set aside your judgment of someone's opinion to wonder about *them*. Your intuition, influenced by sorting, othering, and siloing, will want you to howl, fight, or just walk away. It can take some guts, too, to put your opinion into conversation with an opposing one without any armor. What if people get the wrong idea about where you stand?

And what about where you—and they—have *been*? We get stuck on opinion, too, when we lose sight of the person who holds it—a person who's arrived at that opinion after walking a path we can't see.

Which leads us to the most powerful question any of us can ask across a divide:

Where are you coming from?

Part IV

Paths

I went to the movies a lot growing up. Like, a *lot* lot. I hit fourth grade before it dawned on me that all my friends did not, in fact, go to the movies every weekend. And if there's one thing you learn following all those characters—good and bad, comic and tragic—it's that when you know their stories, people make sense.

One of my favorite classic movies—the French masterpiece *La Règle du Jeu* (*The Rules of the Game*, in English) gets right at this. In a scene where one character tries to explain himself to another, he sums up an inconvenient truth about all human beings: "*Sur cette terre il y a une chose effroyable, c'est que tout le monde a ses raisons.*"* Popularly translated, it means: "The awful thing about life is this: everyone has their reasons."

Everyone *does* have their reasons. They may not be reasons you like or agree with. They may not be reasons you can even learn. But they are there, always. Explaining. And waiting.

---

* Bet you can't guess that Film Studies was my college minor?

And it *is* kind of awful. If you can't understand the characters' motivations in a movie, it's a bad movie. If you can't understand people's motivations in real life, it's just . . . real life. The question is never whether those reasons make sense *at all*. It's whether they make sense *to you*.

I think of each of us as communicating on two frequencies. The first is what we put out there *about* ourselves. The social media posts, the profiles, the public messages and photos and things. Those are the signals we send out to connect with people, and also to ask, in a time of SOS—sorting, othering, and siloing—*Are you with me, or are you against me?*

The second frequency is just . . . us. It's who we really are, if you come up, say hi, and strike up a conversation. It's who we are because of where we've been. The paths we've walked to get here. The ones that tell our story. The ones that actually *can* help explain—better than almost anything else—why we do what we do.

We've explored how to see the complexity of people's beliefs past our overreliance on assumptions, reason, and opinion. Now, that second frequency is the one that we're going to tune to next. We're going to turn it up and listen. Not just to what other people believe but how they've come to believe it. To do this, we'll explore three things: the **experiences** that inform their perspectives, the **values** that underlie their hopes and concerns, and the connections that hold them to their beliefs—something I'm going to call their **attachments**.

11

Experiences

I was a fast test taker in third grade. I'd hand in completed spelling tests or whatever before most anyone else in my class, and since I was the only Latina in my Catholic elementary school in little Dover, New Hampshire, that earned me the nickname "Speedy Gonzales."

Speedy is a Looney Tunes cartoon character, a mouse with an accent who'd go, *"Arriba! Arriba! Ándale! Ándale!"* I wasn't offended, by the way. I was proud.

One day I was talking to my classmate Jessica at her house when the cartoon came up. I told her about Monterrey, Mexico, the city where I was born and where my extended family lived. I told her how Monterrey's name combines the Spanish words for "mountain" and "king." And how, when you're there, you can see my two favorite mountains—El Cerro de la Silla and Chipinque—from the car almost everywhere you go. That's when Jessica got this scrunched up, incredulous look I'll never forget. Then she asked me, real shocked, "They have paved roads in Mexico?"

"Of course they do!" I told her. And malls and restaurants and pretty much everything we have up here!

"OK," Jessica said, and we got back to doodling on the chalkboard in her attic.

After my shock wore off, I realized her surprise made total sense. Speedy Gonzales's Mexico is dusty paths, adobe buildings, and lazy mice-men snoring against the sides of buildings with sombreros over their eyes. *I* knew that was a caricature. But Jessica—and most of my classmates?—probably had no idea.

I remember telling my parents what Jessica had said later that night. I don't remember what they said, but the exchange with Jessica stayed with me for *years*. Thinking back, I'm damn grateful she asked that question and didn't hold back. Kids' curiosity benefits from that: a total, liberating shamelessness. I'm grateful, too, that I wasn't too appalled to answer—and that I was many, many years from even being able to mock or shame her on social media.

We took very different paths to that shared classroom in small-town New Hampshire, and we both learned something from each other that day. Jessica learned that Mexico is more than what you see on TV.

And I learned that people can't know what they've never experienced.

〜〜〜

It's tough to see a person past their opinions and past our own assumptions. It's hard to resist the certainties in our silos in every exchange with people who just don't see important things the same way we do. But when we succeed at it—which we can, and we do—the next step is to direct our curiosity not at *what* they see that's so different, but at the *path* they walked to arrive at that point of view.

Learning about someone else's experiences is the most powerful way to understand them, to see the world as they see it—even for a second—and open your own eyes a little wider to everything as a result.

I'll get mushy and tell you why, though you already know it, and poems and songs and stories have been written for centuries to marvel at it: For all of our differences, we recognize joy and despair and surprise and sadness and loss and triumph in the experiences of other people like we recognize it in our own. I don't just mean that intellectually. We don't follow each other's paths like an argument, parsing logic apart in our minds. This is our intuition at work. We actually *feel* what other people felt as they tell us their stories.

Our experiences—that mix of an event and our personal place in it—tap into something elemental. They tap into what it's like to be *us*. They even get us to help each other, which is why therapists, or friends comforting each other, or strangers attending support groups together, all rely on people sharing their stories to find the right, totally custom way to help. Call it empathy; call it being human. It's just how people work.

In small groups and one-on-one chats where people come together just to tune in to one another, we have little reason to suspect each other of manipulation or bad faith. It's more likely that what we say, we say out of a craving for that big thing we all want, all the time: to matter. Or more practically: to be heard.

Especially by people who don't see things the way we do.

Asking people about the experiences that led them to their beliefs helps us understand them, release "I never thought of it that way" insights, and see our world better. This is because talking about our experiences:

- gives context to our perspectives.

- carries mystery.

- shapes new stories.

We'll explore each of these in turn, then roll out some ways that you can apply the power of experiences to your own conversations.

EXPERIENCES GIVE CONTEXT

One quarantined day in April 2020, I logged onto my first Braver Angels debate. Braver Angels is a national organization out to depolarize the country, and these debates of theirs are, frankly, marvels, the kinds of events you don't think are possible until you attend one for yourself. (And one of several reasons I joined the Braver Angels staff a year later.)

The topic of each debate is a carefully worded resolution meant to help members of the public explore a big issue that divides the political Left and Right. That tumultuous year, the debates had titles like "Resolved: America should embrace radical systemic change to address racism" and "Resolved: The US government should make the process of immigrating to the United States, including achieving citizenship, more difficult."

This first debate I attended was called "Resolved: Government restrictions to combat COVID-19 are worse than the disease; America should reopen for business by April 30."

Hundreds of participants were there, shuffled off into smaller virtual breakout rooms. The moderator of the room I was put into, a woman with the air of a seasoned middle school teacher, previewed how our debate would work. First, she'd call for a volunteer to give a speech in the affirmative—a speech that argues *for* the idea that the government restrictions to combat the coronavirus are worse than the disease. Then, she'd call for a volunteer to give a speech in the negative—someone to argue that this is not true, and that we should not reopen for business by April 30. She would then call on another speech in the affirmative, followed by another in the negative, and so on, back and forth, for the duration of the debate, reducing the (strict!) time allowed for each speech to welcome shorter speeches from more voices. This was not just a series of shortening lectures, though: after each speech, anyone else in the room got a chance to ask questions of the speaker.

These debates are carefully designed to make it tough for anyone to take anything that's said too personally. So before our group got started, our moderator explained a very important rule: whoever asks a question of a speaker *must* (and she would enforce this!) address their question not to the speaker, but to the moderator—"Madam Chair."

To show how this works, she used a lighthearted, low-stakes example. "Let's say the resolution is, 'Resolved: Dogs are better than cats,'" she told the room. "Can I get a speech in the affirmative?" A man (virtually) raised his hand, was called to unmute himself, and said, "Dogs are friendly and meet you at the door. And so dogs are better than cats," keeping it brief, as a demo.

"Do I have any questions for the speaker?" our moderator asked. A woman raised her hand.

I've seen this demo kick off Braver Angels debates again and again since. And it's at this point—when a totally random volunteer raises their hand to demonstrate proper questioning procedure—that something remarkable happens: they always ask the same question. A question of experience.

That day, the volunteer phrased it like this: "Madam Chair, does the speaker have dogs or cats, or have any experience with dogs or cats?"

Our experiences explain our perspectives. Not completely, of course, but they explain enough to give people not just a way to relate to who we are, but a way to *weigh* what we think.

I could tick off a bunch of abstract reasons why I think dogs are 100 percent better than cats—my firm position on this issue. They're more enthusiastic. Energetic. Loving. And, oh yeah, loyal. But if I don't tell you that (a) I am devastatingly allergic to cats, and (b) I owe at least one-fifth of the peace I managed to find in my teenage years to a black toy poodle named Chico who always knew when to bound into my room, leap onto my bed, and lick away angsty tears, well . . . you're missing something pretty important. You're missing where I'm coming from, which will cloud your understanding of where I'm at.

EXPERIENCES CARRY MYSTERY

This brings us to a deeper benefit of sharing our experiences when we talk to people who are different from us. It is maybe the most important benefit, as we try to see things not just through their eyes, but through their *lives*.

Despite sensing, in my journalism, the power of experiences to really grasp people, I struggled to capture this missing element. Then I got to know

April Kornfield, the director of the Braver Angels debates. I kept watching moderators encourage participants to talk about what they've seen and done as they speak about what they think. I wanted to hear her tell me why.

"People think debates are reason only. That it has to be comprised of syllogisms," April told me. "We hammer over and over and over that we love when people share personal experiences."

With a discussion made up of nothing but syllogisms, a kind of deductive reasoning, the problem isn't just that it's tough to *relate* to each other's thinking. It's that it's tough to see that thinking for what it truly is. Logic, reasoning—it all tends to rely on frameworks that are shared, familiar, well articulated. We hang what we learn, in other words, on what we already know, fitting new info to old constructs. But "a map is not the territory it represents," as Polish-American philosopher Alfred Korzybski famously put it. What if someone's perspective is best understood, or *only* understood, with a *different* construct? One that isn't shared or familiar or articulated for you and your silos—or at all? They may sense that construct clearly because they experience it, but they can't point-by-point explain it (because no one could), and that can leave them, and you, stuck. How would you move forward?

Talking to April, we came around to something important: Reasoning alone can't capture the uncharted, unarticulated, un-"reasoned" reality of who people really are and how they really think. But stories somehow can—and sometimes, they can do it surprisingly well. Why?

Sharing experience is essential to understanding each other because it carries "a whole lot of mystery," April said.

I never thought of it that way, I told myself. And then: *Dang. She nailed it.*

People, as we know, and can feel every day, are mysteries. Even the people we know best—our partners, our families, our best friends—are bottomless enigmas. When we flatten out the big, evolving questions of why we believe what we believe and why we do what we do into neat little puzzles, we cheat ourselves out of a broader, clearer view of each other, and therefore, the world of beliefs we construct together. We embrace a false certainty, one that stifles new questions and keeps us from learning more.

What is the mystery that stories can carry? Everything honest that we don't yet understand about other people. Experiences—the stories of what we do, what we've done, and what we've seen—can capture the mystery of who we are on our own scale, in our own lives, and help it travel. We don't need to understand why a story resonates for it to resonate. We don't require some accompanying argument for what it says for the story to say it.

"The shortest distance between two people," said the celebrated Chicago Black youth advocate and entrepreneur Darius Ballinger, "is a story."

EXPERIENCES SHAPE NEW STORIES

Trying to change people's minds when you don't understand them never works and is never worth it. People are harder to move from our positions on things that matter to us for good reason—because our *whole lives* have led us here. Layers and layers of experiences and values have shown us life from a certain angle, and we're not about to be talked out of our deepest beliefs! It *should* take a lot to shake us.

When we *genuinely* change our minds, it's not because we give in to pressure from someone else. It's not because we decide to reject the power of our own experiences. It's because we tell a new story about our experiences that fits us better. You can be moved to craft that new story when new evidence works on you over time, like what happened to David Smith and John Wood Jr. when they changed their deeply held religious beliefs. But you can also craft that new story a lot faster—in an instant—when you see yourself reflected in someone else in a way you didn't expect.

One evening during my freshman year in college, the phone rang in my dorm room. It was my mom. I didn't want to talk with her too long. I had friends to see up and down the hall, bowls of chips to dip into, gaming huddles of guys playing *Goldeneye* to crash. But the chat with my mom got really good really fast. We got to talking about gay marriage. This was 2002, well before the 2015 Supreme Court ruling that legalized same-sex marriage nationwide. And she shared something that had just happened to her and changed everything.

Just the other day, she'd said, she was on a walk home when she saw something that stopped her. She was living in Boston at the time, in a neighborhood called Bay Village that's close to downtown. My father walked to work in the mornings, my mom took public transit to the school where she taught Spanish; it worked out nicely.

Anyway, she was walking home to their little basement condo, and she noticed two people walking ahead of her who looked to be a couple. After a moment, she realized both were men. And very soon after that, she saw one of them lean down and kiss the other one, very tenderly, on the head.

Mom had this intense reaction to that. She'd grown up Catholic—Mexican Catholic, which is its own thing—and on board with the church's teaching on homosexuality. She wrestled all her life with the idea of same-sex marriage. Was it really OK? And here's the weird part: What she felt seeing that kiss between one man and another man was not that it was strange or off or wrong, as she expected. What she felt was something familiar and beautiful and marvelously everyday. Like little kisses with my dad. And us. And between anyone who cares about anyone. *It's love*, she thought. Just love. "*Era tan normal, Mónica*," she told me. *It was so normal*.

She told me this next part with a lot of excitement: Something was growing in her mind that landed with her in that instant, she said. It wasn't a rational argument that planted that seed. It wasn't a point-by-point logical string. It was a moment she felt in a deeper, more mysterious way. An INTOIT moment that changed the way she looked at same-sex marriage by inviting her to change a story she was telling herself.

Before that moment, she told herself a story where same-sex marriage pollutes love. Since that moment, she tells a story where it celebrates it.

WHERE ARE YOU COMING FROM?

One of the best ways to meet people where they are is to ask them where they've been. What paths have they walked to get where they are? What have they seen along the way that changes their landscape, shifts their perspective? What colors emerge that you can draw around yourself to step into their world for an illuminating moment?

We sense all this, naturally, already. I see the most basic evidence of that in a phrase we use almost automatically when some piece of understanding lands with us: "I see where you're coming from." I know where you are. I'm there with you. Sometimes, this phrase comes complete with a slow nod, a look away to a vacant distance while your brain computes the next step to build traction between you.

To release the most insights in dangerously divided times, we need to convert deprivation-based curiosity about ideas to interest-based curiosity about people. That takes meeting people where they are, seeing them past our reliance on assumption, reason, and opinion. Information gaps spark our curiosity, while a base of knowledge provides the kindling. Share stories about the experiences that have brought you to where you are, inspiring whoever you're talking with to do the same, and your generative, self-fueling conversation will build a bond between you as it reveals more mysteries, more gaps, more threads—and more ways to relate.

Asking the question "What am I missing?" reminds us that our perspectives are always limited and we're always missing something, keeping

our curiosity on standby. Asking the question *"Can* I believe it?" helps us approach ideas we don't like with uncertainty and interest.

Inviting these questions is tougher for some folks, on some topics, than others. It all depends on your path. A couple friends of mine have children who have transitioned genders. There's an enormous gulf between their everyday experience with the children they love and the mainstream understanding of trans people. So for them, engaging a certain degree of skepticism on trans issues—particularly online—is like engaging a certain degree of skepticism *about the validity of their own children.* It's not going to happen.

Which leads us to the next big question. Asking "Where are you coming from?" takes us one level deeper, channeling our curiosity toward the paths people have walked to where they are, and the things they've seen and done along the way. As it turns out, sharing personal experiences isn't just *helpful* for understanding people across divides. It's one of the most powerful ways to bridge the divides, period. In fact, fifteen studies across a range of political and moral issues showed that people on either side of the divide "respect moral beliefs more when they are supported by personal experiences, not facts." Especially, the researchers found, when people hear about each other's pain.

Back at Melting Mountains, the event in Sherman County, Oregon, we asked participants to head to different parts of the room to signal one of four choices they made in the 2016 presidential election: Trump, Clinton, another candidate, or no vote at all. As people moved to their respective corners, I remember thinking, *No one's going to stand in the "didn't vote" corner, even if they're supposed to.* Then I glanced toward that corner, and there was Jessica Richelderfer Wheeler.

Jessica is a freelance writer, a mom of twin boys, and a rare nonconservative in Sherman County. She's not exactly liberal, though, either. Over wine one fall evening on my return visit to the county, she told me about her decision not to vote in 2016—and then again in 2020. Not long before this conversation, I'd shared a link on Facebook to a column written by a woman who considers herself "politically homeless" and had decided not to vote. I shared it because I was curious about what would lead someone to choose *not to choose* in such a high-stakes election, and because I found the column insightful on that front. I made the mistake, though, of not being clear about why I shared the column when I shared it, and a bunch of my mostly liberal friends were disgusted. How dare I post a piece about *not voting* just weeks before the most important election of our lives? And who are these horrible enemies of democracy who don't vote, anyway?

The first thing to know about Jessica is that she is not politically disengaged—far from it. We talked for hours about her story: how she grew up in The Dalles before her dad—who rode a Harley in a ponytail in the seventies—moved them to Sherman County to run his family's wheat farm and his dad's parking lot sweeping business. How it felt as if people didn't like Jessica in middle school, branding her a "snobby city girl" even though The Dalles had just 14,000 people. How a distant teenage cousin blurted out to Jessica's father once, "Oh my gosh, you're a Democrat?!" before her mother shushed her: "Honey, we don't say that."

"How did your dad respond to that?" I asked Jessica.

"He laughed," she said. He'd learned to tell the difference between the nasty rhetoric on TV and the good hearts of their neighbors. It would take years, and lots of political angst, before Jessica would learn it, too.

Jessica advocated for liberal ideas at the University of Oregon and voted against George W. Bush twice* and for Barack Obama twice. Things shifted after that. She didn't like what she was seeing from the Left. She didn't love what she was seeing from the Right. With no political group to reflect her mix of political beliefs, she agonized over them in isolation. She stared at her ballot in 2016. She couldn't stomach the idea of voting for either Trump or Clinton. She stared at it some more. She couldn't pretend to care about a third-party candidate. And then she realized: "I would sleep better at night not voting."

And I understood.

---

* She didn't care as much then, she told me, that those votes were *for* Al Gore and John Kerry.

There's an inarguable credibility in what each of us has lived through. What someone *does* as a result of what they've lived can be tough to grasp on its own. But as soon as we walk someone's path alongside them—as soon as we watch a piece of their movie—it's easier to see that everybody has their reasons. That the world, as crazy as it feels, *does* make sense.

SIX THINGS TO TRY

To direct your conversation toward the mystery of where people are coming from, it helps to do what you can to turn everyone—including yourself—into storytellers of their own experience. It's an awesome way for different people to just *connect*, and bonus: some people really enjoy it. How do you dial up the storytelling output of your next bridging conversation? Grab that Traction LOOP and try this:

1. Ask "How did you come to believe X?"
2. Explain yourself with story
3. Pull on examples and details
4. Acknowledge intersections
5. Speak for yourself
6. Share the storytelling role

Reach

Ask "How did you come to believe X?"

To reveal the paths people take on their way to their opinions, don't just ask them why they believe what they believe, but *how* they came to that belief in the first place. Your goal: to elicit stories, not speculation or abstraction.

Explain yourself with story

Most of us default to abstractions. When someone wants to hear why we believe what we believe, the first answer that comes to mind is the direct one: *Because of* X. But with the tricky, complex mysteries that shape, divide, and confound us, that direct answer can't carry all our meaning on its own, and it'll help to tell a story. Plus: offering the personal experiences that have shaped your beliefs helps unlock everyone else's, revealing deeper gaps and keeping the conversation from lingering in a heady, intellectual place that can be tough to relate to or connect around. If you hear a conversation spending too much time in the clouds, it's probably time to pull on people's experiences by pivoting to the personal. Asking "How does this affect you personally?" can be a good way to go.

Pull on examples and details

In conversations about political differences where specifics can get dicey, people will often tell you in vague generalities about something they "always" or "never" see in the political arena, or tendencies that bother them about one thing or another. Listen for when someone begins to describe a pattern they notice without giving you a way to see it yourself, then pull on them to paint a clearer picture by asking them to give you an example of what they mean.

A more direct way to help folks tell their own stories is to prompt them with the language of time and place: "*When* was the last time you felt disrespected for your politics?" "*Where* were you when that happened?" If someone tells you they've read "lots of books" on a particular subject, ask them to tell you about their favorite. If someone tells you they've done a lot of traveling around the country that's informed their views, ask them where, and what's one specific thing they learned. Details fill out the pictures in our minds, which makes people's stories more vivid, powerful, and memorable—and better channels to understanding. Sometimes people drop hints that there's a powerful experience coming to mind about a topic you're tackling in conversation. Listen for those, too. "Oh, I've been there," they might say. Ask them to tell you: "Where?" This again helps turn them into storytellers, and you into someone who—hopefully—can relate.

Grip

Acknowledge intersections

Does a story someone shares remind you of your own? Offer it into the conversation! Every relevant new story shared—so long as it doesn't interrupt, distract from someone's larger point, or hog the mic—helps build traction, momentum, and connection with everyone else who's there.

Speak for yourself

Part of the trouble with thinking we have others figured out is presuming we can speak for them. But if you want to keep curiosity flowing to the most productive places, it really, *really* helps to resist the temptation to speak for others with any confidence—which you can't possibly do—and speak that way only for yourself.

Balance

Share the storytelling role

It can feel pretty good—if you've built up good traction—to tell people about the path you've walked to get where you are. But is everyone being invited to add their stories into the mix, or just the people who seem most eager to talk—or who are being most peppered with questions? In any case, it's good to watch for imbalances: If only one person is opening up, and for too long, they might feel exploited and disengage. Similarly, if someone *wants* to share their experiences but no one seems to want to hear them, they can check out, too, and grow resentful of the conversation. "The only time I see people refusing to acknowledge mystery is when they don't feel they've been heard," April Kornfield told me. A good rule of thumb? Once you've shared your own personal experience around a topic, invite someone else in the conversation to share theirs. And when someone's done telling a particularly vulnerable or hard story, don't forget to thank them.

12

Values

One day around Halloween in 2018, I met my dad for lunch in a suburb of Seattle. We were walking toward a big intersection, talking about the news, when we passed a popular food stand. "Wait a minute," Dad said in Spanish. "Did I tell you what I did there last week?"

He'd marched up to the food stand in the official Darth Vader costume, in full imperial strut. It was the same costume he'd stolen the show with at my daughter's fourth birthday party. The best part, he said, wasn't when he'd used the mask's voice-altering breathing device to place his order. It was when the cashier called out "Vader? Order for Darth Vader?" and everyone in the plaza turned and gawked. One person even asked to take a picture with him. I loved every part of this.

By the time we reached the intersection, we were back to talking about current events. I asked him what he thought of some controversy or other in the headlines, since he'd voted for Trump and all. *"Oye, Moni, no tan fuerte,"* he said. *Not so loud.* I apologized. I get animated when I get into things. But that wasn't what he meant.

"Nadie en mi trabajo sabe por quién voté," he half whispered to me as we crossed the street a couple blocks away from his office. *No one at work knows*

who I voted for. His coworkers are almost all younger than he is—coders fresh out of college, some of them. He tried to tell them once, swiveling his office chair to face a group of his coworkers who were mocking something Trump had said. They laughed his admission off as a joke. They liked working with him; he liked working with them. He wanted to keep it that way. So he laughed along, swiveled back to face his computer screen, and never brought it up again.

Dad can play the bad guy convincingly at a kid's birthday party. There's a video of my daughter taking several steps back as Darth Vader approaches her in the backyard. "Happy birthday." <<Breathing device wheeze>> "I am your grandfather."

Because of his vote, he plays the bad guy in a lot of people's worldviews, too. It hurts me to see it, but I get it. Without repeated evidence to the contrary, it's easy to suspect that the vilest thing you read in a certain point of view hides in the hearts of every person who shares it.

This is why when someone from Seattle asks me why the pair of Mexican immigrants who gave me life voted for Trump, I tell them. For all I know, I might be the only person someone knows who's both close to far-right voters and admits to getting along with them. And if I am, I want to get those who ask past the cartoon villainy. I want to challenge their assumptions and complicate their certainty. I want to give them a peek at what they can't see.

A few months after the 2016 election, I asked Dad if he'd join me for dinner and a show at Dimitriou's Jazz Alley near downtown Seattle. As a kid I'd fall asleep in my room to the sound of Dad on the piano a few feet from my door, tinkering to the intro to Elton John's "Don't Let the Sun Go Down on Me" or playing and singing through my all-time favorite songbooks: *Billy Joel Complete*—volumes 1 and 2. We were not the kind of family that hushed music for anything, and it was with music in the background that I asked Dad to show me more of the path he'd walked to his perspective.

And what I saw was my father growing up as a kid in Mexico, wishing it were as lawful as the United States. A kid who overheard his father's friends teasing him for bothering to pay every cent of his taxes, then committed to following his example. He helped pay for college with money from summer internships at Cervecería Cuauhtémoc, the brewery where his father would work for thirty-five years.* He earned a degree in chemical engineering at Tecnológico de Monterrey, developed a software program to handle payroll for small businesses, and saw his dream come true in 1988 when the company that had hired him to work on its early IT systems had him transferred to its office in Dallas, Texas. As he talks I remember the trip he took the whole family on, years later, to Juarez—across the border from El Paso—to get our green cards. And the nights he and Mom would skip watching *Seinfeld* to quiz each other on key dates in American history, the inner workings of US government—all the stuff they'd need to know to ace the naturalization civics test.

With bass and beats in the background—just a warm-up before the big headlining show—his story played like a jam session to me: lots of improvisation held together by a rhythm, a purpose. "Immigrating here changed everything for us, Dad," I said. "So what worries you about more people immigrating here, too?"

Dad thought a moment. "*Es la ley*," he said. *It's the law.* He doesn't want people to break the law to immigrate here, he told me. He doesn't want people to break the law to do anything. The US government has every right to enforce the laws that make the country fair, functional, and secure, as far as he's concerned. He's got nothing against making the country's immigration policies fairer and more just. But if people want more access to opportunity in this country, they can follow the rules it's set out to welcome them to it.

I wanted to hear more, but Dad fell silent as soon as the lights dimmed over the tables and brightened over the stage. A burst of applause filled the club moments later as the headliners picked up their instruments to play.

---

* And makers of Dos Equis, for the beer nerds among you.

THE VALUES BIAS

One of the simplest definitions of values comes from a tireless researcher on the question of what different people care about—Israeli social psychologist Shalom Schwartz. When we think of values, he says, we think of what is important to us in life.

Seeing each other's values goes a long way toward helping us make sense of each other. The things that matter to us inform everything we believe and every position we take—particularly on the thorniest issues that put our values into tension.

Starting in the 1990s, Schwartz took on a beast of a project. He wanted to study this most abstract of things—human values—and look for patterns that held, even across different cultures. After conducting research in eighty-two countries, Schwartz had the data to back up a pretty amazing claim: There aren't an infinite number of human values out there. There are only ten: stimulation, hedonism, achievement, power, benevolence, universalism, security, conformity, tradition, and self-direction.

According to what's known as the Schwartz Theory of Basic Human Values, values become "infused with feeling" when activated—something any of us can see as soon as certain principles come into a conversation, like being fair (universalism), staying safe (security), and living free (self-direction).

But his most fascinating claim is about how values motivate our behavior: what matters isn't which values each of us holds, but their relative order of importance. Take me as an example. I crave trips to places I've never been before, I didn't drink 'til I was twenty years old because I was terrified of losing control of myself, my grades meant everything to me in high school, and I have zero interest in following my culture's customs just because they're my culture's customs. So it's no surprise at all that my top values are stimulation (I chase novelty), self-direction (I gotta be in charge of myself), and achievement (if I half-ass it, I don't do it), and that my bottom value—way down in tenth place—is tradition (just . . . really not my thing). Take the Schwartz Value Survey online (it's free and easy) and you'll see that relative order for yourself.*

Depending on what values top your list, you may be giving the side-eye to a couple of the "values" at the top of my list, thinking they're anything but. Let's pause on that a bit.

A fun feature of the ten values is that some of them naturally oppose others. Power and achievement don't tend to play well with universalism (concern for all people) and benevolence (concern for people we're close to). The first pair is all "me, me, me" and the second is "us, us, us." Self-direction sneaks around security like a teenager sneaks out of the house to live it up past curfew. And as stimulation's number one fan, I just see the word "conformity" and *cringe*. It makes me think of dystopian novels, the Borg villains in *Star Trek*, and how the "cool" girls in middle school would get up from the cafeteria table to go to the bathroom *all at the same time.*

---

* You can find it at www.yourmorals.org/schwartz_process.php.

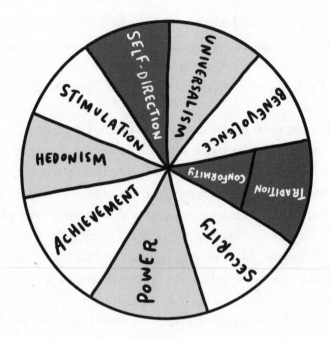

But conformity actually is, like all the others, a handy value. Schwartz describes its goal as "restraint of actions, inclinations and impulses likely to upset or harm others and violate social expectations or norms." Like, you know, not showing up to work with a nasty cold, running red lights, or chewing with your mouth wide open. Loyalty and responsibility are offshoots of conformity. So yeah. I guess those are all right.

The fact that each of us prioritizes values differently matters because it's the "relative importance" of a bunch of values in a certain situation—not just a commitment to any one—that tends to guide what we *do*. To take a simple example, let's say you're getting your driver's license and you have to choose whether or not to designate yourself an organ donor. That might activate your values of universalism (protection of all people by sharing your organs) and tradition (following more customary norms around burial or cremation). Depending on which of those values ranks higher for you—and by how much—you might make a different choice.

This understanding of values has a big implication for how we judge what motivates other people's beliefs. Basically, we're doing it wrong.

To see how, let's say that a Republican wants an immigration policy that ensures strong borders (security) and puts the needs of documented citizens before those of undocumented newcomers (benevolence and conformity). A Democrat, meanwhile, wants an immigration policy that helps people beyond our borders (universalism) and allows undocumented immigrants to pursue citizenship (self-direction).

When they consider each other's stated positions on immigration, the Republican may well believe that the Democrat does not value security or fairness and is therefore morally deficient. Likewise, the Democrat may well believe that the Republican does not value compassion and is therefore morally deficient.

Neither is likely to see that the other is motivated by a different set of top-ranked values. And that's how each of them will miss truly seeing the other: they will mistake a different *ordering* of values for an *absence* of the ones that they think matter most.

And we're right back to that assumption that came up during Melting Mountains, the trip that brought King County liberals together with Sherman County conservatives: *If you're not motivated by this thing I consider good, you must be against it.*

This values bias blocks curiosity. To fix that, we have to stop assuming that people who disagree with us don't value what we value. Instead, we have to redirect our curiosity toward a critical question: What do they value *more?*

~~~

The basic values we've talked about don't map neatly to political issues. But the tensions between them—between security and self-direction, between power and benevolence, between hedonism (pleasure seeking!) and tradition—have everything to do with how the heck we humans manage to live together and make it all worthwhile. And that *is* politics.

One team that tracks the connection between our values and the mess of political issues we citizens are faced with is the Kettering Foundation, a research organization that studies what it takes for democracy to work "as it should"—with people coming together to troubleshoot that democratic ideal of "a more perfect union."

The word "values," to Kettering program officer Brad Rourke, doesn't quite capture these things that matter to us when we consider how we ought to live together. "'Values' suggests a kind of abstract, prescriptive set of ideas," he told me. "But when human beings make the really important decisions together, there's something deeper at work."

These are not just "nice" ideas to aspire to, in other words. They're fundamental to living in society *at all*.

Take, for example, what Rourke refers to as "collective security." We wouldn't bother living in big groups—and towns, cities, states, and so on—if we weren't safer living together than apart, thanks to handy, shared services like fire departments and hospitals. Then there's "being treated fairly." If we work for the benefit of a group, contributing things like taxes and labor, and don't get what we feel is a fair share of the group's baseline resources, like access to education or opportunities to make a living, that's just not acceptable.

Rourke refers to these and other nonnegotiables of a sensible society— like the "freedom to thrive" and "care for others"—as "things held valuable." Our values bias makes us think that people who don't want to do what *we* want to do about a tough issue don't value the same good things we do. But actually, every tough issue that divides and exhausts us—abortion, immigration, gun regulation, you name it—divides and exhausts us *precisely because* it puts some fundamentally *good* values into tension with one another. That tension reveals the most confounding thing of all: trade-offs.

And here's the sucky part: For the most intractable issues, we can't neatly resolve this tension between values or the trade-offs they reveal. Really—we can't! The best we can do is check in with each other, try to approach our diverse value hierarchies as a complicating strength rather than a confusing drawback, and come up with the best imperfect answer to this question: "What is our balance *for now*?"

Sometimes our answer changes a whole lot, real fast. Take one example Rourke brings up: the 9/11 terrorist attacks. That event instantly put two "things held valuable" into tension with each other: our collective security and our freedom to move. Who doesn't miss the days of breezing through the metal detectors at the airport and hugging friends and family right at the gate?* When terrorists hijacked commercial planes and crashed them into the Twin Towers and the Pentagon, everything changed. Our freedom to move gave way to radically deeper anxieties about our collective security. "After 9/11," Rourke says, "collective security was suddenly the paramount concern."

Less than one month after the attacks, we folded no fewer than twenty-two government agencies into a brand-new cabinet department—the Department of Homeland Security. And there were trade-offs. One of them was our freedom to move at airports, which was fine at the time . . . or was it? Because thanks to another value tension that came into play—between fair treatment and collective security—some of us lost more freedom than others. Anyone who appeared to look like the hijackers, including many Muslims, could get held up more often at airport security, unjustly detained, or worse.

We all want to solve our problems for good. I mean, who wouldn't? Seeing things from our own individual point of view, it can seem so darn *possible*. But as long as those problems sit on a fault line between fundamental values in tension with each other, and we live among people who (a) walk different paths, and (b) apply their values to problems in a different order (spoiler alert: both are always the case!), good "solutions" are going to be a lot more elusive than we think.

We may each come up with a solution where the trade-offs seem perfectly acceptable . . . to us.

But what about everyone else?

---

* If you're old enough to remember them, that is!

WHAT ARE YOUR CONCERNS?

You've probably heard it said (or said it yourself) that those *other* people, the ones who disagree with you, "They don't share my values." And maybe, when you say it, you've accepted the assumptions that come with it: that people either hold values or don't hold them; it's a binary, and some people are just value-less and *bad*. You'll see this all-or-nothing framing everywhere if you pay attention. "He has no sense of decency." "She has no empathy." "They just don't care."

But part of embracing complexity and rejecting easy answers is rejecting flat judgments like these—especially when they sneak into our thinking so subtly we barely notice them at all.

When we want to get curious about people's experiences we ask, "Where are you coming from?" When we want to get curious about their values, we become detectives in another mystery: "What are your concerns?"

The question can come in a bunch of flavors. "What worries you about *this*?" "What are you afraid might happen with *that*?" The result is the same and one that I've observed in all my interviews: ask for people's concerns, and they'll show you what they value.

The researchers at Kettering know this, and they make what's learned as a result of asking this question—a process they call "concern gathering"—the first step to exploring the sticky points of every tough social issue. Why? Because when conversations incorporate people's *actual* concerns, they're far more likely to surface the *actual* trade-offs they need to wrestle into balance.

When Kettering researchers gather public concerns, they start where people really are, not where experts or anyone else *thinks* they are. As Rourke writes: "Most contentious issues are framed in expert terms by political and technical elites. People find such framings alien if they do not fully take into account citizens' various starting points and chief concerns. People will not have *one* starting point, but many. The key is to capture them fairly and take them seriously." Otherwise, you're working with assumptions about what people value, not the real values themselves.

〜〜〜

Just for funsies, I sent my dad the link to the Schwartz Value Survey and asked him to take it.

My Schwartz values chart looks like a cityscape dominated by a pair of skyscrapers. I go in big on the top two values in my stack—stimulation and self-direction—and drop off fast for the next three: achievement, benevolence, and universalism.

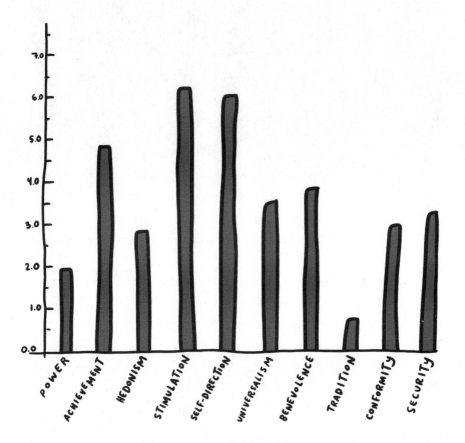

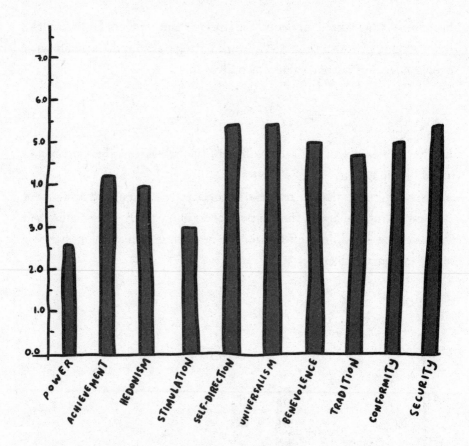

Dad's chart is just something else entirely, with his top six values all strongly held and pretty even. Self-direction, universalism, and security are all tied for first place, with benevolence, conformity, and tradition close behind.

I compared our charts one night when he was over for dinner, and I just geeked out.

Some weeks earlier, about a month before the 2020 election, Dad and I had had a loud, fiery debate about—who else?—Donald Trump. When it started, I was leafing through cookbooks on our kitchen island, wondering what to make for dinner after a day I'd spent working, and Dad, a year into retirement, had helped my third grader and kindergartener with remote school during the pandemic.

When our conversation peaked, my husband had not only gone ahead and made dinner—since it was abundantly clear that I wouldn't—but was eating it in the dining room with the kids while Mom and Tito (short for the Spanish word for grandpa, *abuelito*) carried on, and on, and on.

In the beginning, I had a stupid amount of hope. Trump had done some particularly wacky things that week, in my view—refusing to commit to a peaceful transfer of power, among them—and I figured Dad *might* shift just a *tiny bit* in his support for the guy. But nope: As usual, he had an answer for everything. And as usual, every criticism he threw at me about those awful Democrats left me equally unmoved.

You ever seen videos of rams charging like hell at each other, then crashing? It was like that. Dad sitting on one side of the white quartz countertop, me pacing up and down the other, and every now and then we'd leap, crash, lock horns—gain absolutely no ground—fall back, get up, look for another angle, and leap again.

We're stubborn, the two of us. Not to read too much into this Schwartz values thing—it's a short online survey, after all, and Schwartz's model is just one of *many* well-researched takes out there on how our values might shape our lives. But weeks after that fight, I noticed that self-direction does sit high on both our charts. And holy heck, just look at where we each fall on tradition, conformity, and security. Three of my lowest values are riding tall on his.

Then my eye fell on universalism, the value that aims for "understanding, appreciation, tolerance, and protection for the welfare of all people and for nature." Liberals tend to rate this value higher, on average, than conservatives. And yet, Dad ranks it way higher than *I* do—it's his number one to my number five. His benevolence value, which Schwartz sees as targeted toward "preserving and enhancing the welfare of those with whom one is in frequent personal contact," is also higher. Hmm.

We did finally snap out of it that other night—the constant clashes over the kitchen island. Exhausted from all the insisting, I'd noticed a pattern in what Dad was praising about Trump: How he didn't give an inch. How he didn't make one exception. That observation opened a gap I hadn't seen before.

"Is that your version of strength?" I asked him.

"Yes," Dad said. Trump refused to even imagine defeat. And that, for Dad, is part of what made him a winner.

I cringed and nodded, telling Dad about my version of strength: consensus and compromise, motivating others to be their best. He cringed and nodded back. A moment later, he stood up from the stool where he'd been sitting, and I peeled my elbows off the island. We sat down to a dinner that had gone cold but was still good, critiquing the bird photos he'd taken on his walk through the arboretum that morning and laughing with my five-year-old daughter about the drawing Tito had helped her with for art class. Then he kissed me and the kids goodnight on the cheek at the door* and drove home.

NINE THINGS TO TRY

When we look across our distorted, exaggerated divides, it's easy to mistake a different ordering of values for an absence of the ones we care about most—and judge people accordingly. How can you learn more about people's values while keeping the reach, grip, and balance it takes to explore something so personally raw and meaningful? Going back to our Traction LOOP, here are some strategies to try in your next bridging conversation:

1. Ask for concerns (and hopes!)
2. State your concerns
3. Find values in decisions
4. Pull on values in tension
5. Follow emotion
6. Change the question
7. Listen to anger
8. Offer perspective into confounded questions
9. Pause and persist

---

* A Mexican tradition!

Reach

Ask for concerns (and hopes!)

Asking what concerns people about a tricky topic is the best way to pull out what matters to them. "What concerns you about *X*?" is a solid question for any bridging conversation, especially early on; giving everyone a chance to air out their concerns helps them feel heard right off the bat. Don't want to dwell too much on the negative? You don't have to! As I've learned in my years of interviews and conversations, you can reach for a lot of the same insights about what people value by asking about their *hopes.* That's why we encouraged a question of concern and a question of hope back at Melting Mountains: if a conversation could use more positive moments to find its fuel and make its bond, asking "What do you hope can happen with *X*?" can get people smiling.*

As a bonus, if someone answered that they are not concerned about something or don't have hopes around it, don't be afraid to direct your curiosity at that, too—being careful not to sound too accusatory or demanding: "I'm curious: Why *isn't* that a concern (or hope!) for you?"

State your concerns

Ready to offer your take on something dicey? No matter the topic, making an "I'm concerned about *X*" statement is a *great* way to kick it off. It's not a statement of fact. It's not even really a statement of opinion. Because a *statement of concern* comes from your path, I've learned, it doesn't beg to be argued so much as engaged.

---

* We conducted dozens of research interviews with Seattleites ahead of launching *The Evergrey*. My two favorite questions during these interviews—which came from our colleagues at a media startup called WhereBy.Us—turned everyone into storytellers while getting right at what they valued about their home. They were: "Imagine it's a year from now and you love Seattle more than ever. What had to have happened for you to feel that way?" and "Imagine it's a year from now and you can't stand Seattle and want to leave. What had to have happened for you to feel that way?"

Some conversations won't feel meaningful to you precisely because you skipped this step of putting your own concerns into play. Following the 2020 election, a liberal friend of mine told me about a dissatisfying conversation she'd had with a conservative acquaintance who was skeptical about the results. "I asked all the questions," she told me. Talking more about what

OFFER

happened, she shared that she hadn't offered any of her own misgivings about the election that might have (1) helped reveal knowledge gaps and entry points for her acquaintance, or (2) signaled to him that she, too, was eager to share.

One word of warning about statements of concern: Be careful when you talk about the future. It's the most undeniably uncertain thing we can discuss, but it's dang easy to talk about it with curiosity-crushing certainty. Tempted to say that something bad "will" happen? Try turning it into a statement of concern: *"I'm worried that* X *will happen."*

Find values in decisions

The best personal stories for understanding people's values are stories about the choices we make where values play a starring role. When people tell you about how they came to one of these decisions, listen for how differently ranked values might have wrestled with each other to make it. After the 2020 election—when Latino voters made an 8 percentage point swing toward Trump (as a group they still went 61 percent for Biden)—I stumbled on a news story about why many Latino men voted Republican.

LISTEN FOR

An Arizona man active in Republican politics named Sergio Arellano shared what happened when he approached a voter registration table as a young man and asked about the difference between Republicans and Democrats. A woman at the table told him Democrats are for the poor and Republicans are for the rich. "Well that made it easy," Arellano said. "I didn't want to be poor, I wanted to be rich, so I chose Republican." Whoa.

Pull on values in tension

When you explore the border between your perspective and someone else's, you're bound to discover some of those internal dilemmas that make life complicated. Try listening for values in tension, and if you catch them, name them. This will help pivot the conversation to a context where you can look at the complexity of things more curiously than judgmentally, and it will model the naming of values for everyone else in the conversation, too. If you hear someone getting close to a point of tension, you can also pull on that thread with a question: "It sounds like you're torn on that. Can you tell me more about how?" A note about what to call values: In this chapter I used names that Schwartz and Rourke use, but values can be called a hundred different things. There is no right or wrong one. Just say what you care about!

Grip

Follow emotion

Nothing threatens traction like an emotional outburst. Emotion can be a sign that the conversation is going too far (more on that in a minute), but it can also reveal loads about people's concerns, hopes, and values—telling you you're getting awful close to ideas that are really important to either of you and might be tough to articulate. People will show you when an experience had a particularly deep impact on them; the challenge is to make sure the signal someone's sending is being received. So when you observe anxiety or passion in yourself or others, acknowledge it: "It sounds like you really care about this. Can you say more about it?" In a memorable and wide-ranging bridging conversation I had with a strong rural conservative named Richard, I asked him how he arrived at his deep concern that Democrats and the media were dividing the country. In response, he shared that a particularly impactful moment came when he was watching the hearings to confirm Supreme Court justice nominee Brett Kavanaugh, who'd been accused of sexual assault when he was young. "That's the first time I wanted to yell at the TV," Richard said, with genuine passion, glancing at me. All I had to do to pull on that moment—a big one for him—was to return his look, nod, and let him know I wanted him to continue.

Change the question

The best way I've found to avoid sliding down that toxic assumption spiral that says people on the other side are motivated by something *we* hate is to listen for something *they* love. Why? Because we stack our values in different ways, and if we're going to stay curious in our bridging conversations, we need to change our driving question from "Why don't you care?" to "What do you care about *more*?" When we got to talking about the country writ large, Richard showed me how much it means to him. "I cry with the national anthem, every time," he said, his voice catching. Everything he said afterward made more sense to me because his dedication to his idea of what our country is and means was clear. And thanks in part to my being open to him, I'd received his signal—"I can hear how much the country really means to you"—we kept enough traction to talk for over three hours.

Balance

Listen to anger

"Anger is the force that protects that which is loved," lawyer and Revolutionary Love Project founder Valarie Kaur wrote in her book *See No Stranger*. So before you react to a conversation, shut it down, or run away from the topic, you can take a moment if you can (and it's OK if you can't!) to listen for what anger is showing you about the deeper concerns people are bringing to a bridging conversation.

Feeling *yourself* getting angry and wanting to react? Holding back is not your only option. *If* you think there's enough traction in your conversation to withstand some brutal honesty, you can give an outlet to your anger by labeling your reaction as a reaction as you share it, so people hear it in the right context: "You should know, my first reaction to that is that it's awful. Just the worst. But let me think on it a bit."

Offer perspective into confounded questions

When people are open enough, they might share what confounds them—the walls they're banging their heads against that divide their perspective from those on the other side. *If* this moment comes deep enough into a bridging conversation, and you've built up enough traction, it might serve as an opening to share your perspective precisely where it might illuminate someone else's.

At one point in my conversation with Richard, I observed him getting real heated about one aspect of the protests in the summer of 2020 that just baffled him: "How is it *possible* that people would hurt their own downtown?" Rather than receive it as a cold "*Must* I believe it?" moment, I offered it back as a warm "*Can* I believe it?" invitation. I told him that I had spoken with lots of folks on the left who saw that a different way. Would he like to hear more about that? He nodded, and we dug deeper.

Pause and persist

Values "infuse with feeling," as Shalom Schwartz wrote—sometimes intense feeling—for reasons that may be well beyond the reach of any bridging conversation. If you observe yourself or someone else getting very uncomfortable, maybe not by verbalizing it but shrinking back, or if someone is expressing what sounds like regret for even talking about whatever it is you're talking about, it's probably time to stop. Try switching to a lighter topic or ending the conversation altogether. Do not go too far when people don't want to go too far. That said, I've learned that as long as there are concerns, there are going to be questions—and opportunities to share different perspectives.

The most important thing to do with bridges is to *keep* them, not cross them. So whether it's in an hour or a year—if you can return to this conversation later, you never really left it.

13

Attachments

We've talked about the things that *lead* us to our perspectives—the experiences and values that inform how we interpret the world.

But what about the things that *hold* us to them?

I call these things "attachments." An attachment is anything that causes you to put pressure on yourself to meet a set of expectations about what your beliefs ought to be. That pressure might be good pressure, because the beliefs you're drawn to may add to your life and align with who you are. Or it might be bad pressure, because those expectations push you to conform to something you're not. Some attachments are short-lived or mild. Others are intense and stay with you your whole life. In any case, attachments make it extra hard to lift off from certain ideas to consider them with fresh eyes and look around at alternatives—a big part of being curious. They can even make it hard—as we'll get to—to be and think for yourself.

Sports are an easy example of an attachment that's fun, mostly harmless, and only as intense as your level of commitment. In 2013, my unsporty husband and I made the brilliantly timed decision to try out being local football fans. We read the pregame analyses, hosted weekend watch parties, wore official jerseys on game days, and even got a mini Russell Wilson #3 outfit for our two-year-old. You weren't going to find me getting "curious" about more admirable quarterbacks than Mr. Wilson or better coaches than the incomparable Pete Carroll. What would our fellow fans think? Our unwavering loyalty paid off: when the Seattle Seahawks won Super Bowl XLVIII—clinching the championship *for the first time ever*—the euphoria was intense.*

A person's identity is a common source of attachments—and it isn't something you can simply change. Whether the attachments show up for you, though, doesn't depend on whether you *have* a particular identity, but on how invested you are in it. So if it matters deeply to you that you're a union member, or a Latina, or living with disabilities, or a farmer, or a retiree—you might feel attached to certain beliefs or characteristics that you, as a member of said group, "should" have.

But there's a delicate distinction I want to draw here. Most of the time, we attach to identity-related beliefs because they reflect who we are. But every now and then, we attach to identity-related beliefs because they reflect who other people expect us to be.

Some people have no trouble at all bucking identity expectations loudly and proudly. If that's you, thank you. And keep it up! You're helping to stretch the too-simple storylines out there about different kinds of people, so we don't get so stuck on types and labels in a world of complex human beings. But for most of us, if we sense that what we believe doesn't jibe with what we're *supposed* to believe, it's easier to smile, nod, or just stay quiet.

Which reminds me of one big upset in the 2020 elections involving Latino and Asian voters in California. Everyone expected those two groups would lead the way in easily overturning a twenty-four-year-old statewide ban on affirmative action in education and employment. But nope. The measure failed, big time, 53 percent to 43 percent, not in spite of Latino and Asian voters but because of them. Turns out, a lot of them weren't anywhere

---

* As for what happened the following Super Bowl . . . Let's just say—forgive us, 12th Man!—that our jerseys found a home in the back of a drawer.

near as excited about affirmative action as the "experts" assumed they'd be. An assumption that not a lot of the naysayers, I bet, bothered to correct.

It's easy to see the influence of attachments on other people. *They feel pressure to be Democrats because they're Black. They feel pressure to be Republicans because they're religious.* It's harder, and more important, to notice and be honest about the attachments that influence *you.*

I learned this the hard way when my mom called me out on a big attachment—a bad one—that made me turn against one of my biggest values: telling the truth.

The day after the 2020 election, and before I'd joined the staff at Braver Angels, I gave a talk at a well-attended Braver Angels event about how I'd watched the election results with parents who voted for the other guy. I talked a bit about our background, how we'd come to the US from Mexico, and how we were marking twenty years of being citizens that year. When Braver Angels shared a link to a video of my talk in their newsletter that weekend, they included this passage: "Her parents brought her to this country. They are Mexican immigrants who have experienced the hardships of building a life from scratch in the United States of America. And they voted for Donald Trump."

As soon as I read that, I cringed. My parents did *not* experience hardships building a life in the US, and in my talk, I never implied that they had. As immigrants to a whole new country, my parents had a new culture and set of customs to navigate, sure. But they were a well-educated, upper-middle-class couple in Mexico who were fluent in English and had the resources they needed to make a smooth transition. Their biggest struggle those first few years in the States was missing their friends and super tight-knit family.

I didn't blame Braver Angels for assuming that we'd had the kinds of hardships Americans often associate with Mexican immigration. Lots of immigrants from my native country *do* struggle, *loads*, in a way too few Americans understand. Plus, it's not like there are tons of stories out there filling out the true, wide range of immigrant experiences. The stories of struggle get the spotlight, as, I think, they should.

Now, honesty means everything to me, especially when it comes to people. I had nightmares daily in my beat-reporting days, terrified that I might
have misunderstood a key detail in that day's story or forgotten to check
some lazy assumption of mine with the source. So after I saw the Braver
Angels newsletter, I opened an email compose window and drafted a message to a friend at the organization asking, gently, if they could delete that
part about hardships.

I moved my mouse cursor to the "Send" button on the window . . . then
moved it away.

There's such a strong assumption out there that all Latino immigrants
share an experience of hardship that it's become an expectation, I thought,
not to mention a big source of empathy for Latino immigrants who *do* struggle, who are some of the most vulnerable Americans around. *Do I really
need to stand in the way of that expectation?* I asked myself. *And doesn't it win
me more empathy,* a small, crooked voice in me added, *if I don't?* What's the
harm, really, if people choose to believe this one tiny little lie about me? Isn't
it better, overall, to let it go?

Right then, my phone rang. It was Mom. "Did you see the newsletter?"
she asked in Spanish, breathless. "They said we struggled! We didn't struggle. Not at all! You didn't tell them we *did*, did you, Moni? Have you told
them to correct it yet? You're going to get them to correct it and tell the truth
about us, right? . . . Moni? . . . *Moni?!*"

~~~~~

I've told my mother a few times now that she's my conscience. She thinks
I'm exaggerating, but I'm not. When I get selfish or self-centered, when I
forget what I care about, she's one of the few people in the world who can
set me straight.

Hearing her voice on the phone, I realized why I didn't want to send
the email about correcting our story to Braver Angels. I had an attachment
to the expectation—strongest, I suspected, among my fellow liberals—that
Latino immigrants struggle hard. Playing back the thoughts that had led

to my hesitation, I caught a question—an insecurity, really—that had been hiding beneath the others. It was an absurd, ugly, and totally familiar insecurity, because it's plagued me before. It was there when, after marrying Jason and taking his name, I changed my last name on Facebook from Guzmán to Preston . . . then changed it back. It was there when my daughter was born with blonde hair and I walked around with her, feeling strangely exposed. And it was definitely there when a darker-skinned Latino classmate of mine looked me up and down at the minority retreat in college and said, in a thick accent I don't share, "You're not a real Mexican."

That insecurity, all along, was this: *If an expectation about the Latino experience doesn't fit my experience, am I even Latina at all?*

I sank in my desk chair. When I was very little and still living in Mexico, Mom took me aside after I'd told a big lie about *not* covering my baby brother's hands back and front with dark-blue permanent marker. *"La peor cosa que puedes hacer en la vida es decir mentiras,"* she told me. *The worst thing you can do in life is lie.*

My mom couldn't care less if her story didn't meet someone's expectations or follow some empathy-inducing script. It was *her* story. No one else's. What the hell was I thinking, wanting to hide it? More importantly: How can I possibly seek truth for others if I won't even do it for myself?

"Moni?!" Mom was saying on the phone. "You'll fix this, right?"

"Yes," I told her. "Of course." As soon as we hung up, I hit the Send button on the email window. Within minutes my friend at Braver Angels sent an apology and promised a correction. And I sat at my desk for many long, quiet minutes, trying to understand what I'd almost done.

FACING ATTACHMENTS

Seeing our attachments helps us have stronger conversations about our beliefs because we come into them more self-aware—ready to both connect with others who share our attachments and be wary of anyone who tries to exploit them. Seeing our attachments also helps us see where beliefs get tied together in absurd little bundles, flattening the complexity of who people really are.

My friend Mellina is a mixed-race, lesbian woman living in Seattle. Many folks assume she's liberal, but she's not. She's conservative, and she has to untie those belief bundles in other people *all the time*, trying to show other people that it is both possible and reasonable for one person to hold both *that* sexual identity and *that* set of political leanings.

"What I tell people is, I very much believe in gay rights and gay marriage and all of that," she told me, "but I don't understand what that has to do with *taxes*."

Seeing attachments for what they really are also helps us make tough decisions.

An acquaintance of mine resisted joining Alcoholics Anonymous for years because she was afraid that she would find God. AA is not a religious organization and makes room for people of all faiths or no religious faith at all. Still, its methodology for helping folks get sober is rooted in the belief that there is a power that's greater than each individual, which was enough to make her nervous. The thing that tethered her to the belief that she could not join AA, though, was not an attachment to secular thinking, she told me, so much as an attachment to who her very secular family thinks she is. What if she found faith in God through AA, and it made her sister lose respect for her? Eventually, her alcoholism got so dire she decided to join anyway and accept that risk. She'd been sober for a year and a half when she told me all this. She *had* found God through AA, just as she'd thought she might, but no, her family had *not* abandoned her. In fact, she was as happy as she'd been in a long time.

It's hard work to have conversations with people who disagree with us, but the hardest thing about it isn't *having* the conversation. It's the point in that conversation where you might have to unglue yourself from the expectations society has about who you should be and what you should believe so that you can both think for yourself—for the *actual* mix of opinions, experiences, and values that adds up uniquely to *you*—and consider, with total freedom, a totally different perspective.

STAY SHAKY

As long as we have lives, we're going to have attachments. Loyalties and identities make life interesting. They sweep us up in group victories and bond us in defeat. They give us something to root for, something bigger than ourselves to feel a part of. They grant us that sense of belonging that makes life good. And point out some places where it gets harder to get curious.

So how do you hold your beliefs tight enough to claim them, but loose enough to change them?

I was thinking about this one day when I picked up my smartphone and noticed it had been way too long since I'd cleaned up its applications. As with most smartphones, my digital apps show up as square-shaped icons or groups of icons stacked in a grid across multiple screens. There were a bunch of apps there that I didn't use, plus apps I *did* use—lots—that took too long to swipe to or were just clearly in the wrong place.

I went to edit what apps should appear on my screen, and my phone's operating system responded with the clever little design feature that tells me the apps are ready to be deleted, moved, or regrouped: rather than being fixed in place on my screen, the apps started to *shake in place.*

That's it, I thought. What my phone does to my apps when I want to rearrange them is what I want to do with my beliefs when I'm exploring different perspectives. I don't want them to lock down in certainty. I don't want to have a sure grasp on any of them. Even the ones that stem from a part of my identity. I want to stay curious. I want them to *shake.* So maybe I *know* that I prefer this candidate to that one, or a more porous US border to a more solid one, or sweet foods more than salty. But who knows? Potato chips are *good.*

When my beliefs stay shaky, it's my cue to ask if I can rely on them, if I can move them, if I should delete them altogether, or if I should promote them to my home screen and bump something else out of the way. It gets easier to stay flexible and ask questions of others' beliefs as if theirs are

 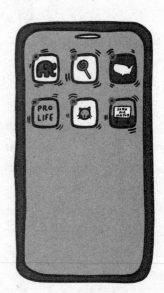

shaky, too. And if they are, then you might open a path where maybe, just maybe, a piece of their perspective jumps from their minds to yours, editing the beliefs around it and making your perspective richer, wiser, or truer to who you are.

FOUR THINGS TO TRY

Just about all of us have some things we feel we *should* believe because of who we are, who we associate with, or some other influential piece of our lives. But do we? To help yourself and the people you're chatting with get some space from their attachments to explore the boundaries between perspectives, consider these few tricks:

1. Get hypothetical
2. Present the strongest argument (for the other side)
3. Acknowledge your attachments
4. Assume absolutely nothing

Reach

Get hypothetical

One easy and very simple way to shake off your own attachments is to pretend, for a moment, to be the proud owner of someone else's. It's the "walk a mile in my shoes" rule: See the issue you're discussing from the perspective of someone with a very different stake in it, and it's almost guaranteed to illuminate something you hadn't considered. Especially when everyone in your conversation approaches a topic from one side: "It makes total sense why tolling the bridge to fund more bus lines sounds like an awful idea to all of us. But what if none of us had cars? What if we had to take the bus from work? Seriously, how would that change our view on this?"

Present the strongest argument (for the other side)

Bridging conversations don't pit arguments against each other so much as they look beyond the arguments to the paths people walk to arrive at their perspectives. To boost your curiosity about the arguments that come up, and to make sure you feed it baseline knowledge from beyond your silos, don't let any discussion of a complex issue stay one-sided or dumbed down. Offer it the complexity it deserves—even if you aren't talking with someone who has a vastly different position—by putting into the room the strongest argument on the *other* side.

This leads to another one of my all-time favorite questions to ask anyone steeped in assurance about their own position, especially when they've just criticized the other side: "What's your most generous interpretation of why they disagree with you?" About half the time when I pull on conversations this way, the person answers by doubling down on their criticism. But then I just double down on the question: "No, really. This wouldn't be controversial if there wasn't *some* reason they thought their position was ultimately good. What do you think that reason is?" That usually does the trick. And hey, this even works on social media. "Seeing lots of tweets today about the push to make Washington D.C. a state, with all the fixin's. My silo being what it is, I'm seeing almost exclusively arguments in favor of this. Which makes me want to know: What are the *strongest* arguments for NOT making this change?" I tweeted in April 2021 when a debate about DC statehood took over the news. The result? A surprisingly curious and nuanced conversation in which a bunch of us actually learned something.

Grip

Acknowledge your attachments

The earlier you offer your own attachments into the room, naming them if they're relevant to what you're talking about, the sooner you can shake off whatever pressure they're putting on you to line up with people's expectations— including your own. Because there's a strong expectation that liberal women are flatly pro-choice, I've gotten into the habit—especially if I'm settling into a conversation on the topic with other liberals—of giving myself room to maneuver around that expecta-  tion early on, saying something like, "You know, I actually have some complicated views on abortion." Once that's out there, I don't worry that I might shock someone with the truth of it, or that the conversation will steamroll ahead under the assumption that every- one is totally aligned on such a charged issue. And there's a bonus, too: drop- ping that little teaser might make someone get curious and pull on my path if they want to learn more.

Balance

Assume absolutely nothing

So your Assumption Assistant has *so many ideas* about this person you're talking to. They wear this, and look like that, and said this interesting thing you heard this other person say once, who was kind of similar to them. We talked about assumptions already. We talked about how we all make them, no matter what. But now that we've talked about attachments, there's something else worth saying: a big part of turning our assumptions into questions is what it does to set people free. What are you assuming about people's beliefs because of the identities they hold? What are they assuming about yours? And how can you help each other wriggle out of those expectations?

Get curious about people's paths, and you'll illuminate more of their perspectives. With enough traction, that'll help you bridge divides you might not have thought you could. Ask where people are coming from, what their concerns are, and what holds everyone to their beliefs, and you'll start telling each other what really matters.

But what if you don't really tell it like it is?

Part V

Honesty

On my second trip to Sherman County, Oregon, riding shotgun with Sandy somewhere among the crisp autumn hills, we got to talking about truth, and Sandy shared an old joke. A boy goes into a barn and sees a man dropping his pants and a woman raising her skirts. The boy runs to the dad and says, "Susie and Chuck—they're going to pee on the hay!"

The boy's dad laughs and says, "Son, you've got the right facts and the wrong conclusion."

And that's exactly it, isn't it? That's how absurd it can be to think we know why people do what they do, when we have no idea.

To question our conclusions across perspectives, we have to get curious. Even stupidly so, because it'll seem like a waste of time in this SOS world of ours where everyone's sorting, othering, and siloing. We direct our curiosity at the mystery of who we are, the gaps between what we know and what we wish we knew, keeping *people* at the center in our conversations, rather than their opinions or our assumptions. Once we're there, we look for the paths people walked to get to their perspectives, the different conclusions they draw about the world.

We'll learn plenty with just that, everything we've covered in this book so far. The steps we've already taken together will help us dodge those us-versus-them showdowns that pit perspective against perspective, as if any of them could achieve total agreement—or cover everything there is to know about why people believe what they believe.

But it's one thing to be curious and another to be honest. Curiosity is worthless without honesty. If people hold back in conversation, release little, put on a mask, is anyone really learning?

If we're not honest together, we're not really together at all. We're not connecting or building traction. We're just *in touch*.

So there are two more things we need to do for our questions to get answers worth reaching for. We need to make it a priority to understand each other's genuine meaning. And then, we need to make it OK for people to share what they really think.

14

Clarity

Each one of us looks at the world with a unique pair of eyes, on a path paved with unique experiences, from our uniquely ranked values. I mean—*unique, unique, unique*—we get the point by now, right?

This is good news and bad news. It's good news because, in theory at least, we should never run out of new things to say to each other. It's bad news because passing meaning from one human being to another is never as easy as we think—especially across big divides.

So apart from resisting the temptation to *other* other people, to accept easy answers about them, to make it all about ideas without the paths you've walked on to get here, we have to do something else to understand each other: we have to make sure we're *clear.*

Does that mean we should all take courses in rhetoric and make sure our vocabulary is as advanced as possible? No. Meaning is in people, *not* words. Words are the best tools we have to try to get our meaning across. But even at the best of times, they fail us.

Listening is about showing people they matter. But people don't feel they matter if their meaning floats out over someone and they get that sense, that sneaking suspicion, that it didn't land right. And sometimes, we hearers will pretend. We'll nod and gesture like we get it when we don't. We'll change the subject before we know what their subject was really about. Traction slips—first reach, then grip, then balance—until you can't pretend anymore, and it's gone.

The earlier chapters in this book ended with lists of things to try as you navigate your own bridging conversations. These final chapters are so full of things to try that you'll find my suggestions throughout.

And we'll begin with our need to listen for what other people *mean*, beyond just what they *say*. We have to *get to* clarity, because it won't just come to us.

REACH: STAY WITH THEIR MEANING

When was the last time someone heard you out on some complex thought until they knew completely and precisely what you meant?

Peter Meyers and Rob Baedeker introduced me to an exercise that got hundreds of people to do it in ten minutes.

Meyers and Baedeker are with a communications firm called Stand and Deliver that boasts clients like Hulu, Twitter, American Express, big names like that.

At the root of the exercise is a sad and simple truth: The experience of being *listened to* all the way on something—until your meaning is completely clear to another human being—is extremely rare in life. It takes an unusual amount of attention, though nowhere near as much as you'd think. The key is just to stay with one crucial question past the point you normally would: What do you *mean*?

The exercise they shared that day is not their own invention, Meyers clarified, but one that openly circulates among gatherings like the one where I encountered it—a globe-trotting arts-inspired leadership conference called the Performance Theatre that played out that year in Seattle. From the stage at the conference, Meyers and Baedeker—whose methods are inspired by improv theater—faced a sea of round tables populated by people in business attire. They got everyone to match off into pairs, then had each person take turns asking the other about themselves with a carefully worded series of prompts. The first two prompts are dead simple, and extremely important for the task of getting people's meaning right:

- Tell me about a problem you're having in your life.

- Tell me everything I need to know to fully understand the problem.

The prompters posing the prompts were instructed not to rush this process. We were to ask for more and more perspective to understand our partner's problem, then test our understanding by checking it with them. "So, you're concerned that you might need to leave your job but aren't sure if you're really ready to jump into the job market without knowing where you're going to land?"

We'll know we have enough clarity, we were told, only when the person answering our prompts can listen to our evolving summary of their problem and say, "Yes, exactly!"

I was paired with the man wearing a tasteful blazer and an easy smile who sat next to me. Let's call him Michael. Michael's job had the immediate unintended effect of making my work as a local media entrepreneur in Seattle feel a bit, well, small. He was the director of corporate communications for a powerful and well-known global organization.

Had it not been for this exercise, I'm not sure we'd have ever connected. But after several minutes, I'd shared some pretty intense stuff with Michael about a problem I was having in my life, and he with me.* We felt not only good about sharing something so meaningful with a person who minutes earlier had been a total stranger, but, we agreed, almost weirdly close. We were invested in each other now. We wanted to know how we worked through these problems we'd just shared. We traded contact info and kept in touch. 'Cause really: How could we not?

The exercise Meyers and Baedeker engaged us in that day was not about bridging the growing political divide between people. It was about bridging the growing divide between people, period. But if it had been about tackling

---

* And a couple additional prompts that went deeper than I'd ever seen at a business conference, including "Tell me who you pretend to be that you're not" and "Tell me what's good about pretending."

more divisive issues, you can imagine the two prompts reading a bit differently. Maybe like this:

- Tell me about an issue you care about.

- Tell me everything I need to know to fully understand your take on the issue.

What would happen if we posed these two prompts to people who are different from us, then kept going, kept listening and pulling meaning out, until we were able to check our understanding and hear, "Yes, exactly!"?

There's a deeper purpose here: When you show people that you want to get their meaning right, you're listening at a level they're not used to. That will not only fuel your curiosity but supercharge the conversation's ability to form a bond between everyone in it.

Every time I've interviewed someone in my career as a journalist to talk *about* them, to thoroughly understand and tell *their* story, it's hard not to come away feeling closer to them. And them to me. That's how important it is to be heard and appreciated. The times when we built tons of traction between us, and I helped them put into words something they'd been struggling to explain—whether it was what it felt like to be eleven years old and Muslim in Michigan just after 9/11, or why people would devote half their waking lives to playing *Defense of the Ancients*, the richest game in e-sports—they appreciated it. Meaning is in people, not words. But when you help them find the right words, it's like you've given them a gift.

Listening is showing people they matter. And when you stay long enough to hear people all the way through on something they care about, you show them they matter *loads*.

GRIP: FOLLOW-THROUGH

When I first learned how to play tennis, one of the toughest things to figure out was how to swing the racket right. And the one thing I kept missing was the follow-through. I stopped swinging the racket after I made contact with the ball. *Why keep it moving in that direction,* I thought, *if the ball is already on its way to the other side of the net?*

Follow-through is a thing we tend to skip in conversation, too. We bounce from asking to listening then to asking again, without the follow-through to make sure we're really grasping for each other's meaning, the way a moving racket changes its grip on the ball. What does the follow-through look like in conversation? It's restating what we've heard and giving the other person a chance to correct us if we're off.

Crucial Conversations, a conflict-training regimen that's popular with the business world, calls this "paraphrasing." You paraphrase to confirm the story you're hearing to make sure you've got it right. Gary Friedman, co-director of the Center for Understanding in Conflict, calls it "looping for understanding" and recommends that you check whether you've understood people's meaning this way every time you hear them say something that seems important to them.

Going back to the techniques in our Traction LOOP,* there are a few ways you can offer this follow-through to something someone says that's worth the attention. "Let me make sure I understand what you're saying . . ." or "Can I repeat that back to you just so I know I've got it?" Then, once you've taken your best shot at summarizing their meaning, you pull to confirm: "Did I get that right?" or "Am I missing anything?" I easily spend a third of my questions during interviews just clarifying. Clarifying, clarifying, clarifying. It is always worth it. Getting someone wrong in journalism, in front of their whole community, can ruin their chance to be seen. I will never forget the pain I saw in the eyes of a new business owner I wrote about for my local newspaper in Dover, New Hampshire, when I was a nineteen-year-old intern there. I'd made so many errors in the feature story I wrote about her and her new shop. I didn't even manage to spell the store's beautiful name right. But even in one-on-one conversation, the cost of carelessness is too high. If you miss each other's meaning, you can lose traction pretty quickly and miss seeing each other.

Which brings us to another step people easily skip in bridging conversations: making sure you understand the meaning of what people are saying

---

* No relation to Friedman's "looping for understanding" tip, by the way! Just a random acronymic coincidence.

as they're saying it. We'd rather not question someone who's really on a roll, or risk seeming like fools when we admit something doesn't make sense to us. But here's a different way to look at it: A strong way to demonstrate that people matter to us is to prioritize getting their meaning, 100 percent, over seeming smart or keeping an easy flow. I've learned this from my time interviewing people at live events with a live audience: Checking people's meaning is good for them, good for you, and good for everyone listening.

Sometimes, it's worth interrupting someone to clarify their meaning, especially if they've just said something that (a) really leaves you scratching your head, or (b) might offend the bejeezus out of you. "Sorry—did you just say you're OK with burning the flag? Oh, you said you're *not* OK with burning the flag. Sorry, go on."

Asynchronous online exchanges make this easy, because you can drop your follow-throughs as comments or in a back channel without ever "rudely" interjecting. I learned early in my digital journalism career that when I respond to comments on my stories with genuine questions of understanding, commenters raise the level of everything they say. They aren't used to hearing from the author of news articles, and my asking about them and their thoughts—even in the unequal exchange of author-commenter—boosted the quality of everything we said next. Being heard made all the difference.

Working to get someone's meaning right can be one of the most direct ways to show you're really listening, and not just faking it with nods, silence, and stillness.

Sometimes, you'll pull for clearer meaning from someone and they won't have it, because they'll still be figuring it out themselves.

This is part of the raw power of conversation—you go places you've never been before and explore them together. When you find yourself sharing still-developing, half-formed thoughts, it can be a good thing! It can mean people are digging deep, pushing new ideas at the boundaries of what they can easily articulate. It means you're excavating something new and covering fresh ground where new insights might be closer to the surface.

It's tempting to think the clear meaning doesn't exist and you should move on. But there's almost always *something* there, and this is where conversations are their most delightfully unpredictable—when everyone's curiosity can pull at the same mystery. "It sounds like you're still figuring that out. What feels important as you think about it?"

To identify these moments when clarity is out of reach, listen for phrases like these: "I'm rambling," "I don't know if this makes any sense, but . . ." And of course, lots of repetitions of a good old "I don't know," followed by stuck, unsure pauses.

Another thing worth mentioning: We all get lost sometimes in conversation. Our minds will wander, and we'll realize that we haven't caught what the other person's been saying. The temp-

LISTEN FOR

tation is to be polite and just pretend, assuming you'll piece it all together eventually. This works well enough a lot of the time—but the stakes are higher in conversations that reach across divides. So when in doubt, clarify. Interrupt and apologize if you have to. One way or the other, it'll be worth it.

GRIP: BUILD MEANING WITH RESPECT

None of us is capable, on our own, of knowing that our meaning is getting through to someone. The only person who can tell us for sure is whoever we're talking to.

To make sure you're *clear* to people, all you have to do is ask.

And mean it.

So that follow-through? It also works in reverse. When you offer your own meaning—particularly one that's complex or cloudy, or a challenge to someone else's position that might be hard to take—you can pull on them with a question: "Does that make sense?"

But don't just steamroll past this checkpoint! Like the boss who asks for questions but enforces a culture of complicity, many of us say things like

"Does that make sense?" not to encourage an honest answer in conversation, but to get tacit permission to monologue. Because this is our default, you have to go out of your way to demonstrate an openness to feedback. You can't control whether other people will get your drift. You can only ensure you don't assume they do.

It is amazing how easily we'll deflect a chance to challenge someone in conversation, especially when the stakes seem high. In the worst live interview I've ever done—a virtual fireside chat with a high-profile figure in the medical industry—we were off the rails and I did not know how to bring us back. While he talked, I put on a straight face for the audience as my brain scrambled to figure out what to do. I wasn't listening to him. At all. So when my guest actually gave me a chance to correct course—"I don't know if I'm answering your question here . . ."—I answered on autopilot. "No, you're fine, go ahead."

So try this: When you ask "Does that make sense?" in in-person conversations, pause your speech, take a breath, and lean your body back. This will make space the other person can step into, not just to give any response but to give the crucial, honest one. Make it as easy as possible for them to say they don't follow if indeed they don't follow.

Should you do this after everything you offer in a bridge-building conversation? No. But you can observe your listeners to direct you. Are they tilting their head? Looking off in the distance, pensive, as you're talking? Are they curling their lip? Shrinking their face? If you see it, offer the opening: "I'm not sure I'm being clear here. What am I missing?"

⌒⌒⌒

Words can make us lazy about shaping our meaning. Sometimes it's easier to give the talking points from our silos than to do the work of pulling out what's really in our heads.

In a timeless 1946 essay, George Orwell described the effect of our constantly borrowing thoughts like this: "When one watches some tired hack on the platform mechanically repeating the familiar phrases . . . one often has a curious feeling that one is not watching a live human being but some kind of dummy," he wrote. "The appropriate noises are coming out of his larynx, but his brain is not involved as it would be if he were choosing his words for himself."

It's easy, too, to casually reach for words and phrases that have become so charged with political meaning from the conflicts that concern them, they can pollute your bridging conversations with messages you did not intend to send. The terms that have this effect are constantly changing, but at the time of my writing, at least, the lexicon included hot buttons like "privilege," "cancel culture," "alt-right," and "socialist."

Sometimes we even hold our silos' jargon over someone else, as if knowing some term's charged meaning gives us the last word on the conflicts that surround it. "That's just your white fragility talking," someone might say. Or, "I don't need to listen to RINOs." This doesn't show people they matter. It shows people how much you think *you* matter.

A term doesn't have to be partisan or hooked to a political issue to jam up your conversation. On an advisory board call for a young nonprofit that was brainstorming its central strategy, I took note of the tip a fellow advisor shared after we'd brainstormed different ideas for the organization's mission. "Put an asterisk next to words that could mean many things," she said. Words like "equity," "justice," "community," and "engagement" got the "star" treatment—so we'd make sure to discuss not just what they mean to each of us, but what they mean to all of us *together*.

It's easy to get caught up in wordsmithing when you don't have to. Here again, George Orwell knew what he was talking about. "Probably it is better to put off using words as long as possible and get one's meanings as clear as one can through pictures and sensations," he wrote. In other words: if you can say what you mean with a story, tell it instead.

BALANCE: SLOW DOWN FOR CHARGED MEANING

When you look for meaning in people, the key question isn't "What does that mean?" It's "What does *that person mean* when they say this?"

This gets hairy when you talk about tough issues, you both use different names for the same things, and the names *they* use feel . . . wrong.

Let's take some terms around immigration as an example. Consider the difference between the terms "undocumented immigrant," "illegal," and just plain "migrant" to describe people who live in the US without being citizens or legal residents. Divisive issues always put values into tension, forcing trade-offs. So depending on which values rank most highly for you when you consider issues around immigration, some of these names will describe key parts of the issue just right, and others will not just fail to capture your concerns but play down their importance.

Among the concerns a range of people have about immigration policy are worries about enforcing our laws (conformity), maintaining strong borders (collective security), and showing compassion and care for all people (universalism). A term like "undocumented immigrant" reflects the values of conformity and security but doesn't lean as much toward universalism. The term "illegal" zeroes in on legality but shows little regard for the person. A term like "migrant" comes closest to reflecting compassion for people's choices and circumstances but doesn't refer at all to concerns around lawfulness.

Let's say you're talking about immigration with someone who's on your "other side" politically. They use a label that makes you cringe. What's next? It'll be tempting to hear it as a rhetorical attack and escalate, but you'll just both lose your balance. If you hear each other's preferred terms as knowledge, though—knowledge to help direct your curiosity toward the other person's values—you can invite them to explore that contrast *with* you, instead of against you. That gives you the opportunity to learn about concerns that don't rise as high for you—concerns others have that you may be missing.

You can listen for a charged term like this, then pull on the conversation to unpack the concerns behind it: "I noticed you used the term 'illegal.' I use the term 'undocumented immigrant.' It makes me wonder about the different concerns we bring to this. What are yours?" When you hit words that could mean many things in your conversations, the same tactic works great. Listen for words where you're unclear on the speaker's meaning, then pull the conversation back, slowing it down to clear things up. "When I hear the term X, I think of Y. When you say it, do you mean something different?"

One way to handle what you suspect might be a tricky term rising in your mind is to offer what you mean piece by piece, instead of tossing the term into the conversation and hoping for the best. So instead of talking about an "illegal," or an "undocumented immigrant," if that's what's about to roll off your tongue, be descriptive and say, "people who cross the border illegally." Yes, it adds syllables, and you don't want to go too far with that,* but describing your meaning in your own words can help unhook it from the partisan vocabulary that gets clicks in the media, which can knock an attempt at an honest bridging conversation way off balance.

But maybe the most critical thing to consider when building balance into your conversation is the *name* you use to refer to a political issue—a name that might be just as divided as the issue itself.

In early 2021, a woman named Wynette Sills decided she needed to do something to help people overcome the biggest force she saw choking understanding between liberals and conservatives: our media. Working alongside colleagues and friends in the local Braver Angels Sacramento Alliance in California, she designed a new program for anyone who wanted to not just talk to someone on the other side, but (gasp!) trade and discuss the news articles that helped shape their political perspectives.

She called the program "Walk a Mile in My News."

During a local pilot of the now-nationwide program in early 2021, Wynette, who is conservative, paired off with a liberal woman she'd just met named Vera. To kick off their bridging conversations, the two women took turns identifying the topics that mattered most to them—the issues they'd spend the next two weeks emailing and chatting about. For Wynette, the Catholic founder of a pro-life advocacy organization called Californians for Life, that issue was abortion. For Vera, who had watched the aftermath of the 2020 election with increasing alarm, that issue was voter rights.

But Wynette saw a problem with the name "voter rights" and pointed it out to Vera. "I felt that was an incomplete name, not a standalone subject," Wynette recalled. Why? Because while people on the left, like Vera, were concerned that Republicans would make voting so hard that it would disenfranchise people—especially people of color—people on the right, like

---

* I've had lively debates with Seattle journalists over the years about the phrase "people experiencing homelessness."

Wynette, were concerned that Democrats would make voting so easy it'd be vulnerable to tampering and fraud. Since the name "voter rights" didn't leave room for the concerns on Wynette's side of the issue, Wynette and Vera agreed to call it "voter rights/election integrity."

Both women would have INTOIT moments exploring the issue from the other's perspective. When Vera shared an article with Wynette about an early version of a Georgia election bill that would have restricted Sunday voting, Wynette had to agree that it looked like Republicans were trying to target Black churches and Black voters who lean Democrat. And when Wynette pointed out that an article Vera had shared referred to voter restriction laws as "Jim Crow 2.0," Vera would realize, some days later, that those words could get in the way. "I came to a place where I could see that for Wynette, for the person she is and what she values," Vera said, "that phrase was a disservice to understanding."

We don't see with our eyes but our whole biographies. The fact that we can transmit even a fraction of that meaning to someone else with language is a marvel.

But how much of that genuine meaning are we interested in passing on to someone on the other side of a big divide? How much of our true perspective will we even let them see?

15

Openness

Want to know my favorite way to see what people really feel when they think no one is looking?

I found it at the movies, in 2003, watching a just-released instant classic by Quentin Tarantino: *Kill Bill: Vol. 1.*

Toward the end of the movie, something crazy happens. One of those twists. (I'd tell you what it is, but I don't want to spoil it if you haven't seen it.) There was a beat of stillness and a couple gasps from the crowd. I was sitting at the very front of the packed theater and suddenly felt this . . . craving. The movie showed a bright scene—lots of light reflected toward the audience. So very quickly, without really thinking, while the moment hung there and before the scene changed, I turned around.

Behind me was the most amazing thing: a room of faces frozen in emotion, in a precise expression of what they felt right then, unfiltered, unprocessed, completely raw. Expressions meant only for the darkness but seen by me.

It was the beginning of a habit, movie after movie. I wait 'til the character hears the devastating news. 'Til the hero finds her deep-down strength at the brink of defeat. At a shockingly sad moment, I turn. At a dark, twisted moment, I turn. At moments of victory, horror, and especially conflict, if I sense that frozen reaction behind me and in me, I turn.

It feels like stealing, every time.

But what I see is more beautiful than anything on the screen.

Honesty.

~~~~

There are *reasons* we are not open with each other all the time about everything. Our minds can think mean, strange, cringeworthy things as they calculate with abandon our take on the world.

Years ago I read a chilling short story about a girl who was frustrated with how the people she knew weren't always honest with her. She got a chance to make a wish, and wished—idiot!—that she could hear precisely what people thought about her, even if they didn't share those thoughts out loud. Within a day the girl was close to suicide. It's just fiction and all, but imagine how *you'd* feel.

Thank goodness for the privacy of our own minds. If we couldn't rely on our ability to divulge precisely the thoughts we want and not the ones we don't—if we couldn't go to dark places and bright ones to suss out who we really are and what we really make of the world—we'd hardly be able to think at all.

The only way to hear, levels deep, what people are really thinking is to earn the privilege. That takes trust, first and foremost, though the relationship doesn't have to be long-lived: Participants in countless workshops I've attended say it's easier to be open about their political positions with strangers than with relatives or friends. The relationship may be shallow, but there's also less of it to lose.

Maintaining a good relationship with someone you're talking to *beyond* the time you're talking to them is outside the scope of this book. But! You absolutely can craft a conversation where it's easier to put it all out there. The trick, as you build reach, grip, and balance, is to raise the potential upside and lower the potential downside of being honest—even when things are drifting or going wrong.

There are four big ways I've found to do this, and I'll break them down for you in this chapter, keeping the Traction LOOP close by. They are:

- Show your work
- Be humble
- Repair with candor
- Ask CARE questions

REACH: SHOW YOUR WORK

You know how math teachers always want their students to show their work? It gives them more information about the students' thinking, helps them see where they might have gone wrong, and can even—woo-hoo!—earn those students partial credit.

There are no final answers in conversation, of course. Some of our calculations we reveal to some people. Some of our calculations we never reveal at all. So you can see where this is going. To make your conversations more open, try revealing *more*. Show your brain at work, not so others can "grade" you, but so that you set the expectation in your conversation that thinking out loud—with all its scrawls, cross outs, and eraser marks—is A-OK and kinda awesome.

Why? Because you have to think out loud before you can think together. And once you show your scratch work, it's much more likely that whoever you're talking to will show theirs, too.

My favorite way to do this, especially when we've bumped up against a particularly complicated question, is to offer this phrase: "Let me think out loud for a bit." Then, unless I observe any hesitation (usually I do this when everyone's leaned in and

OFFER

eager), I give voice to the thoughts in my head.* If this complicates the conversation even more, *great*. As long as we're adding thoughts, we'll find more gaps. And that helps us reach for more insights.

It's worth saying that for this little maneuver to work, you don't need to share information at some high level. Everyone has different natural levels of openness. My husband likes to muse silently on things for minutes on end before he responds (which drives me crazy) while I am—surprise, surprise—more of a quick-speaking, forming-thoughts-as-I-go type of thinker. So all I'd encourage you to try, then, is this: Whatever your natural setting, be just one click more transparent. Allow just a little risk to invite a little more possible reward. This could be as subtle, even, as shifting your body language. Observe yourself: Are you crossing your arms as you talk? Uncross them.

However you choose to take one more step out of yourself, be careful: For this kind of openness to lead you to more insights from others, you'll need to really hold back your criticism. Not silence it altogether, but just . . . give it a minute. Jump in too soon to debate someone who's just opening up and they'll regret having given you a deeper look in.

The more direct approach? If you observe people seeming quiet, or struggling with what to say, offer an invitation to keep it casual. I do this constantly in interviews when I can tell that the person I'm talking to just isn't sure what to let themselves reveal. After several seconds, I put my notebook and pencil down and say, "Feel free to think out loud if you like. I won't hold you to it. Just let me know when you think you've gotten where you want to go." I see them relax, breathe, and go one level deeper with me. When I pick my notebook and pencil back up again, they're digging what they have to say, and so am I. Set a conversational tone where they can shape and edit their thoughts *in real time* with you, and not be so scared of messing up.

〜〜〜

---

* Of course, I'm a raging extrovert. If that's a little too much exposure, buying yourself some time works, too. Just say something like, "Give me a moment to think about this," then, later, give whoever you're talking to a playback of your thoughts.

All this is easier if you think of conversation not just as necessarily unpredictable but also necessarily messy.

If people perfectly articulate every thought that crosses their minds, it's not real life, first of all, and secondly—they're not exploring their thoughts but reciting them. Conversation that searches the intersection between people's raw perspectives can't be that polished or clean. Think of the difference between delivering a prepared speech and falling into spontaneous chatter. The speech is polished only because it's closed. Complete. Done. Like all writing, it's dead on the page compared with the life of a make-it-as-you-go conversation, with its constant restarts, missed turns, and rambles. There's a reason journalists do so many live interviews, and it's not just ratings. Their subjects' rhythms reveal more than their words.

For nearly three years, I emceed the hometown edition of a brilliant grab-bag speaker series that started in Seattle and has since spread to cities all over the world. To kick off each quarterly edition of Ignite Seattle (tagline: "Enlighten us, but make it quick"), I'd do an introductory talk in the same format all the talks had to follow—five minutes, twenty slides that auto-advance every fifteen seconds, no exceptions. And I *never* practiced. In fact, being a much more seasoned speaker than most all of the folks who'd follow me onstage, I'd go out of my way to stumble a bit through the delivery—moving too fast through this slide, too slow through that one— just to set the tone of informality that I knew would (a) relax the speakers so they could be themselves up there, and (b) show every single person in the sold-out crowd of nine hundred that yes, they too could be an Ignite Seattle speaker, opening up about whatever moves them in prepared talks with titles like "Urinals: A Political and Aesthetic Expression," "Traveling Alone and So Can You," and—a personal favorite—"Bluefin Tuna Are Badass Fish."

Curious conversations are always fresh, so you should expect to trip up, at least a little, somewhere. It doesn't matter how smart you think you are, how many articles you've read about the other side, or how amazingly empathetic you think yourself to be.

To keep conversation open, don't treat it like a performance. Embrace it as a fluid, imperfect, collaborative attempt to make sense of the ever-evolving meaning swirling in our hearts and minds.

Do you observe that someone you're talking to is holding back? If the moment's right, help pull it out with a simple, no-pressure invitation. "Any thoughts on this one?"

Observe someone taking a big, resetting sigh? Take one yourself. If you both lift off from the thread for a bit, you'll be better able to see a clearer, more productive way through whatever makes you feel stuck.

And don't confuse honesty for a lack of contradiction! If people contradict themselves, they might be revealing their own messiness, not some inability to think straight. A contradiction doesn't need a correction or confession. Just some curiosity to plumb its depths.

⌣

Speaking of *not* treating a conversation like a performance: the more public the conversation, the less honest the people in it can be.

This is so important, I'm going to say it again.

The more public the conversation, the less honest the people in it can be.

I've talked to so many people now about so many sticky social and political things. Not *one* of our most productive conversations would survive transcription on social media without provoking a scandal in my network. I mean, we all know this, right? We can explore our thoughts together, but we can't explore *all* our thoughts *all* together. Building that much traction across that many different people just isn't possible all at once. But one to one, or in a small, contained group, amazing things can happen precisely because I can share, if I've built the right traction, those thoughts I'm most afraid to share. The ones that might make a stranger listening in wonder if I'm a bad person.

That's how raw, honest conversations work. They go to illuminating places because people feel they can share a portion of the good *and* the ugly that's floating around in their minds.

With enough containment, and enough trust, you don't have to spend time proving your worth in conversation. You don't have to show what side you're on, what goodness you stand for, or, in the group battles that surround you, how decisively you can crush the evil opposition with some killer mic-drop argument. There's no audience to cheer or jeer along—or to give you points for any of it. You get to just be you.

So these are the conversations where change happens *faster*. Because you step out of the internet and the news and the unshared realities to construct a new, temporary reality: the reality of your conversation, and the meaning you make together in it. The more you put what's *really* in your minds and hearts on the table and work with it, the farther you'll actually go.

Can a person who's consumed by hate have influence here? Sure. But so can the person who sets them free of it.

GRIP: BE HUMBLE

Speaking time in a conversation doesn't have to be split fifty-fifty. But if one person is dominating for too long, there's a risk that the quiet folks are feeling ignored, or the talkative folks, overexposed. In either case, you're losing your grip on each other, and someone might lose interest in being open and honest.

Parity is one of the key things to dial up in a strong conversation; one of my favorite ways to correct course for this if you've been hogging the spotlight is just to laugh about it and offer to hand things off as soon as you observe it by pulling out a good question—hopefully before it's too late, and the person you're talking to hasn't already checked out.

I've seen a couple eager event hosts in Seattle be masters at this. They're eager event hosts for a reason: They love people and love to talk. But they're *good* event hosts because they know their limits and how to back off from them. "You know what?" I heard one say, and a not a moment too soon. "I'm doing way too much talking. *You* mentioned figuring out your position on gun issues in college. What happened then that left a mark on you?"

Are you the one stuck with someone who's talking too much? At the next pause after you've observed that (hopefully there's at least *some* pauses!), ask the dominant speaker if you can offer your experience with the topic. Unless they're *really* hogging the stage, they won't say no, and you'll have restored some balance.

Normally, you want your questions to be open and curious rather than all about making space and seeking permission. But desperate times call for desperate measures, and if the conversation is on its way to fizzling out for you, restoring parity is a way to bring it back.

～～～

If you catch yourself *explaining* things at length to people that are not about who you are or what you believe, but about some objective thing out in the world, be careful. At that point, you risk turning a humble, human conversation into a lecture, and your listeners into reluctant attendees.

It gets worse when you treat your side of a debate as the only valid side, explaining as a way of insisting.

One day my friend Nate sent me a whole text thread of an exchange that he, a political "blue," had had with his old high school friend, a political "red." Then he called me up to talk about it. He'd been trying to understand why his friend saw the 2020 election so differently and had gotten, basically, nowhere. Together, we looked at the thread.

One of the first things I noticed? At several points, Nate had responded to his red friend's arguments by sending him links to articles from places like the *New York Times*. His friend would then respond by (a) saying he didn't believe the *New York Times* and (b) sending Nate articles from places like Blaze News. Nate, of course, didn't believe a thing that came from the Blaze. They asked each other to "please" read the articles they traded. But amid all their assertions and challenges, that was about as close as they got to asking any real questions.

"My method has been trying to inform," Nate told me. "Why didn't it work?"

It didn't work because *trying to inform*, like trying to win, can get in the way of trying to listen. Once you drop anchor on a chunk of knowledge you think the other person is missing and try to make the conversation circle *it*, rather than *everyone's* knowledge, you risk turning a bridging conversation into talking-points trench warfare. Wynette and Vera avoided this trap when they traded articles because they agreed to generously explore the other's perspective. When frustrated people start opening links, they're done opening minds.

But hang on. Let's say you have *personal* interesting experience or knowledge of something that's being talked about, something that could level up the conversation if you can drop it into the pool of meaning between you. Do you keep it to yourself? Of course not. But instead of presuming to take the floor and explain it once you've found the opportunity, ask—genuinely—for permission to do so, making the decision a collaborative one to pull the conversation in that direction.

"That's how you avoid arrogance," Peter Meyers of Stand and Deliver told me. "With curiosity."

Want to make sure that experts and nonexperts alike can be open about their perspectives—and find some of that elusive common ground to boot? Pull the conversation in a future-facing, creative direction by asking what good solutions we might find if current constraints weren't an issue.

Matt Camp and Kathy Camp are cousins who both work in politics—Kathy as a Republican political strategist in Florida and Matt as a progressive in government relations in New York. As passionate politicos who don't shy away from debate, they didn't know how to talk politics peacefully with each other until Bill Doherty, the family therapist who cofounded Braver Angels, coached them on how they could listen for each other's meaning instead of aiming to win. Two days after their session with Bill, Kathy got curious and asked Matt to list off the characteristics he'd want to see in his dream presidential candidate, which he did. "I agree with four of the seven things you just said," Kathy remembers telling him. Then the two started scheming: What if they could use their political know-how to help less-polarizing candidates win elections? "We agree on a lot of things even though we vote differently," Matt told me. "We think a lot of Americans feel the same way."

〜〜〜

One of the beautiful things about conversation is that nothing has to hang in the air forever, *including* your mistakes. Let's say that almost as soon as something comes out of your mouth, you know it's off. It disrespects someone you're talking to. It comes off more aggressive or emotional than you meant.

What do you do?

You'll figure out if you need to apologize. You'll figure out what you meant to say and how you can try to better say it (we'll get to how in just a few paragraphs). Before all of that, though, the very second you sense *some-thing's* wrong but before you know what, you take on some humility and say right away, "That's not right."

Why the rush? I'm no fan of sports analogies, but dang it, a football one works beautifully here. It's to throw a flag on the play. Once the flag is tossed onto the field by a ref, all the players stop playing. It's after that—*not* before—that the players and spectators learn why the flag was thrown, what went wrong with the play.

Let a conversation go on when you know you've just stepped in it and who knows? Everything else could just spin out of control. Throw the flag first, *then* let your brain make the call: "I'm sorry. I shouldn't have called you that." "I don't mean it that way at all. Let me try again." If on review, every-thing's golden, just say so. "You know what, I think we're good, actually. As I was saying . . ." But, more often than not, some repair may be in order.

BALANCE: REPAIR WITH CANDOR

Sometimes a person feels so put off by what is or isn't being said that they either lash out or check out. And just like that, you've lost them. Or they've lost you.

Both things can suck. But at least when people lash out, you know they're upset. You have that knowledge to work with. When they check out, it's another story.

Once on a team-wide call at a company I used to work for, an executive passed on tough news in a way that seemed to glaze over things that people on my team were super concerned about. When she asked if people had any questions, she got that heavy silence, not of satisfaction, but silent protest. Everyone was relieved when the call ended, then they rushed to have private conversations where they felt free enough to say what they were really thinking.

In a curious conversation that can, in theory, work with most anything, checking out is the worst. It's invisible, for starters, and tough to catch in the act. You can't know what people are *not* expressing, and there *are* alternative explanations. Maybe whoever's being weirdly quiet at this meeting just decided they have nothing of substance to say?

Here's how I think of it. When people check out like this, their silence is not really silence. You just can't hear their fed-up internal scream.

Despite a few examples like the one I just gave (we had our fair share of startup shake-ups, toss-ups, and cleanups), the executives at this company taught me a lot about how to get ahead of silent disengagement. They built a culture that was more human than most when it came to disagreeing openly. They would say they wanted to hear people's honest reactions to what they knew were shitty situations. They kicked off the conversation by admitting their own concerns and doubts, named whatever exhaustion and resentment folks across the company were feeling, and validated and *thanked* people who stepped up to say more—with no judgment—using what was learned to make some legit changes. It didn't fix all our problems. But it made us more resilient and willing to be honest about what those problems were and how much they sucked.

The same thing works in conversation across divides. If stuff starts to feel uncomfortable, offer that you're sensing that, and that you're more interested in hearing what others really think than in keeping things calm, cool, and dishonest. If you observe a sign that somebody might want to object but isn't sure how, offer that observation—knowing you might be wrong—"I saw you shaking your head at that," then pulling on the honest reaction. "What's on your mind?"

Sometimes things feel way off and you don't know why. Just like when we talked about admitting mistakes, in this case, too, the key thing is to throw the flag as soon as you're ready. This takes some guts to do, no joke. But I've seen it work absolute wonders.

In 2016 I was lucky enough to take a class with Harvard professor Chris Robichaud and hear him talk about his infamous "Patient Zero" simulation. Designed to train graduate students and government executives in the principles of adaptive leadership, it's an intensive, hours-long simulation where participants are split into teams of about seven, told that each group is running the government of a different fictional country, and made to role-play within their groups through a scenario you'll have to read twice to believe: a worldwide zombie apocalypse.

Curious as all heck (I mean *come on*), I asked Robichaud if he'd let me watch the next run of the Patient Zero simulation. By all means, he said. And there I was, a little spectating pip-squeak in a room of dozens of high-level government folks from all over the world who didn't have a clue what they'd signed up for.

The scenario is not about testing expertise. It's about zombies—and not a conceivable disaster like, say, earthquakes—specifically so that no one could possibly claim technical prowess in knowing how the hell to resolve the many intractable dilemmas that would arise during the course of the simulation. Do you, the national government, try to covertly assassinate the leader of an uncooperative but beloved religious group (awful!), or allow the massive religious parade he's insisting on leading tomorrow that is *guaranteed* to turn millions of *your* citizens into flesh-eating creatures (aaah more awful?!)? Or here's another one: Do you send your armies to shoot down the zombies infecting more of your citizens (die, zombies, die!), or do you try your darnedest to *quarantine* them, since you might find a cure someday and wouldn't want to go down as having murdered your citizens (but in your defense, *they were flesh-eating freaks!*)?

So yeah. The simulation sharpens intragroup communication and collaborative leadership skills for those moments when all hell breaks loose, no one has any idea what to do, but *someone's* got to do *something*.

In the group I observed, a funnyman sat at the middle of the table and caused trouble. He was cynical and resistant to the exercise but kept his group's attention by cracking jokes. It was leading the group toward some seriously neglectful decisions. I was starting to give up on them.

But then, another person at the table, an older man with a white goatee who'd been quietly observing everything, for the most part, spoke up. With confidence, calm, and absolutely no aggression, he changed the fate of this group's doomed fictional country with one mighty phrase: "I am not comfortable with this conversation."

The effect was magic. All eyes at the table turned away from the funnyman and toward him. He took a breath, looked around the table, and got to work—helping everyone deliberate the awful trade-offs they were faced with, helping them frame the issues so they could make better decisions. In the introductions, a bunch of other folks at his table had seemed more impressive to me at the start. Their résumés had, anyway. But who would I want in charge of my country if aliens invaded or something? This guy.

No one even looked at the funnyman after that.

I've seen it over and over again since. It's yet another version of the "throw the flag" principle, with a gutsy twist: "I'm not comfortable with this conversation" can be a great thing to offer when any conversation loses its way.

But sometimes, a conversation just loses *you*. When we talked about experiences, we talked about how stories are good for bringing the mystery of who people are and what they think into an exchange that could otherwise get stuck on what's already known, named, and articulated. What do you do when a conversation goes one way, but you are squarely somewhere else?

First, observe when you're feeling dismissed or neglected. It's toughest to troubleshoot in group conversations. When it happens to me, I'll start resenting the people speaking, who are of course completely oblivious to that resentment, or dart a look toward the exits. Can I go to the bathroom, then *disappear*? If I can't escape, I'll reset my body posture a bunch of times—shifting in my seat, recrossing my legs, leaning forward and back. When I pull out my phone—which I *can't stand* seeing other people do in an engaged conversation, I mean it just burns me—I know I've lost all hope.

After I go home, I'll regret not having tried. Every time. How can the people in a conversation know they've lost you if you don't, you know, *say* anything? What do I blame them for? *Not reading my mind?* That regret is what's given me the guts to, more and more over the years, make my own space in a conversation that is supposed to include me but doesn't. "I hear what you all are saying, but I see this differently. Let me try to explain what I mean . . ." Or: "I come at this another way, I think." Or, if I have a more specific idea of what to bring up: "We're talking about *X*, but aren't we missing *Y*? I think it's important."

This works in reverse, too. Do you observe someone looking lost or left behind? The difference between someone who is patiently listening and someone who's unwillingly disengaged can be subtle. Do they look impatient? Are they scowling a bit? If so (making sure you're not being a jerk or anything): pull on that and check! "Just taking a step back, I'm wondering if the way that we're talking about this gets to where you're coming from. Is there something we're missing, do you think?" Someone did this to me in a conversation where I was quickly checking out, and I couldn't believe it. I stepped in, said my piece, and the conversation made way, way more sense to me after that.

One of the hardest things to monitor in conversation, especially if you are really invested in it or feel a lot of momentum, is recognizing when the gig is up.* Tender topics can be so illuminating and make a conversation so valuable and insightful. But observe who you're talking to for signs that you're going too far. Might the person be feeling overexposed? Taken advantage of? Like they're being held to something they said they're not even that

---

* I speak very much from personal experience on this one because—surprise, surprise!—I can be way too curious for my own good, or anyone's else's.

sure about yet, and the whole conversation's starting to feel weird and like a big mistake? Take a break into a different topic when needed—especially an easy one to connect with where you have something in common—or just offer to stop altogether.

Wynette Sills, the creator of the cross-partisan "Walk a Mile in My News" program, told me that as a pro-life advocate working in California—a very Democratic state—she's learned to be quite careful with this when she has bridging conversations with liberals about abortion. "I never want to push beyond a person's comfort level," she told me. "Whenever I sense we're getting to a cringing, soft place where somebody's sensitives are being stretched, I'll say, 'Let's pause there and reconcile and refresh and maybe come back to it at a different time.'"

ASK *CARE* QUESTIONS

Jacqui Banaszynski, my onetime journalism teacher, put a phrase in my head at that workshop years ago that never left: "Live life in the form of a question." So here we are, at the point where—in a book about being curious—we talk about what it takes to ask your own *good* questions. And the first thing to know is this: Good questions don't follow a script. They don't come in order. You don't even know if it was a *good* question, really, until you see what comes out of it.

The main test of a good question, for the purposes of crossing the big divides in our world, is whether it leads to better understanding between people. In a big way or a small way. That's it. A bad question gets you away from understanding by costing you traction, compromising trust and goodwill.

In any case, questions have this incredible and incredibly obvious power that I didn't appreciate until I'd spent years asking them for a living: When you ask a question, people feel compelled to answer it. Ordinary people. Powerful people. It's super hard to dance the dance that keeps you from confronting whatever a question presents. Questions, in other words, put intense pressure on people to release information. They can be tactless.

Exploitative. Abusive. Or, they can be refreshing. Liberating. Revelatory in a way you would never expect.

Only you can know when a question is a good question. But to give you a little guidance, here are four characteristics I've learned make for not only better questions, but much more fulfilling conversations. I call it the CARE check: if your question is curious, answerable, raw, and exploring, you're on the right track.

Curious

You'd think it would be a given, but not all questions are curious! Questions are curious only when they are driven by one primary goal: to fill the gap between what you know and what you want to know with new knowledge.

Some questions are driven by other goals. Among them: making a statement, stumping or cornering someone, deflecting attention, making an accusation, seeking affirmation, baiting a confession. Watch enough high-profile exchanges on TV or the internet and you'll run into so-called gotcha questions. These are not curious questions. They're questions meant to put pressure on someone to hold them to some judgment, responsibility, or challenge. Sometimes it's a public service. Other times, a partisan performance. "Oh, so you believe protesters *should* destroy someone's property to make their point?"

You might want to ask a gotcha question yourself if you believe that whoever you're talking to, in a much more casual conversation, is not being accountable to some critical role or obligation of theirs, like, say, being a good parent or friend or citizen. But when you do, watch how it changes the conversation. It puts the person you're talking to on the defensive and makes the whole conversation look more like a battle than an "unrehearsed intellectual adventure."

The stronger your relationship or level of trust with the person, the more it can withstand and even grow when you turn up the heat this way. We're all accountable to something, right? But if you're serious about understanding someone, gotcha questions are not going to get you there.

Answerable

Ask someone a question you know they can't answer in the moment and you're not really asking a question at all. It can be the equivalent of a physical shove: you're daring them—showing off your presumed expertise or superiority or pushing the person to a place where they'll feel less valued for what they can contribute.

"Oh yeah? What was the US GDP in 2017?" is not an answerable question in a conversation unless you're asking an economics expert or are sitting in front of a textbook, flipping through charts. Bridging conversations are more about trading and exploring meaning than suddenly doing research. Ever seen someone reach for their phone to look up something that comes up in a fast-moving conversation, and someone else roll their eyes in response? Don't get me wrong: Research is obviously critical for finding out what's true! It's just not easily done in groups, and it can weigh down or pretty much halt an engaging conversation. The exception to this would be asynchronous conversations over email or social media that already have a lot of built-in breaks, where calls for some research—given in the right tone—are not so out of place.

An answerable question is one that a person doesn't need anything outside themselves to explore, and so it doesn't expect anything from them they can't provide. All the questions we've talked about to explore people's paths to their beliefs, plus questions that help clarify or bring out stories, definitely qualify.

Another *unanswerable* question to avoid, by the way, is the one that picks a fight: "Name *one time* that politician didn't mess everything up!" In this case, the question signals closed-mindedness, intimidation, and—most likely—a commitment to sounding right at all costs. Asking the question is like telling curiosity to hold your beer, basically. It turns the conversation into a duel where nothing is learned and no one is listening.

Raw

This brings us to the biggest thing no good question can carry: assumptions. Many of the questions we ask across the divide incorporate opinions, accusations, or frustrations. But questions are most powerful when they're raw—when nothing else is baked in. Raw questions don't try to get a two-for-one deal: If you want to share your opinion—cool—share it in a statement! But if you want your curiosity to do its best work for you, it's more productive to ask questions that prompt answers, not an objection or defense.

This is an insight that's been well thought through by the bridge builders at Braver Angels. In one of the workshops the organization is best known for—the Red/Blue Workshop—a group of politically "red" and "blue" participants come together to better understand the perspectives on the other side.* My favorite part of the two-day experience comes when the blues craft questions for the reds and the reds craft questions for the blues. But they don't just think about the questions and ask them on the fly. Oh no. Each group goes off into separate rooms to take the time to prepare them.

I participated in one Red/Blue Workshop on the blue side, and later, my parents participated in another Red/Blue Workshop on the red side. So to show you precisely how a loaded question becomes a raw one—and how you have to *see* the assumptions you carry before you can toss them aside and get curious—I'm going to walk you through how one of my questions for the red side shed its assumption, and then, how one of Dad's questions for the blue side did the same.

"I want us to ask about democracy—concerns about the state of democracy and what's happening to it," I told the blues in our closed breakout room

---

* And we know it works: A 2021 study of the Red/Blue Workshop found that people who take it are 22 percent less hostile toward the other side one week later, with some depolarization effects lasting more than six months. "If effects of this magnitude were extrapolated to the US adult population, they would be large enough to reverse more than half of the increase in polarization observed over the past three decades," the researchers wrote.

in my virtual Red/Blue Workshop, which took place just one month before the 2020 election. "I want to try to separate policy from what's happening to our democracy. Can anyone help me come up with that question?"

The other blues jumped in, acknowledging that they knew exactly where I was coming from. Emboldened by their encouragement, I saw my deepest, bluntest concern spelled out: "I want reds to answer for what I see as a degradation of our democratic institutions as a result of this administration's behavior," I told my fellow blues, my pulse racing, their heads nodding. "That's what I want to get to."

We knew it would do no good to directly share those frustrations and accusations with the red participants. And that's where the magic happened: Once we saw our sincere, loaded judgment, we could see past it to the question that had the best chance of filling the gap between what we knew and what we wanted to know. We saw how to leave room for people we didn't understand to tell us what we were missing. We started by stripping out the assumption that our democracy was being degraded, leaving room for the possibility that it's more resilient than we think. Then, we took out any assertion that this administration was to blame. The raw question we emerged with was, simply, this: "What concerns, if any, do you have about the health of our democracy?"

A similar thing happened with the red participants in a separate Red/Blue Workshop when Dad proposed a question on climate change. Much like his daughter, he started out polite: "I have an idea for a question about climate change and how certain people are when they say something like, 'The world is going to end in twelve years if nothing changes,'" Dad told his fellow reds. "Is that really just hyperbole, exaggeration?"

And sure enough, the folks in his silo helped him see the bluntest version of his concern—plus an amusing dose of sarcasm: "So is the question something like, 'Do you still really believe this climate-change nonsense, even though all of your predictions, you know, from 1970 still have not come true?'" one of his fellow reds asked, smiling.

Dad laughed. "Right. I don't know if that's a little rude," he said to tension-releasing chuckles from the group,* "but that's kind of the question now, yeah."

Knowing what they needed to take *out* of their question, the group of reds got to work. They started by dropping the assumption that blues were just caught up in doomsaying, leaving room for the possibility that the alarm around climate change was justified. Next, they removed another assumption they had that there was no practical way to address a planet-sized problem. The raw question they ended up with was this one: "How great is the threat of climate change? How can we reasonably fix it given the economic consequences?"†

Do you need to huddle up with people on your side for minutes on end just to prepare a great question to bring to your next bridging conversation? Of course not. Workshops slow down the mechanisms in our minds so we can examine them closely. Real conversations are always better at full speed, with all the risks and rewards that come. Besides: The assumptions we strip out of our best raw questions also show us what those questions should be about. Notice what assumptions turn up in your next conversation, turning up new questions and gaps, and trust yourself. You'll know what to do.

Exploring

Curiosity needs you to *not know*. But then here comes certainty, beckoning from every corner, offering cognitive closure, a resolution, an easy answer, an escape.

---

* I laughed, too. *Of course it's rude*, I thought, listening in as one of the workshop's silent observers. *It's honest!*

† Dying to know how reds and blues would answer raw questions like these? Go find someone to ask! Pro tip: Braver Angels workshops are free and open to anyone who's ready to be curious.

Sometimes questions can be too demanding of answers. So, you want to ask exploring ones. Demanding questions carry an expectation that the person should have some satisfying answer for you right here, right now. But if your goal is to understand across divides, you don't want to pressure people to tell you what they think you want to hear, or to defend a position they earnestly have. You want them to be honest about where they stand, especially if it's complicated.

A question that pushes people toward certain answers is often called a leading question. Think about the difference between "What's your take on background checks for buying guns?" and "You don't think there ought to be more background checks, do you?" If people don't have an answer you're pining for, in terms you want to understand right now, well, that's OK. There's always the next conversation.

EPILOGUE

No One Is Beyond Understanding

My second-favorite word in Spanish that has no translation in English is *"convivir."* It's a verb that means "to live together." The closest we get to it in English is the verb "coexist," which in my humble opinion aims a bit low. All we need to do to coexist is not kill each other. Co-*living* takes more.

I've covered a lot of protests in my career. I see a democratic beauty in all of them, no matter the issue or anyone's judgment of the ideas, and I approach them with a kind of reverence for the frustration, courage, and hope people bring to each one. I carry a notebook, a pen, and a camera or smartphone as I walk alongside them, but not a poster. *Never* a poster. My duty is to document, not partake.

So it was strange and unnerving when a friend invited me to make signs at her house for the next day's 2017 Seattle Women's March, which I would cover for *The Evergrey*. I said no . . . then called back and said yes. I brought black and silver Sharpies and a thick square of foam board I set on my friend's kitchen table. I looked at it while she decorated her poster—a liberal message I could sympathize with but was not my biggest concern. Not even close.

Staring at that blank uncertainty, I let my mind wander to my conservative parents and my liberal friends, to the divides ripping truths and stories and people apart all around me. I pictured in my mind the assumptions filling our silos and gathering strength. What would it take now, I thought, to not just live *my* life in the form of a question, but for everyone who's walked a different path with different concerns to different opinions to live *some* questions *together*? How can we do that before our fears of each other and our certainties about each other solve unsolvable mysteries and close the gaps we dare leave open, before it becomes *too* hard for *too* many to see past the caricatures to who and what is really there?

Before, in other words, it's too late?

I carried my sign in the January sun in a street-soaking sea of political slogans, surrounded by hundreds of thousands of people's own frustration, courage, and hope. The three simple words on it got odd looks. They seemed out of place in an angry, anxious time, but I believe to my core that they weren't then and aren't now. That while each of us fights and rages for our own convictions, we can choose to leave room for what we're missing and the people who can show us different views on the same shared world. Not to change our minds but challenge them, one "I never thought of it that way" moment at a time.

Not everyone has to do this. But enough of us *must*.

When I knew I had to write this book, I took out that sign from the closet I'd stored it in and propped it on a wall near my desk. The three words stared at me as I stared at the blank uncertainty of these pages, attempting to fill them with whatever questions and tools and stories might flesh out their promise, if we can hold them up as high as our perspectives and our pride:

"Honesty, curiosity, respect."

The way we sort, other, and silo in dangerously divided times is an SOS. But it's also an opportunity, for two big reasons. First: it's making us confront our complexities and contradictions, pushing us to see each other as fully as we can, helping us be honest together so we can be together at all. And second: it's making us want to share what we think and feel with all kinds of different groups and communities as the world shifts around and through us. What a perfect time, then, to try new ways to listen—to begin with the radical idea that no one is beyond understanding and see what it reveals.

Building a bridge to the other side isn't easy, but it's also likely that it's not as hard as you think. Take the first step out of your silo, and the gulf you've been afraid to span might look more like a gap and feel more like an invitation. And even when the divide *is* as big as you feared, the most important thing to do with a bridge is to keep it, not cross it, because the strength of these bridges lies in people, not ideas. This is not a book about relationships. It's a book about being curious. But I guarantee that when you are more and *more genuinely* curious, it will strengthen all the relationships that matter to you—whether they're with your relatives, your colleagues, your country, or yourself.

So here's your mission, dear reader, if you choose to accept it:

Surprise yourself.

Take one step closer to someone who disagrees with you—whether that means spending time with a friend or relative you've been drifting apart from, reading an opinion from an earnest voice on the other side, or sparking a conversation you've been both eager and hesitant to have. When you want to explore why they're wrong, explore what you're missing. When you want to determine whose view wins, determine what makes each view understandable. When you want to discover *why* someone believes something that confounds you, discover *how* they came to believe it. When you want to know what their problem is, try to know what their concerns are. When you want to demand why they don't care about what you care about, learn what they care about *more*. When you want to trap them into saying what you want to hear, free them so they say what they honestly mean.

And when you want to stop listening so you can react or respond or judge—which will be often!—mind that gap between what you know and what you most certainly don't and ask *one more* curious question.

Want all in? Awesome. Set yourself the challenge to think or say "I never thought of it that way" in response to a different perspective every day—and do whatever it takes to get there.

Whatever you do to reclaim curiosity, I want to hear about it and help you along! You can reach me via email at moni@reclaimcuriosity.com, on Twitter @moniguzman, or plug in to a whole new curious community by signing up for my newsletter at bit.ly/reclaimcuriosity.

This isn't the end, folks. It's just the beginning.

With honesty, curiosity, and respect,

Moni

ACKNOWLEDGMENTS

I knew writing a book was hard work but now I *know* writing a *book* is *hard work*! There's no way I could've done this without the mountain of support I got from family, friends, colleagues and collaborators, and several amazing people I can't believe I'm lucky enough to know, let alone learn from.

Some authors end by thanking their spouses, but F that. Jason Preston, it is a dream to have you as a partner in all the things. You're patient when I'm not. You believe in me when I don't. You share in my ambition but with that touch of *chill* that keeps me from burning. Thank you.

Mi mami y papi. I still remember the moment I told you I wanted to write this book, fully expecting you to freak out in that unfiltered way of ours about my wanting to share your story as well as my own. And all you said was what roughly translates in my memory to, "Hell yes, Moni, go for it!" I don't know what I did to deserve you two. *Los adoro.*

Matt Belford: In our first conversation, I barely knew what a book agent *was.* Having such a relentless champion helping me fill all the gaps in this journey means the world. Claire Schulz: Who knew editors could be so dang approachable? I can't tell you how many times one of your comments made me smile big with some fresh new angle. The team at BenBella Books—Lindsay, Sarah, Jessika, Alicia, Glenn, and more—plus copyeditor Scott Calamar: Thank you for making this newbie author feel so dang supported. And Haley Weaver: How fun to watch these concepts come to life in your illustrations! You draw out the beauty, richness, and potential of everyday *humanity* like no one else. Thank you for giving your enormous talent to this book.

Big thanks to my Circle Rock Sisters, Susan Lieu and Julie Pham, for the dig-deep critiques and *delicious* dinners; to Marika Malaea for guiding me through drafts and doubts with honesty and wisdom; to Danny Goodwin Jr. for the weekly writing huddles that never failed to perk me up; to my D&D crew and pandemic podmates for keeping me (mostly) sane in insane times; and to all my colleagues in curiosity who said *yes* to reading my manuscript, participating in a wild framework-testing experiment, or listening to me present a first draft of a chapter *live* to you as a *talk* because that's how my brain works and you totally rolled with it (*or all three!*): Buster Benson, Bill Boyd, Rossilynne Culgan, Kayla DeMonte, Justin Eckstein, Warren Etheredge, Nedine Hall, Tim Hay, Carlos Hernandez, Peggy Holman, Alexandra Hudson, Philippa Hughes, Jihii Jolly, Jessica Jones, Kevin Loker, Kathie Marchlewski, Traca Savadogo, Mellina White, and Sara Winge.

To my kids, Lina and Julian: It was inspiring to watch you two learn and grow up close this year. I'm glad you got to see Mami do the same.

Special thanks to my mentors Tom Rosenstiel and Dean Miller for helping me see past my own blind spots to what I really wanted—and needed—to say; to Sam Ford for the *amazing* conversations that helped launch this book; to everyone at the Nieman Foundation for Journalism, the Henry M. Jackson Foundation, the Kettering Foundation, and Hedgebrook for seeing something worth elevating in these wacky ideas I get into my head; and of course to my fellow scrappy innovators at WhereBy.Us and *The Evergrey*—for helping to show what *magic* can happen when we insist on putting people first.

To all the brave bridge builders from across the country who have opened their arms to me and shared their stories—you've taught me more than you know, and we're just getting started. And to everyone at Braver Angels, especially my colleagues Mary Beth Stibbins, John Wood Jr., April Kornfield, and Ciaran O'Connor: you're teaching me what it means to do right by people who see the world differently—and have given my once wandering faith in *all* of us a warm and perfect home.

And finally, a hearty "Good morning!" to Sandy Macnab, who opened his big world in Oregon to a little liberal from Seattle and ended up changing her life.

NOTES

Introduction

xvii **the biggest threat to our country's** Anthony Salvanto et al., "Americans See Democracy Under Threat—CBS News Poll," CBS News, January 17, 2021, https://www.cbsnews.com/news/joe-biden-coronavirus-opinion-poll/.

xvii **the number one issue facing** "New Poll: Voters Rate Political Division as Top Issue Facing the Country," Georgetown Institute of Politics and Public Service Battleground Poll, June 15, 2021, https://politics.georgetown.edu/2021/06/15/new-poll-georgetown-institute-of-politics-and-public-service-releases-june-2021-battleground-poll/.

1: Sorting

5 **the "birds of a feather"** Miller McPherson, Lynn Smith-Lovin, and James M. Cook, "Birds of a Feather: Homophily in Social Networks," *Annual Review of Sociology* 27, no. 1 (August 2001): 415–444, https://doi.org/10.1146/annurev.soc.27.1.415.

5 **We bond more easily** Julianne Holt-Lunstad, Timothy B. Smith, and J. Bradley Layton, "Social Relationships and Mortality Risk: A Meta-Analytic Review," *PLoS Medicine* 7, no. 7 (July 2010): 7, https://doi.org/10.1371/journal.pmed.1000316.

6   **Just one in every eight** Gus Wezerek, Ryan D. Enos, and Jacob Brown, "Do You Live in a Political Bubble?," *New York Times*, May 3, 2021, https://www.nytimes.com/interactive/2021/04/30/opinion/politics /bubble-politics.html.

6   **address-level research** Jacob R. Brown and Ryan D. Enos, "The Measurement of Partisan Sorting for 180 Million Voters," *Nature Human Behaviour* 5 (2021): 998–1008, https://doi.org/10.1038/s41562-021 -01066-z; Emily Badger, Kevin Quealy, and Josh Katz, "A Close-Up Picture of Partisan Segregation, Among 180 Million Voters," *New York Times*, March 17, 2021, https://www.nytimes.com/interactive/2021/03 /17/upshot/partisan-segregation-maps.html.

6   **Those voters—so about** Reuters staff, "Fact Check: '133 Million Registered Voters' Argument Uses Flawed Logic," Reuters, January 1, 2021, https://www.reuters.com/article/uk-factcheck-voters-133-million /fact-check-133-million-registered-voters-argument-uses-flawed-logic -idUSKBN296284.

7   **"Each election becomes, not just"** Lilliana Mason, "Best Of: The Age of 'Mega-Identity Politics,'" interview by Ezra Klein, *Vox Conversations*, Vox, re-aired November 28, 2019, audio, 1:15:59, https://radiopublic.com /Ezra/s1!e039b.

8   **Between 1972 and 2000** Lilliana Mason, *Uncivil Agreement: How Politics Became Our Identity* (Chicago: University of Chicago Press, 2018), 28.

8   **As for race, in 2012,** Mason, *Uncivil Agreement*, 37.

9   **As of 2021, 72 percent . . . at least once a day** "Social Media Fact Sheet," Pew Research Center, April 7, 2021, https://www.pewresearch .org/internet/fact-sheet/social-media/.

11   **Gingrich hoped Republicans** Peter T. Coleman, "Lawmakers, to Repair Our Polarized Congress, Make DC Your Home," *The Hill*, May 16, 2018, https://thehill.com/opinion/campaign/388007-lawmakers -to-help-repair-our-polarized-congress-make-dc-your-home; Lawrence Lessig, "Newt Gingrich, the Man Who Changed Washington," CNN, November 21, 2011, https://www.cnn.com/2011/11/19/opinion/lessig -gingrich-change-washington/index.html.

12   **Former Democratic representative David Skaggs**   Evan Philipson, "Bringing Down the House: The Causes and Effects of Personal Relationships in the U.S. House of Representatives," *CUREJ: College Undergraduate Research Electronic Journal*, University of Pennsylvania (April 2011): 32, https://repository.upenn.edu/curej/141.

12   **"I take it we're all"**   David Burkus, "How Criticism Creates Innovative Teams," *Harvard Business Review*, July 22, 2013, https://hbr.org/2013/07/how-criticism-creates-innovati%20/; Peter F. Drucker, *Management: Tasks, Responsibilities, Practices* (New York: Harper Business, 1992).

13   **In the 1980 presidential election . . . 1,726 landslide counties**   Max Rust and Randy Yeip, "How Politics Has Pulled the Country in Different Directions," *Wall Street Journal*, November 10, 2020, https://www.wsj.com/graphics/polarized-presidential-elections/?mod=article_inline.

14   **Sixty-five of our least populous**   Christopher Ingraham, "Look at the Jaw-Dropping Emptiness of America," *Washington Post*, January 20, 2016, https://www.washingtonpost.com/news/wonk/wp/2016/01/20/americas-emptiest-places-42-of-the-land-1-of-the-people/.

14   **"If it feels like Republicans and Democrats"**   Rust and Yeip, "Different Directions."

2: Othering

18   **More than half of Americans**   "APA Public Opinion Poll—Annual Meeting 2018," American Psychiatric Association, interviews conducted March 23–25, 2018, https://www.psychiatry.org/newsroom/apa-public-opinion-poll-annual-meeting-2018.

18   **a win by the other side**   Michael Dimock and Richard Wike, "America Is Exceptional in Its Political Divide," *Pew Trust Magazine*, March 29, 2021, https://www.pewtrusts.org/zh/trust/archive/winter-2021/america-is-exceptional-in-its-political-divide.

18   **One mental health services provider found**   "Mental Health in a Pandemic Winter," *Vida Health* (blog), January 11, 2021, https://blog.vida.com/blog/2021/1/11/mental-health-in-a-pandemic-winter.

19   **In 1954, social psychologist Sherif**   Muzafer Sherif et al., *Intergroup Conflict and Cooperation: The Robbers Cave Experiment* (Norman: University of Oklahoma Book Exchange, 1961; Classics in the History of Psychology), accessed July 10, 2021, https://psychclassics.yorku.ca/Sherif/.

19   **"wander within hearing"**   Sherif et al., *Robbers Cave Experiment*, 78.

20   **"The boys revealed"**   Sherif et al., *Robbers Cave Experiment*, 79.

21   **"I soon discovered"**   Henri Tajfel, *Human Groups and Social Categories: Studies in Social Psychology* (Cambridge: Cambridge University Press, 1981), 1.

21   **In one experiment, Tajfel showed**   Henri Tajfel, "Experiments in Intergroup Discrimination," *Scientific American* 223, no. 5 (November 1970): 96–102, https://faculty.ucmerced.edu/jvevea/classes/Spark/readings/tajfel -1970-experiments-in-intergroup-discrimination.pdf.

22   **In a modified follow-up study**   Tajfel, "Experiments in Intergroup Discrimination."

23   **"To know what has come before"**   Jon Meacham, *The Soul of America: The Battle of Our Better Angels* (New York: Random House, 2018), 10.

23   **hate group's membership**   Jennifer Mendelsohn and Peter A. Shulman, "How Social Media Spread a Historical Lie," *Washington Post*, March 15, 2018, https://www.washingtonpost.com/news/made-by-history/wp/2018 /03/15/how-social-media-spread-a-historical-lie/.

24   **an estimated 750,000 Americans died**   Guy Gugliotta, "New Estimate Raises Civil War Death Toll," *New York Times*, April 3, 2014, https:// www.nytimes.com/2012/04/03/science/civil-war-toll-up-by-20-percent -in-new-estimate.html.

24   **"The dogmas of the quiet past"**   Andrew Glass, "Lincoln Defends His Emancipation Policies to Congress, Dec. 1, 1862," *Politico*, December 1, 2017, https://www.politico.com/story/2017/12/01/this-day-in-politics -dec-1-1862-268420.

25   **"When the beans supposedly"**   Sherif et al., *Robbers Cave Experiment*, 146.

25   **Democrats are off**   Daniel Yudkin, Stephen Hawkins, and Tim Dixon, "The Perception Gap: How False Impressions Are Pulling Americans Apart," More in Common, June 2019, https://perceptiongap.us/.

25   **They thought just half**   Yudkin, Hawkins, and Dixon, "The Perception Gap."

25   **A 2020 study**   "America's Divided Mind," Beyond Conflict, June 2020, https://beyondconflictint.org/americas-divided-mind/.

26   **In a 2018 study**   Douglas J. Ahler and Gaurav Sood, "The Parties in Our Heads: Misperceptions About Party Composition and Their Consequences," *The Journal of Politics* 80, no. 3 (July 2018): 984, https://doi.org /10.1086/697253.

26   **people discriminate against**   Shanto Iyengar and Sean. J. Westwood, "Fear and Loathing Across Party Lines: New Evidence on Group Polarization," *American Journal of Political Science* 59, no. 3 (July 2015): 701, https://doi.org/10.1111/ajps.12152.

26   **three kinds of polarization**   Anne E. Wilson, Victoria A. Parker, and Matthew Feinberg, "Polarization in the Contemporary Political and Media Landscape," *Current Opinion in Behavioral Sciences* 34 (August 2020): 223, https://doi.org/10.1016/j.cobeha.2020.07.005.

26   **And the further someone is** [in footnote]   Samantha L. Moore-Berg et al., "Exaggerated Meta-Perceptions Predict Intergroup Hostility Between American Political Partisans," *Proceedings of the National Academy of Sciences* 117, no. 26 (June 2020): 14864–72, https://doi.org/10.1073/pnas .2001263117.

27   **Hillary Clinton beat . . . 53-point spread**   Gene Balk, "Even Some of Washington's Reddest Counties Were Bluer in 2020," *Seattle Times*, December 10, 2020, https://www.seattletimes.com/seattle -news/politics/even-some-of-washingtons-reddest-counties-were-bluer -in-2020/.

27   **"Seattle's Only Trump voter™"**   Danny Westneat, "Four Months In, 'Seattle's Only Trump Voter' Has His Doubts," *Seattle Times*, May 24, 2017, https://www.seattletimes.com/seattle-news/politics/four-months-in -seattles-only-trump-voter-has-his-doubts/.

29   **Don Lemon, told his viewers that he**   Joe Concha, "Don Lemon: 'Had to Get Rid of' Friends Who Support Trump," *The Hill*, October 30, 2020, https://thehill.com/homenews/media/523535-don-lemon-had-to-get -rid-of-friends-who-support-trump.

3: Siloing

34 **One reason this happens is** Mónica Guzmán, "To Conquer the Digital Jungle, Your Brain Needs Your Help," *Seattle Times*, June 21, 2014, https://www.seattletimes.com/business/technology/to-conquer-the -digital-jungle-your-brain-needs-your-help/.

34 **In a groundbreaking 1999 study** Cass Sunstein, "The Law of Polarization," *Journal of Political Philosophy* 10, no. 2 (December 2002): 175–95, https://doi.org/10.1111/1467-9760.00148.

34 **a 2005 experiment where liberals** Cass R. Sunstein, David Schkade, and Reid Hastie, "What Happened on Deliberation Day?," *California Law Review* 95, no. 3 (2007): 915–40.

35 **"One of the characteristic features"** Cass Sunstein, *Why Societies Need Dissent* (Cambridge: Harvard University Press, 2003), quoted in Stephen Miller, *Conversation: A History of a Declining Art* (New Haven: Yale University Press, 2007), 267.

35 **The Markup, a nonprofit newsroom** [in footnote] Corin Faife and Alfred Ng, "After Repeatedly Promising Not to, Facebook Keeps Recommending Political Groups to Its Users," Markup, June 24, 2021, https:// themarkup.org/citizen-browser/2021/06/24/after-repeatedly-promising -not-to-facebook-keeps-recommending-political-groups-to-its-users.

37 **"What information consumes is rather"** Herbert A. Simon, "Designing Organizations for an Information-Rich World," in *Computers, Communications, and the Public Interest*, ed. Martin Greenberger (Baltimore: Johns Hopkins University Press, 1971), 40–41.

37 **"Our brains are most productive"** Sherry Turkle, *Reclaiming Conversation: The Power of Talk in a Digital Age* (New York: Penguin Putnam, 2014), 62.

38 **"people who said they read"** Daniel Yudkin, Stephen Hawkins, and Tim Dixon, "The Perception Gap: How False Impressions Are Pulling Americans Apart," More in Common, June 2019, https://perceptiongap.us/.

39 **2020 study looking at empathy** Elizabeth N. Simas, Scott Clifford, and Justin H. Kirkland, "How Empathetic Concern Fuels Political Polarization," *American Political Science Review* 114, no. 1 (2020): 258–69, https:// doi.org/10.1017/S0003055419000534.

39   **2020 Northwestern University study . . . 67 percent**   Steve Rathje, Jay
J. Van Bavel, and Sander van der Linden, "Out-Group Animosity Drives
Engagement on Social Media," *Proceedings of the National Academy of Sciences* 118, no. 26 (June 2021): e2024292118, https://doi.org/10.1073/pnas
.2024292118.

40   **some of the one hundred protesters**   Allan Smith, "Tea Party-Style
Protests Break Out Across the Country Against Stay-at-Home Orders,"
NBC News, April 16, 2020, http://www.nbcnews.com/politics/donald
-trump/tea-party-style-protests-break-out-across-country-against-stay
-n1185611.

40   **"If Congress doesn't get it"** [in footnote]   Mónica Guzmán, "Braver
Angels Goes to Washington, Testifies at Hearing to Depolarize Congress,"
Braver Angels, June 27, 2021, https://braverangels.org/braver-angels
-goes-to-washington-testifies-at-hearing-to-depolarize-congress/.

41   **a *New York Times* story . . . "frustrated with the choice."**   Julie Bosman,
Sabrina Tavernise, and Mike Baker, "Why These Protests Aren't Staying
Home for Coronavirus Orders," *New York Times*, April 23, 2020, http://
www.nytimes.com/2020/04/23/us/coronavirus-protesters.html.

42   **In her book *The Happiness Hack***   Ellen Petry Leanse, *The Happiness
Hack: How to Take Charge of Your Brain and Program More Happiness into
Your Life* (Naperville, IL: Simple Truths, 2017).

45   **powell's response to the pastor**   Public Affairs, "Berkeley Talks Transcript: john powell on Rejecting White Supremacy, Embracing Belonging," *Berkeley News*, September 6, 2019, https://news.berkeley.edu/2019
/09/06/berkeley-talks-transcript-john-powell-400-years/.

45   **chatting in person with someone from**   Thomas F. Pettigrew and Linda
R. Tropp, "A Meta-Analytic Test of Intergroup Contact Theory," *Journal
of Personality and Social Psychology* 90, no. 5 (May 2006): 751–83, https://
doi.org/10.1037/0022-3514.90.5.751.

45   **powell doesn't capitalize his name** [in footnote]   Cathy Cockrell, "To
Berkeley Civil-Rights Scholar, Race Is Uppercase Concern," *Berkeley
News*, December 11, 2021, https://news.berkeley.edu/2012/12/11/john
-powell-profile/.

46   **when liberal and conservative judges**   Cass Sunstein, David Schkade,
and Lisa Michelle Ellman, "Ideological Voting on Federal Courts of

Appeals: A Preliminary Investigation," *Virginia Law Review* 90, no. 1 (March 2004): 301–54, https://doi.org/10.2307/3202429.

Part II: Curiosity

50   **"I'm as guilty as the next person"**   David Weinstein, "Opinion: Outside In," *Laguna Beach Independent*, July 2, 2021, https://www.lagunabeach indy.com/opinion-outside-in-16/.

50   **"These are challenging times"**   Lenny Mirra, "Letter to the Editor ~ Letter: It's Time to Start Listening to Each Other," *Valley Patriot* (North Andover, MA), June 5, 2021, http://valleypatriot.com/letter-to-the -editor-letter-its-time-to-start-listening-to-each-other/.

50   **"knowledge emotion"**   Paul J. Silvia, "Confusion and Interest: The Role of Knowledge Emotions in Aesthetic Experience," *Psychology of Aesthetics, Creativity, and the Arts* 4, no. 2 (May 2010): 75–80, https://doi.org/10 .1037/A0017081.

4: Perspective

51   **One model that does a decent**   Daniel C. Hallin, *The Uncensored War: The Media and Vietnam* (Berkeley: University of California Press, 1989).

55   **And you want to reach**   Maria Konnikova, "Why We Need Answers," *New Yorker*, April 30, 2013, https://www.newyorker.com/tech/annals-of -technology/why-we-need-answers.

60   **opposition party that never won**   David A. Shirk, "Mexico's Victory: Vicente Fox and the Rise of the PAN," *Journal of Democracy* 11, no. 4 (October 2000): 25–32, https://doi.org/10.1353/jod.2000.0086.

5: Friction

64   **you post the pic on social media**   https://www.reddit.com/r/Seattle /comments/4x3n0e/does_anyone_know_the_deal_with_the_empty_lot _on/. [Post no longer exists.]

64   **"The first time I"**   Anika Anand, "'Once Land Is Gone, It's Gone for Good': A Tribute to Seattle's Cass Turnball," *The Evergrey*, February 1, 2017, https://theevergrey.com/land-gone-gone-good-tribute-seattles-cass-turnbull/.

64   **consolidated modern curiosity**   George Loewenstein, "The Psychology of Curiosity: A Review and Reinterpretation," *Psychology Bulletin* 116, no. 1 (1994): 75–98, https://doi.org/10.1037//0033-2909.116.1.75.

65   **a story that solved this**   Anika Anand and Mónica Guzmán, "Why There's a Bunch of Stuffed Animals in a Vacant Lot," *The Evergrey* (email campaign), November 2, 2016, https://us7.campaign-archive.com/?u=8adcb05347121ec911dc897b6&id=da8f73fa44&e=8967beef5f.

66   **Beth Anderson got us thinking**   Caitlin Moran, "Money, Politics, and Earthquake Safety: Why Haven't We Retrofitted Pioneer Square's Brick Buildings?," *The Evergrey*, June 20, 2019, https://theevergrey.com/money-politics-and-earthquake-safety-why-havent-we-retrofitted-pioneer-squares-brick-buildings/.

66   **the history of one of our**   "Is Seattle 'Dying'?," *The Evergrey* (email campaign), March 19, 2019, https://theevergrey.com/newsletter/2019-03-19-is-seattle-dying/.

69   **"Does Seattle get an influx of"**   Ana Sofia Knauf, "Are People Flocking to Seattle for Our Homeless Services?," *The Evergrey*, July 19, 2018, https://theevergrey.com/seahomeless-coming-to-seattle-for-services/.

69   **As the legendary broadcast journalist**   "Edward R. Murrow," Wikiquote, last modified September 11, 2020, https://en.wikiquote.org/wiki/Edward_R._Murrow.

70   **"like a lawyer's opening statement"**   Amanda Ripley, "Complicating the Narratives," *The Whole Story* by Solution Journalism Network, last modified January 11, 2019, https://thewholestory.solutionsjournalism.org/complicating-the-narratives-b91ea06ddf63.

71   **Not just so we can know**   Michel de Montaigne, *Essais de Montaigne* (Paris: Périsse Frères, 1847; Wikimedia Commons), 105, https://commons.wikimedia.org/wiki/File:Montaigne_-_Essais,_Musart,_1847.djvu.

6: Conversation

81 **Litman calls the parched type** Jordan A. Litman and Paul J. Silvia, "The Latent Structure of Trait Curiosity: Evidence for Interest and Deprivation Curiosity Dimensions," *Journal of Personality Assessment* 86, no. 3 (2010): 318-28, https://doi.org/10.1207/s15327752jpa8603_07.

7: Traction

93 **if a conversation has three** Amanda Ripley, "Make America Talk Again: The Lab Teaching Sworn Enemies to Have Decent Conversations," *Guardian*, June 27, 2018, https://www.theguardian.com/world /2018/jun/27/make-america-talk-again-how-to-bridge-the-partisan -divide.

94 **"I think of the analogy"** Anika Anand, "Why This Seattleite Started a Project to Bring Trump Voters and Hillary Voters Together," *The Evergrey*, March 2, 2017, https://theevergrey.com/seattleite-started-project -bring-trump-voters-hillary-voters-together/.

96 **One of its foundational tips** Ronald Heifetz, Alexander Grashow, and Martin Linsky, *The Practice of Adaptive Leadership: Tools and Tactics for Changing Your Organization and the World* (Boston: Harvard Business Press, 2009), 8.

8: Assumptions

103 **"Can You Tell a 'Trump' Fridge"** John Keefe, "Quiz: Can You Tell a 'Trump' Fridge from a 'Biden' Fridge?," *New York Times*, October 7, 2020, https://www.nytimes.com/interactive/2020/10/27/upshot/biden-trump -poll-quiz.html.

104 **"The current scores suggest"** Keefe, "Quiz: Can You Tell a 'Trump' Fridge from a 'Biden' Fridge?"

104 **"Puzzles are orderly"** Ian Leslie, *Curious: The Desire to Know and Why Your Future Depends on It* (Toronto: House of Anansi Press, 2014), 46.

108 **"small American farmers are nearing"** Alana Semuels, "'They're Trying to Wipe Us Off the Map.' Small American Farmers Are Nearing Extinction," *Time*, November 27, 2019, https://time.com/5736789/small -american-farmers-debt-crisis-extinction/.

109 **About 99 percent of all American job** Semuels, "'They're Trying to Wipe Us Off the Map.' Small American Farmers Are Nearing Extinction."

9: Reason

119 **In Buddhist scripture . . . people seeing one side.** Thānissaro Bhikkhu, *Udāna: Edclamations* (Valley Center: Metta Forest Monastery, 2014), 106–108.

122 **Haidt marshals decades of research** Jonathan Haidt, *The Righteous Mind: Why Good People Are Divided by Politics and Religion* (New York: Pantheon Books, 2012), 53–54.

123 **more like its press secretary** Haidt, *The Righteous Mind*.

125 **Haidt and others have deduced** Haidt, *The Righteous Mind*, 98.

126 **"Those of us who've been"** Lili Loofbourow, "Illiberalism Isn't to Blame for the Death of Good-Fair Debate," Slate, July 12, 2020, https:// slate.com/news-and-politics/2020/07/illiberalism-cancel-culture-free -speech-internet-ugh.html.

10: Opinion

135 **"When you feel you won"** Elizabeth Grace Saunders, "How to Stop Getting Into Pointless Arguments Online," *Wired*, October 28, 2020, https://www.wired.com/story/how-to-stop-arguing-online/.

135 **"Are you coming to bed?"** Randall Munroe, "Duty Calls," *xkcd*, no. 386, accessed July 19, 2021, https://xkcd.com/386/.

137 **Going back to our intuitive elephant** Haidt, *The Righteous Mind*, 80.

138 **"political identities are not"** Ezra Klein and Alvin Chang, "'Political Identity Is Fair Game for Hatred': How Republicans and Democrats

Discriminate," *Vox*, December 7, 2015, https://www.vox.com/2015/12 /7/9790764/partisan-discrimination.

140 **"We are more intimately bound"** Charles D'Ambrosio, "By Way of a Preface," in *Loitering: New and Collected Essays* (Portland: Tin House Books, 2016), 22.

143 ***"Le cœur a ses raisons"*** Blaise Pascal, *Pensées de M. Pascal sur la religion et sur quelques autres sujects, qui on esté trouvées après sa mort parmy ses papiers*, édition de Port-Royal (Paris: Guillaum Desprez, 1670; Wikimedia Commons), https://fr.wikisource.org/wiki/Pens%C3%A9es/%C3 %89dition_de_Port-Royal/XXVIII.

144 **He advised the graduates** Bill Adair, "Facts, Community, and Bears," Medium, May 1, 2019, https://billadairduke.medium.com/facts -community-and-bears-3d7587423ec0.

11: Experiences

153 **We actually *feel*** Tania Singer and Claus Lamm, "The Social Neuroscience of Empathy," *Annals of the New York Academy of Sciences* 1156, no. 1 (March 2009): 81–96, https://doi.org/10.1111/j.1749-6632.2009.04418.x.

157 **"The shortest distance between two people** Darius Ballinger quoted in slide presentation at #WeaveThePeople, Weave: The Social Fabric Project, Aspen Institute, Washington, DC, May 14-16, 2019, https://www .aspeninstitute.org/events/weavethepeople-gathering-at-union-market-in -washington-dc/.

160 **"respect moral beliefs more"** Emily Kubin et al., "Personal Experiences Bridge Moral and Political Divides Better Than Facts," *Proceedings of the National Academy of Sciences* 118, no. 6 (February 2021): e2008389118, https://doi.org/10.1073/pnas.2008389118.

12: Values

168 **When we think of values** Shalom H. Schwartz, "An Overview of the Schwartz Theory of Basic Values," *Online Readings in Psychology and Culture* 2, no. 1 (December 2012): https://doi.org/10.9707/2307-0919.1116.

169 **values become "infused with feeling"** Schwartz, "Theory of Basic Values."

174 **"Most contentious issues are framed** Brad Rourke, *Developing Materials for Deliberative Forums* (Dayton: Kettering Foundation, 2014), 11.

180 **Republican politics named Sergio Arellano** Jennifer Medina, "A Vexing Question for Democrats: What Drives Latino Men to Republicans?," *New York Times*, March 5, 2021, https://www.nytimes.com/2021/03/05/us/politics/latino-voters-democrats.html.

182 **"Anger is the force that"** Valarie Kaur, *See No Stranger: A Memoir and Manifesto of Revolutionary Love* (New York: One World, 2020), 107.

13: Attachments

186 **Everyone expected those two groups** Michael Powell, "Liberals Envisioned a Multiracial Coalition. Voters of Color Had Other Ideas," *New York Times*, November 16, 2020, https://www.nytimes.com/2020/11/16/us/liberals-race.html.

14: Clarity

203 **"looping for understanding"** Amanda Ripley, "Complicating the Narratives," *The Whole Story* by Solution Journalism Network, last modified January 11, 2019, https://thewholestory.solutionsjournalism.org/complicating-the-narratives-b91ea06ddf63.

206 **In a timeless** George Orwell, "Politics and the English Language," in *Princeton Readings in Political Thought: Essential Texts Since Plato*, edited by Mitchell Cohen and Nicole Fermon (Princeton: Princeton University Press, 1996), 597.

207 **"Probably it is better to"** Orwell, "Politics and the English Language."

209 **a woman named Wynette Sills** Mónica Guzmán, "Do You Have What It Takes to 'Walk a Mile in My News'?" Braver Angels, May 30, 2021, https://braverangels.org/dare-to-walk-a-mile-in-my-news/.

210 **"I came to a place"** Guzmán, "Do You Have What It Takes to 'Walk a Mile in My News'?"

15: Openness

228 **"If effects of this magnitude"** [in footnote] Hannah Baron et al., "Can Americans Depolarize? Assessing the Effects of Reciprocal Group Reflection on Partisan Polarization," Braver Angels, accessed July 19, 2021, https://braverangels.org/library/resources/can-americans -depolarize-assessing-the-effects-of-reciprocal-group-reflection-on -partisan-polarization/.

INDEX

ABOUT THE AUTHOR

Mónica Guzmán is a bridge builder, journalist, and entrepreneur who lives for great conversations sparked by curious questions. She's the director of digital and storytelling at Braver Angels, the nation's largest cross-partisan grassroots organization working to depolarize America, the host of the Crosscut interview series *Northwest Newsmakers*, and a cofounder of the award-winning Seattle newsletter *The Evergrey*. She was a 2019 fellow at the Henry M. Jackson Foundation, where she studied social and political division, and a 2016 fellow at the Nieman Foundation for Journalism at Harvard University, where she researched how journalists can rethink their roles to better meet the needs of a participatory public. She was named one of the fifty most influential women in Seattle, served twice as a juror for the Pulitzer Prizes, and plays a barbarian named Shadrack in her besties' Dungeons & Dragons campaign. A Mexican immigrant and dual US/Mexico citizen, she lives in Seattle with her husband and two kids and is the proud liberal daughter of conservative parents.